The Law of the School

A Parent's Guide to Education Law in Scotland

Prepared by **Graham Atherton**
Senior Research Officer,
Scottish Consumer Council,

with the assistance of
Joan Aitken   Robert Brown   Alexander Fraser   Susan Kreitman,
and Norman MacEwan

Scottish Consumer Council

Edinburgh
Her Majesty's Stationery Office

Scottish Consumer Council
314 St. Vincent Street
Glasgow G3 8XW

© Crown copyright 1987
First published 1987

Illustrations by 'Larry'

ISBN 0 11 492484 8

Contents

Preface   5
Acknowledgements   7
Introduction   9

Parents' responsibilities and rights   13

Admission to school   17
Advice and assistance   20
Assisted places   25
Attendance   30
Bi-lingual education (inc. Gaelic)   34
Boarding accommodation   36
Books, equipment and materials   38
Children's educational rights   40
Children in care   43
Children's hearings   46
Choice of school   50
Class size and staffing   61
Clothing and uniform   64
Complaints   66
Curriculum (what is taught)   73
Denominational schools   78
Discipline and punishment   81
Education authorities   88
Employment of schoolchildren   92
Examinations and assessment   95
Exclusion from school   100
Fees and charges   105
Finance and funding   107
Grants and financial help   110
Guidance   116
Holidays   119
Home education   121
Homework   123
Independent schools   125
Information for parents   128
Inspections and inspector's reports   134
Leaving age   137
Legal action   139
Meals and milk   142
Medical attention   144

Migrant and other mobile children   146
Parent-Teacher and parents' associations   149
Post-compulsory education (after 16)   152
Pre-school education   155
Property loss and damage   158
Racial discrimination   161
Religious education and observance   165
Residential (former 'List D') schools   167
Safety and supervision   172
School buildings   176
School closures and changes   179
School councils   186
School records and reports   189
School rules   193
Scottish Education Department   194
Sex discrimination   197
Special abilities and aptitudes   201
Special educational needs   204
Teachers' conditions of service   221
Transport   224

Acts of Parliament, government regulations and circulars   227
Educational and legal terms explained   232
Periodicals and other publications   240
Useful addresses   242
Index   248

Preface

Parents have long been recognised as playing a very crucial role in their children's educational development. Encouragement and support from the home can affect children's educational progress in a very positive way. The Scottish Consumer Council believes that one way of helping this to happen is to make parents aware of the duties and rights the law now gives them to see that their children are properly educated.

Recent years have seen a considerable expansion in the law to do with education. The Education (Scotland) Act 1981 gives parents new rights to written information about their children's schooling, to ask for a choice of school, to appeal against certain education authority decisions, and to be consulted about school closures and certain other changes. Each of these areas is covered in detail in this Guide.

There are, however, many other areas of education law, found mainly in the Education (Scotland) Act 1980 but also hidden away in other statutes and detailed regulations, which parents may be less aware of but which may still be of importance to them. In addition there are a number of "grey areas" of education about which the law has relatively little to say, such as what should be taught at school, but which a Guide of this kind cannot afford to leave out.

Altogether some 56 different educational topics are covered by this Guide, prepared and checked by a team of experts to whom the SCC is greatly indebted. Although the Guide should not be regarded as an authoritative statement of the law, which only the courts can rule on, we do believe it will be a valuable source of reference for parents in their dealings with the educational system. We also think that the Guide will be of interest to teachers, education officials, teacher educators and anybody else whose work brings them in touch with parents.

Barbara Kelly
Chairman
Scottish Consumer Council
1986

Acknowledgements

The Scottish Consumer Council is grateful to the many individuals and organisations who commented on drafts of this guide. We would especially like to thank staff or members of the following bodies for their assistance and support:

Convention of Scottish Local Authorities
Grampian Regional Council
Law Society of Scotland
Lothian Regional Council
Scottish Education Department
Scottish Parent Teacher Council
Strathclyde Regional Council

We are greatly indebted to Miss Margaret Walker, formerly of the Solicitors Office, New St. Andrew's House, who spent the start of her retirement checking and rechecking drafts.

Valuable comments on particular sections were also provided by staff or representatives from the Advisory Centre for Education, British Association for Early Childhood Education, Campaign for Freedom of Information, Catholic Education Commission, Church of Scotland Education Department, Comhairle nan Eilean, Commission for Local Authority Accounts in Scotland, Commissioner for Local Administration in Scotland, Commission for Racial Equality, Education Otherwise, Educational Institute of Scotland, Equal Opportunities Commission, Geilsland School, Gifted Children's Information Centre, Independent Schools Information Service, Kerelaw School, National Association of School Meals Organisers, National Association for the Welfare of Children in Scotland, National Union of Students, Parents for Gaelic-Speaking Education, Professional Association of Teachers, Society of Teachers Opposed to Corporal Punishment, Scottish Joint Negotiating Committee for Teaching Staff in School Education, SCOPE—Scottish Pre-school Playgroups Association, Scottish Examination Board, Scottish Ethnic Minorities Research Unit, Scottish Society for the Mentally Handicapped, Scottish Secondary Teachers' Association.

We would like to single out the following individuals who provided much valued assistance:
Rosemary Burnett, Scottish Parent Teacher Council, in helping us to get feed-back from parents on the readability and usefulness of the text.
Margaret Burns, Legal Advisory Officer, Scottish Consumer Council.

George Currie, St. Andrew's College of Education. Jean Lawson,
Scottish Education Department, who provided very extensive
comments on the section dealing with special educational needs.
Alastair Macbeth, University of Glasgow. Struan McCallum and
colleagues at Balrossie School, in commenting on drafts dealing with
Residential (former List D) schools. David McNicoll, HMI, Consultative
Committee on the Curriculum. Beti Wyn Thomas, National Consumer
Council.
The text was edited by Finella Wilson, Scottish Consumer Council.
Typescripts: Muriel Adam, Patricia Hassan and Margaret Sloan.

What does the guide cover?

This guide is the first of its kind on education law in Scotland. If you are a parent of a school age child (ages 5-16 approx) then it should prove especially useful in helping you to understand and deal with the sorts of decisions, difficulties or problems you may be faced with. Parents of children under 5 or who have reached school leaving age will also find a number of the topics of interest.

The Guide covers a wide range of matters connected with children's education. It starts off by explaining your basic rights and responsibilities as a parent. You are told about your legal duty to see that your child is properly educated, for example. The Guide then goes on to deal with these matters in more detail, under topic headings in alphabetical order. Questions dealt with include:

Can you be forced to send your child to school?

Do you have any choice of school?

Do you have any educational rights if your child is in care?

What legal rights do school pupils have?

Must certain things be taught at school?

Can your child be made to wear school uniform?

What punishment can schools give to your child?

Are schools allowed to charge you for anything?

Can you insist on homework being given?

What sort of information about schools are you entitled to?

How much responsibility do schools have for your child's safety?

Is there anything education authorities must do before they are allowed to close down a school?

What can happen if the school rules are disobeyed?

What is your legal position when teachers go on strike?

And many more!

Special sections cover getting advice and help, making a complaint, and taking legal action. The role and duties of official bodies like the Scottish

Education Department and education authorities are also covered. Other sections deal with things like the employment of schoolchildren, school inspections, racial and sex discrimination, and special educational needs. For further information about these and other topics, you are referred to various other publications as well. A good background introduction to the Scottish educational system is to be found in Factsheet 15, "Scottish Education", issued free by the Scottish Information Office.

What does this Guide do?

The Guide attempts to:

tell you about your legal rights and responsibilities over a wide range of matters to do with your child's education. The Guide also says what education authorities and schools must do and what they need not do — in connection with your child's education.

indicate what sorts of services and arrangements you can expect to be provided for the education of your child over and above what the law requires. A lot of these services and provisions — such as how your child is taught at school — are not laid down by law at all, but result from the policies and practices of education authorities or schools.

point to steps you could take on your own or with other parents to make sure that your legal rights and responsibilities are properly respected — and what to do if they are not. Bear in mind, though, that a lot of matters to do with your child's education are not legally enforceable at all but depend on the amount of co-operation or goodwill between education authorities, teachers and parents — such s whether or not a school has a parent-teachers' association.

You should find answers in this Guide to a lot of the questions you are likely to ask about your legal rights and responsibilities in education. Not every single problem or difficulty that may arise can of course be covered, mainly because there are no clear-cut answers to many of the questions parents ask. Certain issues, like the safety and supervision of pupils, have not been clearly resolved in a legal sense, and where this is the case, we say so. This Guide should not, in any case, be regarded as the "last word" in the law — this rests with the courts. You will find a special section in the Guide about where to go for further advice and help. The SCC regrets that it cannot itself deal with individual enquiries. Every effort has been made, at the time of going to press, to bring this Guide up to date with the latest or impending changes in the law, but readers should consult a solicitor or other legal adviser about any further changes in the law since the date of publication.

How to use this Guide

Topics are arranged alphabetically. If you cannot find the topic you are looking for, look in the index at the end.

Cross-references If the topic does not cover what you are looking for, you may find it is dealt with under another topic instead, and this will be listed at the end of the section.

Legal and educational terms are used as sparingly as possible, but a list of common terms is given at the end. Occasionally special terms have to be used in the text. An explanation of these is then given.

Acts of Parliament References to the appropriate Acts of Parliament are given at the end of most sections on different topics. These refer to the Act by date, chapter and section(s); relevant acts are listed in full at the end of the Guide. For example, *1980, c.44, s.30* refers to the Education (Scotland) Act 1980, chapter 44, section 30 ("duty of parents to provide education for their children"). You should be able to get copies of Acts of Parliament through HMSO and in most central reference libraries.

Regulations (or "statutory instruments") A lot of law is too detailed to put into Acts of Parliament and is found in regulations derived from these Acts instead. Again these are referred to where appropriate at the end of each section; relevant regulations are listed in full at the end of the Guide, together with any amending regulations. For example, *SI 1975/ 1135* refers to Statutory Instrument No. 1975/1135, The Schools General (Scotland) Regulations 1975. You should be able to get copies of the relevant regulations through HMSO; central reference libraries may also stock some of these. You should quote the date, number, and title when asking for the appropriate statutory instrument.

Circulars and memoranda These are documents published from time to time by the government to give guidance to bodies such as education authorities in carrying out various laws, although they cover a lot of non-legal matters as well. They do not carry the force of law but can only advise or recommend what should be done, not what must be done. They are nonetheless important in giving you an indication about how the government expects particular laws or policies to be put into practice. Relevant ones are mentioned (again in abbreviated form) at the end of many topics and listed in full at the end of the Guide. For example C 1100 refers to Scottish Education Department Circular 1100 "Corporal punishment in schools" (1983).

Other publications At the end of some sections, mention is made of important official reports and other useful publications giving further information about particular topics.

Useful addresses A list of education authorities, official bodies and voluntary organisations which may be able to provide further information, advice or assistance is found at the end of the Guide.

Parents' responsibilities and rights

"It shall be the duty of the parent of every child of school age to provide efficient education for him suitable to his age ability and aptitude either by causing him to attend public school regularly or by other means."

"In the exercise and performance of their powers and duties under this Act, the Secretary of State and education authorities shall have regard to the general principle that so far as is compatible with the provision of suitable instruction and training and the avoidance of unreasonable public expenditure, pupils are to be educated in accordance with the wishes of their parents."

Education (Scotland) Act 1980

What are your basic responsibilities?

Parents are legally responsible for making sure that their children are properly educated once they reach school age (ages 5-16 approx). You normally do this by seeing that your child regularly attends a school run by the education authority. But it is possible for your child to be educated at home, at an independent school or somewhere else instead. The law does not say exactly what sort of education should be provided. It uses the word "efficient education" without saying what this means other than that it should be according to your child's age, ability and aptitude.

Parents' legal responsibilities continue until school children reach leaving age (age 16 approx). If your child has certain special educational needs, some of your legal responsibilities may extend to age 18, or even beyond in certain circumstances. You can give your children a good start by sending them to play groups or nursery school, or simply by spending time playing with and reading to them. When your child has started school, you can continue to give him or her as much encouragement and support as possible by:

taking an interest in your child's schoolwork.

stimulating your child's interests and abilities through books, hobbies, outings, etc — and by talking to your child.

visiting school to discuss your child's progress — the school will arrange for you to do so at least once a year and may want to involve you in other ways.

Research has shown that the children who get encouragement at home tend to do better at school later on.

On reaching the legal school leaving age (age 16 approx) young people normally become responsible for their own education. Parents may be expected to contribute towards their maintenance if they decide to carry on at school or college after 16, but grants or bursaries may be payable.

Normally, it is the responsibility of *both* parents to make sure that a child is properly educated. Where parents are separated or divorced and there is a court order for custody of the child, responsibility rests with the parent given custody. Where there is no court order for custody both parents continue to have responsibility even if they are separated. If the child is illegitimate, the mother is usually solely responsible, except when the court gives custody to the father. If a child is in care, parents may share the responsibility with foster-parents or whoever else is in charge.

What else do parents have to do?

As a parent, you have a number of special legal duties in connection with your child's education. These duties include:

making sure your child is properly educated, either through regular attendance at school or "by other means", for example, by arranging for your child to be educated at home.

seeing that your child obeys the school rules.

making sure that your child attends school properly dressed, although not necessarily in school uniform.

arranging for your child to be medically or psychologically examined if asked to do so.

making proper arrangements for your child's safety and supervision outside school hours.

You will probably want to visit the school to discuss your child's progress, subject choice, future career, and so on, although you are not under a legal obligation to do so. To find out more about how you can become involved in your child's education, you could contact a member of school staff, attend meetings of any parents' groups at the school, or read the written information for parents provided by the school and other publications.

The basic rights of parents

Parents' have the right to choose the kind of education they want for their children. This is stated in the United Nations Declaration of Human Rights, but this right is limited by Scots law. In Scotland this means that the education authority need only "have regard" to your wishes. The authority does not have to go along with them if it thinks that the instruction you want is unsuitable for the child or that unreasonable expenditure might be needed for extra staff or accommodation.

You also have the right to ask for a choice of school, although your child may only be offered a place at another school if certain conditions are met. The law is rather less clear, however, about the extent to which you can choose particular courses or exams, although you should certainly expect your views and preferences to be considered carefully.

Do parents have other rights?

You also have a number of specific rights. If education authorities, and in some cases school staff, fail or refuse to observe them, they risk being taken to court. You have a right to:

receive certain written information about schools.

be consulted about school closures and other changes.

have your child educated without having to pay fees, although charges may be payable for certain items and some education after school leaving age.

be consulted about or appeal against decisions made about your child's special educational needs.

be represented on school councils.

appeal if your child faces exclusion from school.

withdraw your child from religious education and observance.

have your child taught in Gaelic if you live in a Gaelic speaking area.

freedom of your child from racial or sex discrimination.

assistance with clothing, boarding accommodation and education, meals and milk, grants and other financial assistance in certain circumstances.

receive free medical care and services like guidance for your child.

Although not obliged to by law, many education authorities and schools offer a range of other opportunities and services which parents or children may be entitled to.

These could include:

nursery and other forms of pre-school education.

arranging for you to meet school staff at parents' days or evenings or join parent-teacher and parents' associations.

running extra-curricular and other activities for your child out of school hours.

keeping you informed of your child's progress at school.

entering your child for public examinations.

If you have any problems about services which must be provided by law, it is advisable to discuss them with the school staff first. If this is not satisfactory, you could complain to the school or education authority, or even to the Secretary of State. The rest of this Guide provides detailed information on all of the above-mentioned responsibilities and rights of parents.

Where to find out more
1980, c.44 especially ss.1, 28 and 30; 1981, c.58, ss.1-6.

Admission to school

Starting school

Education authorities are allowed to fix their own starting dates at schools which they run. They can set different starting dates for different schools in their area if they want to. They can also fix more than one starting date for a school in a calendar year, although the practice in recent times in Scotland has been to have a single starting date in the year so that classes are not disrupted in the middle of the school session. The general practice in Scotland is for the school session to start in the middle of August and finish towards the end of June or early July.

Some months before your child is due to start school or transfer to secondary school, you will normally be told by the education authority which school he or she can attend. You will also be informed of your right to ask for a different school should you want to send your child somewehere else. You must be automatically supplied with written information for parents about the school at which your child is offered a place. It is your duty to see that your child goes to school regularly. This means making sure that the education authority has your child's name and address well before the school starting date. This is normally not necessary if your child has already been attending nursery school or is transferring to secondary school, as the authority should already have your child's name and address. The authority must give details in the local press about school starting dates in time to allow you to enrol your child. You should let the authority know if you intend to move to another area, so that your child can transfer school if necessary. Independent schools fix their own starting dates.

School starting dates

There are *two* types of school starting date which affect when your child can start school for the first time:

1   The date when your child is actually due to start school. This is known as the "school commencement date". In Scotland, this is usually sometime in August.

2   The date by which your child must have reached 5 in order to start school at the previous "school commencement date". This is known as the "latest appropriate date". It may not precede the *next* school commencement date by more than six months and seven days.

The table below gives examples of how this works (the school starting dates will of course vary slightly from year to year and between education authorities).

	Start of school ("school commencement date")	Date of 5th Birthday	Date by which child must be 5 ("latest appropriate date")	Age on that date	Allowed to start school	Age on starting school
Child A	25 Aug 1986	25 Feb 1987	28 Feb 1987	5 years 0 months 3 days	Yes	4 years 6 months
Child B	25 Aug 1986	25 March 1987	28 Feb 1987	4 years 11 months 3 days	No	5 years 5 months
Child C	25 Aug 1986	1 March 1987	28 Feb 1987	4 years 11 months 28 days	Doubtful: education authority would decide	4 years 5 months 28 days

Child A has reached five just three days before the latest appropriate date and so is entitled to start school on the previous school commencement date even though he/she has not reached *school age* by then. The parent cannot be *forced* to send the child to school until the next commencement date, however — this could be in another year's time — and the law on school attendance would not apply until then. If your child is in this position, you could get guidance from the education authority about whether your child would benefit from starting school before five or waiting until the next commencement date.

Child B has not reached the age of five by the latest appropriate date and so would have to wait until the next school commencement date before starting school — this may not be until August 1987, when he or she would be five years and five months old.

Child C was born one day "too late" and so may have to wait until he/she is almost five-and-a-half years old before starting school. If born a day earlier, on 28 February, the child would have been entitled to start school a year earlier at exactly age four-and-a-half years old.

Under-age admissions

It is possible for your child to begin school earlier than the normal age for starting. This could happen if your child has just failed to reach five by the "appropriate latest date" for starting school, as with child C in the table. Some authorities take a more relaxed attitude than others in this question. It could also arise if your child is advanced and mature enough to benefit from starting school earlier. Before deciding whether to offer a place the education authority will probably want your child to be expertly assessed, by its child guidance staff, and will need to work out whether there are enough spare places or staff to justify your child starting school at an earlier age. You could ask the authority what its policies are on this matter.

To get your child admitted to school at an earlier age, you will have to write to the education authority asking for a place at the school(s) you are interested in. You can do this through the same procedures used for choosing a different school; this then allows you to appeal against the authority's decision if your request is refused. You may be asked to give convincing reasons why your child should start school earlier than normal. Get expert advice, if necessary, from child guidance staff.

If your child has certain special educational needs it is possible that the authority will in any case arrange for your child to begin school earlier.

Introducing your child to the school

The school may arrange for you and your child to visit school and perhaps spend a few days in the ordinary classroom before the official start of term. Many schools arrange special meetings or provide booklets of their own for parents of children starting school for the first time. Similar arrangements may also be provided for parents of children about to transfer to secondary school.

Transfer to secondary school. Your child will normally transfer to secondary school at age 11 or 12, after the seventh year of primary school. Your child will usually be offered a place at the secondary school which normally receives pupils from the 'feeder' primary school he or she has attended. You must be given the opportunity to ask for a place at another secondary school, however, in the same way as for children starting primary school.

See also
ADVICE AND ASSISTANCE
ATTENDANCE
CHOICE OF SCHOOL
GUIDANCE

HOME EDUCATION
INDEPENDENT SCHOOLS
INFORMATION FOR PARENTS
PRE-SCHOOL EDUCATION
SPECIAL EDUCATIONAL NEEDS

Where to find out more
1980, c.44, ss.1, 31, 32 and 135 as amended by

1981, c.58, s.28A; SI 1975/1135 as amended;
C 614 and C 1108.

Advice and assistance

When parents need help

You may from time to time want advice and help about various matters to do with your child's education.

This could, for example, arise when you want to:

choose a school for your child.

appeal against a decision by the education authority rejecting your choice of school or excluding your child from school.

claim some cash benefit or service which you or your child may be entitled to, such as free school meals or maintenance or school transport costs.

object to matters such as school closures and certain other changes, which the education authority may have to consult you about.

defend yourself against some legal or other action taken against you, for example in connection with school attendance.

make a complaint or take legal action about something to do with your child's schooling.

obtain practical help with something, like writing a letter, filling in a form, or preparing for an interview or appeal.

How to go about getting help

When you are seeking advice you should:

take with you any correspondence or other documents, including application forms, which your adviser may want to refer to (keep photocopies or carbons of anything you post).

not necessarily expect to obtain an answer or solution to your problem straight away — further enquiries may have to be made and you may be referred to somebody or somewhere else.

note down the names of anybody you speak to, especially when dealing with officials by telephone, in case you have to contact these people again.

be ready to listen to points of view other than your own — this does not mean you should always agree with them!

Do not automatically assume that a legal or other remedy exists — it may be that a change in the law or established practices are required before anything can be done to help you.

Where to go for help

You should be able to get advice and assistance from:

School staff, including any secondary school guidance teachers who are responsible for your child. You will nearly always need to approach the school first (or the school may approach you) about any personal difficulties affecting your child, and only if the school fails to deal with the matter satisfactorily should you turn to other sources of help.

Education authority officials, who must in many cases inform you about their policies and practices on particular matters whenever you request written information for parents. They should also be able to refer you to any specialist sources of advice, for example to do with any special educational needs your child might have.

If there is a parent's group at your local school, it may be willing to advise you in some cases or refer you to somebody who can. Some voluntary organisations are often in a position to help specific groups of people with special problems, such as the schooling of children with special needs or special abilities. Some may agree to represent you in appeal, court or other proceedings (see address list of voluntary organisations at the end of the Guide).

When a problem affects a whole group of parents, such as the closure of a school, it may be worth turning to school councils, local councils of social service, community councils and other community organisations for support.

Local advice centres, such as citizens' advice bureaux, which are to be found in most major towns and cities. Staff and volunteers there are trained to deal with a wide range of enquiries and problems, including ones to do with education, and their services are normally free. They can give you basic legal advice and information, and may be able to help you to prepare an appeal or make a complaint. In some cases they may arrange for you to be represented at appeals and other legal proceedings. Ask at your local library or post office, or look in the yellow pages for the address and phone number of your nearest advice centre.

Solicitors who should be able to advise you on the law to do with education in Scotland, but you could ask your advice centre to put you in touch with solicitors specialising or interested in your sort of case. Many solicitors belong to a scheme in which you need pay no more than £5 for the first half hours' worth of advice, regardless of your income. This half hour will be important in helping you and your solicitor to decide whether you have a case. If your income (after tax, insurance, etc) and savings are below a certain level and after allowing deductions for the ages and number of dependents you have, you automatically qualify for legal advice and assistance free of charge or at a reduced charge.

Advice covers

interviewing you and giving you verbal and written advice.

writing and answering letters on your behalf.

checking documents, etc.

A solicitor can also represent you in court, but the financial help you get for this is covered by a separate legal aid scheme which you may qualify for. Before legal aid will be given in civil cases, your solicitor has to convince the local Legal Aid Committee, or the Supreme Court Committee in Court of Session cases, that your case (as pursuer or defender) has a chance of success. The Department of Health and Social Security also has to work out whether you are entitled to legal aid on grounds of financial hardship. In criminal cases, when you wish to plead not guilty, the court itself will decide whether or not you qualify for criminal legal aid.

Legal aid does not cover representation at appeal committee hearings to do with choice of school, exclusion of your child from school, and so on. It does, however, cover representation if you decide to take your appeal to the sheriff court. It does not cover legal action taken into the European Court of Human Rights, although the European Commission may grant legal aid of its own. Ask at your advice centre, or most solicitors' offices for leaflets telling you about the legal advice and legal aid schemes. In some towns and cities, you can go for legal advice and assistance to a free 'legal dispensary' run by qualified lawyers in their spare time — ask at your advice centre or library for details of opening times, etc.

Other specialist groups or organisations can provide advice, information or assistance of their own, as in the following cases:

Bursaries, grants and other financial assistance	Scottish Education Department (Students' Awards Branch) Dept. of Health & Social Security (supplementary benefits for school leavers).

Children in care	Social work department of your local authority, or your child's social worker.
Guidance	Child guidance and careers guidance services of the education authority.
Independent schools	Independent Schools Information Service.
Racial discrimination	Commission for Racial Equality (and local community relations councils).
Sex discrimination	Equal Opportunities Commission.

See the address list of these and other organisations at the end of the Guide.

Publications

Various publications booklets, leaflets and other materials — may be worth reading as well for advice and information. A good starting point is *Education A-Z: where to look things up* published by the Advisory Centre for Education, and updated regularly. It is an A-Z of sources of information on all major educational topics, with names and addresses of relevant organisations, including Scottish ones. You should look at any of the following publications:

booklets and leaflets written specially for parents by bodies such as the Advisory Centre for Education and the Scottish Parent Teacher Council. Education authorities issue information of their own for parents in booklet or leaflet form. The Scottish Information Office publishes a series of "factsheets" and other booklets on different educational topics.

periodicals for parents, including the bi-monthly ACE Bulletin, published by the Advisory Centre for Education, the Scottish Parent Teacher Council Newsletter (three times a year), and Parents and Schooling, published by the Campaign for State Education.

articles in the weekly education pages of papers like *The Scotsman, Glasgow Herald,* and *The Guardian* and in *The Times Educational Supplement Scotland.* The BBC and independent broadcasters regularly produce programmes on education, often with parents in mind.

inspectors reports on various educational topics and on individual schools.

Scottish Office and other official reports, for example on what is taught at school and teaching methods.

library books and periodicals on educational topics for lay or professional audiences. Ask your librarian to refer you to suitable books.

Less accessible but still available to the public are acts of parliament and government regulations concerned with education. Some of the larger public libraries should, however, stock their own copies. Copies can also be ordered through Her Majesty's Stationery Office (address in telephone book). The National Library of Scotland in Edinburgh and some large public libraries keep a comprehensive collection of these. You may also be able to get hold of government circulars, giving guidance to education authorities, from these libraries (or you could write to the Scottish Education Department, Room 323, 43 Jeffrey Street, Edinburgh 1, asking for the copy you want). A list of the relevant acts, regulations and circulars is given at the end of the Guide.

Rather than trying to read all of these documents on your own, you should get an advice worker or lawyer to help you. The relevant acts of parliament, regulations, circulars and other publications are listed at the end of each of the topics covered in this Guide.

See also
COMPLAINTS
GUIDANCE
INFORMATION FOR PARENTS
LEGAL ACTION
PARENT TEACHER AND PARENTS' ASSOCIATIONS

Where to find out more
Guide to Legal Aid in Scotland, Legal Aid Committee The Law Society of Scotland, (current edition).
You and Your Rights: an A-Z Guide to the Law in Scotland, Readers' Digest Association, 1984.

Assisted places

Help with School Fees

If your child is offered a place at an independent school belonging to the Assisted Places scheme, you may be entitled to have all or part of the fees and other expenses, except boarding costs, paid for out of public funds, depending on your income.

To belong to the Assisted Places Scheme, schools must satisfy school inspectors that they meet certain standards of achievement, provide a broad range of subjects taught at secondary school level and have suitably qualified staff and proper facilities.

Over 40 Scottish independent schools now belong to the Assisted Places Scheme, most of them in the central belt of Scotland. You can get a list of these schools from the Scottish Education Department or the Independent Schools Information Service (see the address list at the end of this Guide).

Who is entitled to an assisted place?

Certain basic conditions must be met:

i.   Your child must have been ordinarily resident in the British Islands* or other countries of the European Economic Community** in the two years immediately before January 1 in the calendar year an assisted place is due to be taken up. Refugee children are also eligible provided that they have not been ordinarily resident outside the British Isles since being granted refugee status or political asylum.

ii. Your child must have reached the age of 10 before taking up an assisted place as the places are intended for secondary education. Different schools have varying ages of entry — usually between 11 and 13 — and some offer "preparatory" schooling for younger entrants.

iii. You must have given the school you want to send your child to details of your "relevant income" (see below).

An assisted place can be taken up regardless of whether your child already attends an education authority or independent school. Assisted

*including the Channel Islands and Isle of Man.
**Belgium, Denmark, France, German Federal Republic, Greece, Italy, Luxembourg, Netherlands, Portugal, the Republic of Ireland, and Spain.

places can be offered to children for as long as they are receiving secondary education, but only up to the age of 20.

Schools offering assisted places must advertise them at least once a year in a national newspaper. You can apply to as many schools as you want to. Simply write to the school(s) you are interested in for an application form. Your child may have to satisfy the school's entrance requirements before an assisted place can be taken up. The school must tell you what its entrance requirements are when sending you its written information for parents. Your child could be asked to attend an interview or sit an entrance exam.

What does the assistance cover?

i.   *All or part of your school fees*

You can get help with the payment of school fees in accordance with a statutory scale, which is adjusted from year to year. In the 1985-6 school year, for example, you would not have to pay anything in school fees at all if your "relevant income" (see below) was not above £6376. For higher incomes, you pay a "parental contribution" in school fees based upon your relevant income. The table below gives examples of parental contributions for 1985-6.

Relevant income	Parental contribution
£ 6,376	Nil
£ 7,000	£ 78
£ 8,000	£ 219
£10,000	£ 615
£12,000	£1,092
£14,000	£1,728
£15,000	£2,058

The difference, if any, between the school's fees and what you contribute is met out of government funds. For example, if your relevant income is £10,000, you would pay the first £615 in fees out of your own pocket, and any remaining amount in fees would be claimed by the school from public funds.

If you have more than one child with an assisted place, you pay only 1½ times (two children), 1.8 times (three children) or twice (four or more children) the amount laid down in the sliding scale. Your contribution is also reduced if your child holds an assisted place for only part of a school year. You are normally expected to pay your share of the school fees in three equal instalments at the start of each school term.

ii. *Travel costs*

You can receive in advance or claim back a grant to cover all or part of the costs of providing transport for your child to attend school. The school has to be more than three miles walking distance away by the nearest available route from your home. The grant will cover the cost of transport for daily journeys of up to 25 miles each way. Grants can also be claimed for a limited number of journeys by boarders at schools within or beyond this distance. Your child is expected to take advantage of any season tickets or reduced or concessionary fares, since the grant will not cover the "excess" portion of higher fares.

If your income is not above a certain level (£6,389 in 1985-6) the grant covers the whole of your eligible travel costs. Otherwise it is equal to the amount by which your travel costs are greater than one twelfth of your income over £6,210. For example, if your income is £9,000 and your child(ren's) travel costs amount to £400, you can claim back £400, less the difference between £9,000 and £6,210 divided by 12 (rounded down to the nearest multiple of 3), which comes to £400 — £231=£169.

iii. *Clothing and uniform*

If your income is below a certain level you may be entitled to a grant towards school uniform and other school clothing such as sports clothing. The amount of grant you get depends on how low your relevant income is and how much you have spent or expect to spend on school uniform or other clothing. In 1985-6 school year, for example, you could claim the £108 maximum if your income was below £6,210, with lesser amounts payable for incomes up to £7,075. The grant is payable for the first school year of the assisted place, but a lower grant may also be payable in following years if your income is below a certain level. In needy cases, the grant can be paid out in advance.

iv. *School meals*

If you are on supplementary benefit or family income supplement, the school must provide your child with a mid-day meal free of charge. Your entitlement continues until the end of the school year even if you are no longer receiving these benefits by then. If your income is not above a certain level (£5,400 in 1985-6) your child is entitled to a school meal at half price.

v. *Charges for field study courses*

You will not be charged for field study courses away from school which your child may have to take part in to prepare for SCE, GCE or similar examinations in biology, botany, geology, zoology or other approved subjects.

How is your 'relevant income' worked out?

In working out how much, you should pay towards your child's school fees and other expenses, the school will ask you to give details about your family income and the number of dependents you have. You must declare:

i. **Any earned and unearned income** (except child benefit and mobility allowances) *from any source* for the financial year immediately before the school year in which your child is offered a place. Normally this year will be your income tax year (from 5 April to 4 April in the following year). Any income of your spouse or dependent children up to age 20 must be included, as must any family income from annuities, gifts, investments, or pensions, and so on. No allowances are made for deductions from family income, such as income tax, mortgage or superannuation payments.

ii. **The number of dependents you have** For each dependent you have, except the child(ren) with the assisted place(s), £900 (1984-5) of your income is disregarded. Not only do your children and spouse count here, but also any other people wholly or mainly dependent on you, such as elderly relatives, separated or divorced partners.

If you deliberately give false information about your income or circumstances when applying for an assisted place, the Secretary of State can order the school to charge you for the school fees in full, including the fees for any other children of yours who already have assisted places. Should this happen, you must be given a chance to object to the Secretary of State, before he decides whether you should be charged in full.

If you are unable to provide information about your income before the beginning of the school year, then the school can ask you to give an estimate of your income for the year concerned, or failing that, details of your income for an earlier financial year. You are expected to give the school more up-to-date information about your income as soon as the school thinks it possible for you to do so. Under-or overpayments in fees will then be adjusted accordingly.

What happens if your income suddenly drops?

If you become unemployed or suffer a drop in family income in some other way, your contribution towards your child's school fees and other expenses will be reduced. The assistance you get is then based on your relevant income for the current financial year instead of the previous one. Any likely loss of annual income by 15 per cent or more would count for assistance on this basis. Even a smaller loss in income could count if the school thinks that hardship would result, although the school would need government approval first before adjusting your contribution.

See also
CURRICULUM (WHAT IS TAUGHT)
INDEPENDENT SCHOOLS
INFORMATION FOR PARENTS

Where to find out more
1981, c.58, s.5; SI 1986/1104.
Assisted places Scheme: a brief guide for parents current edition), Scottish Information Office.

Attendance

Making sure your child goes to school

Parents have a legal duty to see that their children are properly educated once they are of school age (ages 5-16 approx). You normally do this by making sure that your child regularly attends a school run by the education authority. But it is also possible for your child to be educated at an independent school, at home or elsewhere so long as the education is suitable. You are breaking the law and risk prosecution for failing to send your child to school without a "reasonable excuse", however.

If your child is over 14, you can ask the education authority for permission to keep your child away from school to help out at home for example if you are taken ill and there is nobody else to look after you or other members of your family. The education authority may only give permission if satisfied that exceptional hardship would otherwise result. Permission need only be granted up to the next school starting date, and your child could be required to attend school later on up to school leaving age at 16 approx.

Non-attendance at school

You have a reasonable excuse if:

illness prevents your child attending school or being educated. The education authority can require you to have your child medically examined if necessary.

your child lives beyond the statutory walking distance to school and the education authority has made no proper arrangements for transport.

there are other circumstances which in the opinion of the court count as a reasonable excuse. For instance the education authority has already agreed to your child being educated at home.

You should let the school know as soon as possible why your child cannot go to school. You should also write to the education authority for permission to educate your child at home or elsewhere: your request may not be turned down without good reason. Being excluded from school for misbehaviour does not count as a reasonable excuse for non-attendance.

Failure to attend school without good reason

If your child fails to attend school without a reasonable excuse or if the education authority is not satisfied that you have made proper alternative arrangements of your own for your child's education, you can be required to give an explanation. You will probably be given an opportunity to discuss the matter with school staff or education authority officials. You can be ordered to give a formal explanation (with or without your child) before an official or an attendance sub-committee of the education authority or school council. If your child has been kept away from school or the authority has already agreed that your child can be educated elsewhere, you may be allowed to send in a written explanation instead. You must give details of the alternative arrangements you have made to educate your child where appropriate.

If not satisfied with your explanation or convinced that your own arrangements are adequate, the education authority can:

issue an attendance order, naming the school your child must attend. You can be prosecuted for ignoring this order, which stays in force until withdrawn by the education authority or court. However, you can appeal against this order or the school named in the order (see below).

warn you that a decision will be made within six weeks' time whether or not to prosecute you unless your child starts to attend school regularly.

refer your child's case to the reporter of a children's hearing to decide whether your child is in need of special care or protection; this is most likely to happen when children truant from school.

take you to court. You can be fined up to £50 if found guilty of failing to send your child to school without a reasonable excuse or for ignoring an attendance order. For third or subsequent convictions, you can be fined *and* imprisoned up to a month. The court may also refer the matter to the reporter of a children's hearing.

Attendance orders

Before deciding whether to issue an Attendance Order, the education authority must have considered any views you might have about the school (if any) you want your child to attend. You could take this opportunity once more to justify your child's non-attendance at school if necessary. You must be given 14 days in which to appeal to the sheriff court against the attendance order once it has been served on you.* The sheriff can agree with the education authority's decision by confirming the order, cancel the attendance order, or change the school named in the order. The sheriff's decision is final; you have no further right of appeal. The order stays in force until the education authority (or the court) decides it should end so long as your child continues to be of school age. At any time the order is in force, however, you can ask the education authority to:

> withdraw the attendance order on the grounds that you have made alternative arrangements to educate your child.

> change the name of the school in the attendance order, for example as a result of you moving house.

The education authority may also do either of these things without waiting for you to ask it to do so.

The education authority must grant your request, but need not do so if it thinks that either the alternative arrangements are not satisfactory or the change of schools is unreasonable or not in the best interest of your child. You can again appeal to the sheriff if your request is turned down.

The above procedure was sometimes used in the past by parents to get a choice of school, but as a result of changes in the law it is no longer necessary for parents to withdraw their children from school in order to do so.

Truancy

If your child has been staying away from school, you could face the same consequences as other parents of children who have failed to attend school without good reason. Nowadays, however, much greater emphasis is given to providing help and support to the families of

*You are expected to obey the attendance order while waiting for your appeal to be heard by the sheriff. Your appeal does not count as a reasonable excuse for your child not to go to school.

children who persistently stay away from school. Attendance orders are seen by some education authorities only as a last resort. Children may stay away from school because of such things as unsettled family life or difficulties they are having with pupils or staff at school.

If truancy is suspected, any of the following steps are likely to be taken:

the headteacher may arrange for a school attendance officer or education welfare officer to visit your home and report back to the school.

guidance or other staff from the school or the education authority may arrange to interview you and your child, either separately or together.

other agencies like social work departments, the police, or medical services might be asked to make enquiries of their own and report back to the school.

you may be required to appear with or without your child before the attendance sub-committee of the school council, or the education authority.

Attendance order proceedings, prosecution or referral to the reporter of the children's hearing are only likely to take place if the above steps have already been taken and the child is still not going to school.

Registration and daily attendance

Schools must keep a daily register of admissions, morning and afternoon attendances, absences and withdrawals of pupils on their roll. Your child must normally attend school on each day it is open for education, normally 200 days in each school year. Your child need not be allowed in school as a result of circumstances beyond the school's control, however, for example closure of the school owing to industrial action, or fire damage. This does not necessarily mean that your child should stop being educated — the education authority may make alternative arrangements, for example in temporary classrooms. Your child's attendance record should appear in the school report issued to you each year. Authorised absences from school to visit the doctor, or attend interviews, etc. count as attendances. Being excluded from school for misbehaviour counts as absence.

See also
CHILDRENS' HEARINGS
EXCLUSION FROM SCHOOL
GUIDANCE

LEGAL ACTION
SCHOOL COUNCILS
TRANSPORT

Where to find out more
1980, c.44, ss.30-31, 33-44; SI 1975/1135, sch.1, C816.

Bilingual education (including Gaelic)

Speaking a different language

There are several other languages spoken in Scotland besides English so that it is possible for bilingual education to be provided in schools. There are nearly 83,000 people in Scotland who speak or understand Gaelic, including most people in the Western Isles and some Highland areas. Some Gaelic speakers are also found in southern and central Scotland, including around 10,000 in greater Glasgow. About 13,500 Gaelic speakers are under 20. There are also smaller numbers of people who speak Asian languages such as Urdu, Bengali and Cantonese.

Gaelic

Education authorities must provide for the teaching of Gaelic* at schools in Gaelic-speaking areas. Although the law does not say where these areas are, in practice most of the instruction in Gaelic should be provided by all schools in the Western Isles, many in Skye and Lochalsh and some schools in other parts of the Highlands. A few schools in other areas offer Gaelic instruction as well, mainly only as a subject option. You will probably have to convince the education authority — and the courts if necessary — that you are living in a Gaelic-speaking area before the school will agree to provide Gaelic teaching which is not provided already.

The law does not say how much instruction should be provided in Gaelic. Nor does it say whether Gaelic should be taught to pupils from non-Gaelic speaking homes as well. Since education authorities have a general duty to consider your wishes concerning your child's education, you should at least expect your views about whether you want your child taught in Gaelic to be taken into consideration.

The education authority must provide written information for parents about any schools in its area which provide for the teaching of Gaelic. This information, must be published in Gaelic as well as in English where appropriate. This means that schools in Gaelic-speaking areas should publish their handbooks for parents in both languages. In these areas, the authority may also agree to provide progress reports on your child in Gaelic. Appeal committee and other proceedings, on such

*The law does not explain what "the teaching of Gaelic" means but it probably refers to Gaelic being used in teaching as an everyday medium of instruction, not Gaelic simply being taught as a "school subject".

matters as choice of school or consulting parents about school closures, may also be in Gaelic.

Languages other than Gaelic

The law does not mention any other specific language in which children must be taught. Migrant children of workers from EEC and other countries are entitled to some teaching in their host country in their own mother tongue. It is by no means clear, though, whether other children who are born and brought up in Britain but speak a foreign language are entitled to bilingual education, for example, children of parents from "new commonwealth" countries. It might be argued that these children should be given bilingual education so that they get most benefit from school education or that their circumstances are exceptional enough to justify special instruction. On the other hand, the law does not consider that these children have special educational needs if their learning difficulties are simply a result of speaking a different language.

In practice, education authorities can provide some bilingual instruction for pupils at schools with sizeable numbers of pupils with limited English, as in some urban areas with ethnic minorities. They may be able to get government grants for extra teachers to do this work. In addition, the Secretary of State has power to pay grants to local authorities with substantial numbers of children of parents from new commonwealth countries to cover extra tuition in their own language (he has not, so far, made use of this power). The authority must provide written information for parents in other languages, besides English, which are widely spoken in its area.

See also
CHOICE OF SCHOOL
INFORMATION FOR PARENTS
MIGRANT AND MOBILE CHILDREN
SPECIAL EDUCATIONAL NEEDS

Where to find out more
1966, c.51, s.11; 1980, c.44, ss.1, 28 and 50;
1981, c.58, s.3; SI 1982/950; C1071.

Boarding accommodation

Living away from home

In some circumstances children have to stay in hostel or other accommodation away from home in order to attend school. This could happen when:

your child lives too far from the school for daily travel to and from home, as in some highlands and islands areas.

your child is living in exceptional circumstances, for example if your work forces you to live away from home a lot and there is no one else to look after your child.

the nearest suitable school is beyond daily travelling distance. This could arise where your child has special educational needs or special aptitudes which cannot be catered for properly by local schools.

Education authorities must issue written information for parents about their provision of boarding accommodation. Accommodation may be school-based or in separate hostels, private homes or wherever else the authority thinks suitable. You cannot normally be charged for accommodation and meals, but you may have to pay for these if your child is living away from home in order to attend a different school from the one selected by the education authority.

There are no rules or regulations saying what standard of accommodation should be provided, other than those to do with statutory overcrowding, fire prevention and health and safety. Authorities should, however, have their own policies about the type of accommodation to be provided and how hostels, etc, should be staffed and equipped. They will have their own arrangements for providing out-of-school supervision of boarders and must take reasonable precautions to ensure their proper safety.

You must be consulted by the education authority about any arrangements for your child to be boarded out. Although the law does not go into any detail, you should expect to be consulted about:

the choice and whereabouts of the accommodation.

the kind of facilities provided for sleeping, private study and recreation.

any special diet or medical care your child needs.

out-of-school supervision.

arrangements for weekend and holiday leave.

Your religious beliefs must also be respected. Boarders must be allowed to attend church and take part in other religious activities outside school hours as long as education authority expense is not involved.

See also
CHOICE OF SCHOOL
INFORMATION FOR PARENTS
RELIGIOUS EDUCATION AND OBSERVANCE
SAFETY AND SUPERVISION
SPECIAL ABILITIES AND APTITUDES
SPECIAL EDUCATIONAL NEEDS

Where to find out more
1980, c.44, ss.1, 7(6), 10, 13, 17(5), 50 and 52.
Pupils and Staff in residence Scottish Council
for Research in Education, 1979.

School books

Pupils who go to education authority schools must be provided with free books, equipment and materials. Each authority is left to decide what sorts of book and other items to provide and how much to spend on them. Basic equipment and materials must, however, include paper and jotters, pens and pencils, mathematical instruments and material needed for practical classes such as art, craft, and technical subjects. Things like computers need not be provided, but nearly all schools in Scotland do now have the use of one or more. Most schools have their own libraries and secondary schools are usually equipped with laboratories and workshops.

Schools are given a certain amount per pupil, with which to buy books and materials. This is called their capitation allowance. The amount varies from one authority to another and is generally higher for secondary than primary schools. In deciding what sorts of books and materials to buy, schools are usually influenced by guidelines drawn up by the authority and by educational advisors. There is nothing to stop schools raising funds of their own to pay for additional books, equipment or materials — or asking parents to make donations — but it would be unlawful for the authority to *rely* on school funds for the purchase of essential books, equipment, and materials.

The books and materials provided at school are normally the property of the education authority. Schools do not have to let your child take them home, but if they do so, you and your child will be responsible for taking reasonable care of them. A charge could be made for damage not due to ordinary wear and tear, although schools often take a sympathetic view of accidental damage. The school can also charge for articles which pupils wish to keep, such as things made in craft and home economics, but it cannot make you pay for the raw materials used in classes. These charges are often nominal and may not be made in needy cases.

Pupils are often allowed to bring in their own books, materials and equipment, such as encyclopaedias and calculators, but the school may forbid certain articles to be brought in such as felt-tipped pens, sharp instruments or poisonous substances. The school is responsible for taking good care of books or materials which pupils have been asked to bring into school for project work, displays, and so on.

If your child goes to an independent school, you will probably have to pay for the books and materials yourself, except if your child has an assisted place or is there by arrangement with the education authority.

See also
ASSISTED PLACES
INDEPENDENT SCHOOLS

Where to find out more
1980, c.44, ss.5, 11 and 12.
Schoolbook Spending Series, Educational Publishers Council, (current Scottish edition).

The basic right to education

> *"Everyone has the right to education. Education shall be free, at least in the elementary and fundamental stages. Elementary education shall be compulsory. Technical and professional education shall be made generally available and higher education shall be equally accessible to all on the basis of merit."*

> *"Education shall be directed to the full development of the human personality and to the strengthening of respect for human rights and fundamental freedoms. It shall promote understanding, tolerance and friendship among all nations, racial or religious groups and shall further the activities of the United Nations for the maintenance of peace."*

> *Article 26(i) and (ii)*, Universal Declaration of Human Rights, United Nations, 1984.

Every child has the right to be cared for by their parents. Parents also have certain rights and responsibilities to see that their children are properly educated once they have reached school age, for instance making sure that their children go to school regularly. The education authority must see that proper education is provided for children of school age. It must also cater for childrens' special educational needs. These duties continue until your children reach school leaving age at 16 approx., when they then become responsible for their own education.

What rights do children have?

While at school, your child has few specific rights of his or her own which are not already part of those mentioned above. Your child is, however, entitled to certain fundamental human rights supported by national and international law and enforceable through the courts. These include:

Freedom from unnecessary suffering and ill treatment

The European Convention on Human Rights says that "no one shall be subject to torture or to inhuman or degrading punishment or treatment." Under Scots law it is a criminal offence, to neglect or ill treat a child under 16 in any way that is likely to cause unnecessary suffering or affect their health.

Liberty and freedom of movement

Children cannot be detained anywhere by force except:

by order of a court or children's hearing.

if they are arrested by the police in order to prevent some offence being committed, or to protect somebody from injury.

when they are under the care of their parents or teachers and need supervision.

Children can move about the school or classroom provided that this is not against school rules or prevents them being properly educated. Schools are entitled to keep pupils in classrooms during school hours in order to educate or discipline them, but pupils cannot be kept in after school if parents object. Schools have a right to declare parts of the school premises out of bounds for safety or other reasons.

Freedom to have and express personal views

Your child is not legally obliged to accept or practice whatever is taught at school; nor can your child be prevented from expressing his or her views. The European Convention on Human Rights gives everyone freedom of thought, conscience and religion, and freedom to express or practice these, limited only by the interests of public safety, the protection of public order, health and morals and the protection of the freedom and rights of others.

Freedom to join organisations

Pupils are entitled to run their own organisations, clubs and societies as long as they involve activities which are lawful and do not cause a breach of the peace. Pupils will, however, probably need official permission to run any of these activities on school premises. The headteacher may use the school rules to ban certain activities, although pupils can ask for a proper explanation when this happens, making a complaint at a higher level if necessary. Most schools encourage pupils to set up and take part in a wide range of out-of-school activities. Some schools have their own "pupils' councils" giving pupils opportunity to make their views known and take part in the running of the school. Some education authorities allow pupils to be represented on school councils. *Article 11* of the European Convention gives everyone the right to join groups and hold meetings in a peaceful fashion, including the right to form or join political parties and trade unions.

Legal Action

Under Scots law, boys under 14 and girls under 12 (legally known as "pupils") cannot enter into any legally binding agreements of their own or take anyone privately to court, but their parent or guardian is entitled to do so on their behalf. Older children, boys from age 14 to under 18 and girls from age 12 to under 18 ("minors") can do any of these things but usually only with the consent of their parents ("Curators").* Between 16 and 18, however, your child as a "young person" assumes all of the rights that you as a parent had to do with his or her education. Under common law though, you are as parent still entitled to advise your child and represent them in dealings with the education authority, appeal committees, etc. At 18, your child becomes fully legally responsible as an adult.

See also
ATTENDANCE
CHILDREN IN CARE
CHILDREN'S HEARINGS
LEAVING AGE
PARENTS' RIGHTS AND RESPONSIBILITIES
SCHOOL COUNCILS
SCHOOL RULES
SPECIAL EDUCATIONAL NEEDS

Where to find out more
1980, c.44, esp ss.1, 28 and 30; c.58 1981, ss.1-4; SI 1975/1135.
Convention for the Protection of Human Rights and Fundamental Freedoms and Protocol, Council of Europe, 1953.
Universal Declaration of Human Rights, United Nations, 1984, Articles 3, 9, 11.
International Covenant on Economic, Social and Cultural Rights, United Nations, 1966.
International Covenant on Civil and Political Rights, United Nations, 1966 Ratified by the UK government in 1976.

---

*The Scottish Law Commission has recommended that the age of legal responsibility should be changed to 16 for boys and girls, with those under 16 having no legal capacity at all in most matters.

Children in care

When parents cannot look after their children

Parents or guardians are legally responsible for bringing up their children, taking care of them and seeing that they are educated. If parents either fail or are no longer able to take care of their children arrangements may be made for the children to be received into care by the local authority, through its social work department. This is only likely to happen, though, if other sorts of help, such as living with another relative, are not thought suitable enough. If your child is to be taken into care you will still continue to hold some or all of your rights and responsibilities to do with education, depending on the sort of care your child is under. The social work department will consult both you and the education authority about your child's education.

Your child can be taken into care in the following ways:

Voluntary Care. This may happen when there is no parent or guardian to look after your child properly, for example due to the death, illness or other temporary incapacity of one or both parents. You can also ask for your child to be taken into care for a limited period if you are having great difficulty coping at home. Your child can normally be taken out of voluntary care at your request, although after six months in care you may be requested to give up to 30 days' notice. The local authority will then arrange for your child to be taken out of care if it considers that this is in his or her best interests. The local authority must in any case take all possible steps to return your child to you or someone else suitable, such as a close relative, when this is in the best interests of the child.

Your child will usually continue to attend school in the ordinary way. If your child is being looked after at a foster home or a children's home in another area and is likely to remain in care for some time, a change of school may be necessary. You have the same rights and responsibilities as a parent as before, and your wishes concerning your child's schooling will be discussed with you when your child is received into care.

Compulsory Care. This could happen if your child has committed a criminal offence, is beyond your proper control, has fallen into bad company, is in moral danger or has been truanting from school. It could also arise if the health, safety or welfare of your child is at risk. Your child can normally only be taken into compulsory care by order of a children's hearing, through a supervision order.

Your child may continue to go to the same school but in some cases your child may have to attend a school somewhere else. This could happen if your child is being looked after at a foster or children's home in another area or is sent to a residential (former List D) school. Most of your rights and responsibilities as a parent will continue as before, but the social work department in carrying out the supervision order from the children's hearing, will be in charge of your child's day-to-day welfare. In practice this means that your educational responsibilities and rights will be exercised by the person actually in charge of your child on behalf of the local authority, for example the foster parent or the head of the children's home or residential school. You cannot, for example, remove the child from the home or school where he is placed without permission. You can from time to time, however, ask for the supervision order to be reviewed by the children's hearing; this could result in your child being taken out of care or child care arrangements being altered in some way.

By a local authority taking over parental rights. In some circumstances where a child is in compulsory or voluntary care, the local authority may take over all of the rights and responsibilities of the parent, except ones to do with religious upbringing and adoption. This is done through a "parental rights resolution". This is only likely to happen if the local authority is satisfied that this is in your child's best future interests. Your parental rights may only be taken over if your child has been in care for three or more years, if both parents are dead (or the child abandoned) or if your child can no longer be looked after because of some permanent disability, mental disorder or lifestyle of the parent(s). You must be given a chance to appeal to the sheriff court if you object to your parental rights being taken away. The parental rights resolution can stay in force until your child reaches 18 if necessary.

In this case, whoever is responsible for maintaining or has care and possession of the child bears the educational rights and responsibilities of the natural parent. In practice, though, the natural parent, if known or still alive, may still be encouraged to take an interest in the child's education even after the natural parents' rights and responsibilities have been taken away if this is thought to be in the child's best interests. The natural parents could be encouraged to visit the school to discuss their child's progress, for example, or be allowed to see school progress reports on their child. They might also be asked for their preferences about the school they would like their child to attend. A lot would depend on the circumstances of the case and whether it is in the child's best interests to involve the natural parents.

The local authority must always give first consideration to the need to safeguard and promote the welfare of a child in its care until he or she is grown up. It must also find out and consider what the wishes and feelings of the child are, as far as is possible, appropriate to the child's age and understanding when decisions are to be made about a child's future in care. This would include any decision to take your child out of care and return him or her to you. It could also presumably refer to any decisions which might affect your child's educational well-being, such as a choice of foster parent, children's home or residential (former List D) school.

See also
CHILDRENS' HEARINGS
RESIDENTIAL (FORMER 'LIST D') SCHOOLS
PARENTS' RESPONSIBILITIES AND RIGHTS

Where to find out more
1968, c.49, parts II-III; 1980, c.44, s.28, 30 and 135; 1983, c.41, s.7.

When children have difficulties

Children may be brought before a children's hearing if they have been truanting from school, if their behaviour is out of control, or if they have broken the law or are in other serious difficulties. The hearing has to decide whether any compulsory measures of care, protection, guidance or treatment are needed. In some cases this could result in a child being sent to a residential (former List D) School.

Social background reports

Before your child can be brought before the hearing, an official called the Reporter will arrange for a background report to see if any of the above reasons for referral exist. In cases of truancy, you should already have had the chance to discuss your child's difficulties with school and other educational authority staff before the matter is referred to the Reporter. A social worker will visit you and your child and possibly the school to prepare the background report. Although you do not have to answer any questions, in most cases it is probably in everyone's best interests that you do so. The social worker will tell you the gist of what the report contains. You could also be shown a copy of this and be asked to comment or correct anything in it, but you are not legally entitled to see it.

Decision of the Reporter

After studying the social background report, the Reporter may decide to:

take no further action if no proper reasons for referral exist or no longer exist — this could happen if your child has started attending school regularly again.

arrange for your child and family to have a social worker to turn to for advice, assistance and guidance if you agree to this.

call a children's hearing but only if a reason for referral exists and if your child is thought to be in need of some kind of compulsory care and protection.

If the Reporter decides to refer the case to the hearing, you will receive a written statement saying when and why your child is to attend.

What happens at a Children's Hearing?

The aim of the hearing is to get everybody concerned to discuss your child's difficulties openly and constructively in order to decide what can be done in his or her interests. Proceedings are informal and not heard in public. The press can attend but rarely does so, and is not allowed to publish anything that could reveal the identity of the child concerned. Ordinary court procedures are not followed and no witnesses are called.

Both you and your child must normally attend the hearing — it is against the law not to do so, but if you have good reasons for not being able to go, you should get in touch with the Reporter straightaway. There is no need for you to be legally represented at the hearing and you cannot in any case claim legal aid except when the case goes to court. You can, however, get somebody such as a friend or advice worker, to come along with you to speak on your own or your child's behalf. The case will be considered by three people drawn from a local "children's panel" of trained but unpaid volunteers appointed by the Secretary of State. The only other people normally present, besides yourself and your child, will be the Reporter and the social worker who has prepared the background report.

Both you and your child will first be asked if you have properly understood and accepted the reasons why the case has been brought before the hearing — if either of you do not, then the matter must be referred to the sheriff court. The members of the hearing will then talk to you both about the child's difficulties and what should be done about them. Your child may not be spoken to alone without your permission. The hearing must also consider the social background report on your child and any other reports which might have been asked for, such as reports from the school. You can also submit reports or written statements of your own or get someone else to do so, such as a friend or professional person who knows your child. Seek expert advice as well before you go to the hearing.

Decision of the hearing

Having discussed the case and considered all the reports the hearing must decide whether to:

take no further action, dismissing the case on the grounds that no compulsory measures of care, etc, are needed.

arrange for your child to be put under the voluntary care of a social worker or take part in some voluntary activity.

order your child to come under compulsory care, under what is called a "supervision requirement". This could be either supervision under a social worker while your child continues to stay at home. Or it could involve your child living away from home for a time, with a relative or foster parent, at a children's home or at a residential (former List D) school.

The decision will be announced to you at the hearing — clear reasons for it must be given to you, in writing if you want or intend to appeal. Sometimes the members of the hearing may not reach a decision straightaway but might want to obtain further information or reports about your child, for example from the child guidance service, before finally deciding what should be done at a later date.

Referrals and appeals to the Sheriff

Your child's case must be referred to the sheriff if:

i. **you or your child do not accept the reasons given for holding the hearing or have not properly understood why the case was brought before the hearing.** The sheriff then has to decide in private whether there were proper reasons for referring the case to the hearing. If there were not, the case must be dropped, otherwise the hearing is allowed to continue.

ii. **you or your child disagree with the decision of the hearing.** You have to appeal to the Sheriff within three weeks. The Sheriff is allowed to question the Reporter and anyone preparing the necessary background and other reports. He can also call for additional reports. After carefully considering everything to do with your child's case, the sheriff will decide whether to:

support your appeal;

order the hearing to reconsider its decision. You can appeal to the sheriff again within 7 days if you are still not satisfied with the result; or

agree with the decision of the hearing.

You have a further right of appeal to the Court of Session, but only against an interpretation of law or the way in which the case was conducted, not against the decision itself. You should get legal advice before the case goes to court. The Reporter or social worker should be able to give you more information about how to appeal. You may qualify for legal aid.

The time for reviewing a case

Your child may not be under compulsory care for any longer than the hearing or court considers necessary. The compulsory care does not last for any fixed length of time, but the hearing must reconsider your child's case:

within a year of the supervision order being made, otherwise the compulsory care ends automatically.

whenever you or your child ask the hearing to do so, so long as the supervision order was made at least three months ago. You must wait another six months before you can ask for another review.

if the social work department asks for a review of your child's case to be carried out. It must carry out reviews of its own every six months.

As before, the hearing must discuss the case with you and your child and consider reports from social workers and others concerned. It must decide whether your child should continue to be under compulsory care or not and may decide whether the type of care should change, for example from residential to non-residential care. You have the same rights as before to appeal to the sheriff. Any compulsory care stops once your child reaches 18.

See also
ATTENDANCE
ADVICE AND ASSISTANCE
GUIDANCE
RESIDENTIAL (FORMER LIST D) SCHOOLS

Where to find out more
1968, c.49, pts II-III; 1980, c.44, s.36(3); SI
1971/492 as amended.
Children's Hearings, Scottish Education
Department/Social Work Services Group,
HMSO, 1984.

Choice of school

You are allowed by law to ask for a choice of school for your child. You can do this by asking for a place at the education authority school of your choice or by sending your child to an independent school. However you may do neither of these things and arrange for your child to be educated at home instead. In deciding at which of its own schools to offer your child a place, the education authority must "have regard" to the general principle that your child is to be educated according to your wishes. It need not, however, offer a place at a school which cannot provide suitable education* for your child or if too much extra public expense is involved, such as having to employ an extra teacher. The authority may in certain cases refuse to let your child go to the school of your choice, but you can appeal against this.

The law allows you to ask for a place at the education authority school of your choice at any time. This includes nursery schools. You must be given the opportunity to do so before your child is due to start primary school for the first time and before your child is about to transfer to secondary school. You may also be given the chance to send your child to a denominational school. Parents of children with special educational needs can make a choice of school as well, but the procedures for doing this may be somewhat different. Pupils are entitled to make their own choice of school once they have reached school leaving age.

How to make a choice

When choosing a school, you should seriously consider which school:

is best suited for the education of your child, including any special educational needs your child might have.

fits in with your own views about such matters as the school's relationships with parents, the curriculum, discipline, homework, and so on.

is most convenient to reach by public transport or other means. The authority does not have to provide free transport if the school you send your child to is different from the one it originally selected for your child.

is desirable for other reasons, for example if older brothers and sisters or friends, already go there or because of out-of-school activities.

*according to your child's age, ability and aptitude and any special educational needs your child might have.

In some cases your choice may coincide with the school the authority has selected for your child; where it is different, you have to make what is called a **placing request**. Only a very small number of parents in fact request a school different from the one selected for their child, but when they do so, in the great majority of cases (95 per cent in 1983-4, for example) their request is granted.

read the written information for parents issued about the school(s) you are interested in, including any recently published inspectors' reports.

visit the school(s) concerned and speak to staff there about the school — many schools run "open days" for parents to give you a chance to meet staff and find out what the school is doing. Take the school's information handbook for parents with you.

seek advice from the education authority, especially if your child might have special educational needs.

Do not simply rely on hearsay or gossip about schools in your area, since this may be based on misleading information or misunderstanding about what the schools are doing.

Placing requests

Before your child is due to start primary school or transfer to secondary school, you will receive a letter from the educational authority — usually in January or February before offering a place at a school selected for you. The school selected will often be one in your immediate neighbourhood but does not have to be. You will also be told at this time of your right to ask for another school. You do this by making what is called a 'placing request' for a 'specified school'. You name the school you want your child to go to either by letter or by filling in a form given to you. You do not have to give reasons for your choice, but your request may stand a better chance if you do so. You can name more than one school, but only your first preference has to be considered. Alternatively, you can put in several requests naming only one school at a time, to make sure that each of your preferences is considered.

You can put forward a request for a choice at any time you want to, but to be sure of a place for your child in the next school year your request should normally reach the education authority by March 15 (for August admissions). Requests can still be dealt with after this date, but your child has less chance of being offered a place if places are limited.

You can also make a placing request to transfer your child to another school at any time. You may want to do this if you are moving to another area, your child is unhappy at his or her present school or for some other reason such as a change in domestic circumstances like a family separation. Again, you do not have to give reasons for wanting a transfer, although your request is likely to be considered sympathetically if you do so. It is best to ask for guidance from the school or education authority about the advisability of moving your child to another school during term time, since this could disrupt his or her education. You can also make a placing request to send your child to a nursery school of your choice, but in this case you do not have right of appeal to an appeal committee.

When schools do not have enough places

Education authorities must draw up and publish their own guidelines for deciding which children should be admitted to schools at which there are more requests for places than places available. The guidelines may be the same or may be different for each school affected. You may be given a copy of these at the time you are given an opportunity to make a placing request or at any other times you ask for information. You have a right to be consulted about changes to these guidelines — this is explained in the section on school closures and other changes.

Guidelines are likely to give priority to children:

living in area(s) from which the school normally admits pupils, including the areas served by "feeder" primary schools where the school is a secondary school.

with brothers and sisters at the school or whose parents were educated there.

with medical or special educational needs which can be best catered for at the school.

They may also include other considerations, such as ease of transport from home to school or availability of particular courses or subjects your child wants to follow.

Education authorities may set aside a limited number of spare places at schools for future incomers into their areas. They cannot, however, refuse placing requests simply in order to keep spare places. There is no guarantee, on the other hand, that if you move into an area, your child will automatically get a place there. The school may be full already and you may have to accept a place at a school in another area instead. In this case the authority must meet your transport costs if the school is beyond statutory walking distance. You can, of course, still make a placing request for the school you want. You may also be told that your child will be transferred there are soon as a spare place becomes available.

Opportunities to make a placing request

To give you the opportunity of making a request for a place in the school of your choice the education authority must do three things:

(a) **The education authority must put an advertisement in a newspaper in your area, giving a date by which you must normally make your placing request.** This should normally appear in January or February each year, at least six months before the start of the next school year. The advertisement will have to appear more than once a year if there is more than one admission date. The advertisement must first appear at least four weeks before the final date for making placing requests. It must give the addresses and telephone numbers of local education offices, schools or libraries which provide further information for parents. The advertisement may also contain other information such as school enrollment dates for parents of pre-school children. The education authority may advertise as often as it wants to and can use other methods of advertising, such as local radio.

(b) **When offering a place at the school selected for your child, the education authority must inform you of your right to make a placing request at another school** — this must normally be at least six months before your child is due to start there. You must be given a date by which to make your request — this date must normally not be less than four weeks away. These time limits may be shorter if you have just moved into the area or the authority proposes an immediate change of school for your child. You must be given information about the school offering a place, and the telephone numbers and addresses of places which give information about other schools.

(c) **The education authority must allow you to ask for a choice of school at any other time of the year.** In this case, you simply send in your placing request to the authority or ask for a form with which to do so. Again, you are entitled to ask for information about the schools you are interested in.

How to make your request for a choice of school

You should address your request to the education authority, not to the school you want your child to go to. Once your request has been received, the authority must tell you in writing:

(i) the name of the person or body (education authority official, school council, etc) dealing with your request.

(ii) whether you will have a chance to put your case in person or in writing.

(iii) the name of a contact person who can answer questions about how the education authority actually considers your request.

(iv) the date by which you must assume that your request has been refused if you have not by then heard from the education authority.

(v) the reasons for which your request can be refused.

(vi) about your right of appeal if your request is turned down.

The education authority should tell you whether or not your request has been granted either by: April 30 (for admissions at the start of the next school year in August), or within two months of receiving your request (for admissions at any other time of the school year). The authority must write and give you the reasons for its decision.

Refusal of a placing request

The education authority can refuse your request for a school if granting it would result in:

the employment of an additional teacher, although the education authority can transfer staff to other schools.

spending a lot of money on alterations like building new classrooms. One court has ruled, however, that the need to convert accommodation like cloakrooms into classrooms does not justify the refusal of a placing request.

serious harm to the continuity of your child's education, for instance if your child has already had several changes of school.

serious upset to the discipline or welfare of pupils at the school.

the education normally provided at the school requested is not suited to the age, ability or aptitude of your child.

the school requested caters only for pupils of the opposite sex to your own child.

your child has already been excluded from the school you want your child to go to.

the school requested is a special school and your child does not have the special educational needs catered for there.

At least one of these reasons must be given to you in writing when the education authority turns down your request. It may give other reasons not listed here as well, such as ones to do with its own priorities for dealing with admissions to schools which have no spare places. The education authority does not have to refuse your requests if any of these grounds exist, however. It may decide that your child's special circumstances justify admission to the school you want, even if this means, say, employing an extra teacher there.

What to do if your request is turned down

If your request has been turned down, you are entitled to appeal against the education authority's decision. Your appeal will be considered by an appeal committee set up by your education authority. The appeal committee has to be convinced that the authority was justified in turning down your placing request on one or more of the grounds for refusal mentioned above. Otherwise your request must be granted. The committee consists of three, five or seven people appointed by the authority. At least one of these people must be drawn from each of the following two groups:

(i) members of the education authority or education committee, including "co-opted" members.

(ii) parents of children of school age *or* persons who in the opinion of the education authority have "experience of education" or are familiar with the educational conditions in the authority's area — such as school council members.

The chairman of the appeal committee must not be a member of the education committee of the authority, which may not have a majority of more than one of its own members on the committee. None of the appeal committee members must be education authority officials or advisers or have been involved in the decision to turn down your placing request. Nor may any of them be parents, teachers, school council members, etc. from either of the schools you or the authority want your child to attend.

You should try to get all the advice and help you can both in deciding whether to appeal and in preparing your appeal. You should remember that although you can make as many requests for a choice of school as you want, once you have made an appeal, you are not allowed to appeal again for the same child until at least another twelve month's time. You may therefore prefer to make more than one placing request before deciding whether to appeal or not. In 1983-84, for example, 37 out of 230 appeals by parents were successful.

How to go about making your appeal

There are three stages: *before* the hearing, *during* the hearing, and *after* the hearing.

(i) **Before your appeal** You must inform the appeal committee of your wish to appeal within 28 days of receiving the education authority's refusal of a place. You should also do this if you have not heard from the authority by April 30 or after two months. You should already have been given an address to write to. In your letter you should give:

> your name and address.

> the name of your child.

> the name of the school you want your child to attend.

> the date of the education authority's letter refusing your placing request (or when it was deemed to have done so, if you have not heard from the authority within the above mentioned time limits).

> a statement saying that you want to appeal against the education authority's decision. You do not have to give reasons for wanting to send your child to a particular school, although it may help all concerned if you do so.

The appeal committee must acknowledge your letter and let you know within two weeks when and where your appeal "hearing" will be held. The hearing should not normally take place within 28 days of you being told, unless you and the education authority agree to the date being brought forward. *You will need this time to prepare your case.* If the date chosen is inconvenient, you can ask the committee to fix another date, although it does not have to do this if other parents or committee members would be inconvenienced. You can arrange for somebody to speak on your behalf if you cannot attend the appeal yourself. The hearing can be held at any time of the day and in any place, but the committee is expected to arrange some or most hearings outside normal working hours and within reasonable travelling distance.

When preparing your case, you can decide whether:

i. to put your case wholly in writing without having to attend the hearing yourself;

ii.   speak at the hearing yourself, or arrange for someone to speak for you. You can send in a written appeal as well.

iii.   to do neither of these things but simply let the committee reach a decision based on information given by the education authority.

If you decide to put your case in writing, you must send a copy of this to the appeal committee and another copy to the education authority within ten days of the hearing. The education authority must also send to you, within ten days, copies of any information it considers relevant to its decision. It is best to start preparing your case as soon as you have decided to appeal without waiting until you are told the date of the hearing.

When preparing your case, you should consider whether:

the education authority was told everything you think it needed to know before it made its decision — for example, have all the reasons for your choice been given?

there have been any changes in your circumstances since your placing request which are worth letting the education authority know about.

Do not wait until the hearing itself to give this information — make sure it reaches the appeal committee and the education authority in good time — at least 10 days beforehand so that the hearing does not have to be adjourned.

The appeal hearing

Regulations lay down special rules about how hearings should be run. The education authority is expected to give you as much help and guidance as possible about the proceedings. If you decide to attend the hearing in person, you can take up to three people with you. One of these people can speak on your behalf if you want.

The Committee is allowed to hear appeals from several parents at the same time if these parents are appealing against the refusal of a place at the same school, at the same stage of education, and based on basically the same reasons. This could mean that the hearing has to be delayed beyond the normal waiting period so that appeals can be heard together. You must be given an opportunity to speak to the committee privately if you ask to do so.

The hearings are not open to the press or general public, although the committee may allow certain people such as official representatives, trainees, school inspectors to attend as "observers". The chairman is expected o behave in an informal way and can limit the number of observers present. The following things will normally happen at the hearing:

First, the education authority will be asked to say why it turned down your request and may ask other people to support what it has said.

Next, you or your representative will be given the chance to question the education authority's officials there.

Then, you or your representative will be asked to say why you think your child should be given a place at the school you want and why you think that the education authority should not have turned down your request. You can call your own witnesses to support what you have said. If you have already written down your reasons and sent them to the appeal committee and the education authority, you can simply say that you have nothing to add to what you have written.

Now it is the turn of the education authority to ask you, your representatives or your witnesses any questions.

The education authority will then sum up its case.

You or your representative will sum up your case.

The chairman of the appeal committee may allow you or the education authority to present any relevant documents to the committee, which both sides are entitled to see and take copies of. The chairman can disallow any statements or questions which he thinks are repetitive or too complicated, for example if several appeals are being heard at once and the issues and questions have already been well aired.

When the hearing may be adjourned

The hearing can be brought to a halt and adjourned until a later date if:

you or the education authority request an adjournment and the committee agrees that you or the authority need time to consider any significant additional information which the other side was not told about before.

the committee needs further information or advice; it is the duty of the education authority to provide any legal advice which is asked for.

the committee is satisfied that you or the education authority need to get further information relevant to the case.

the committee is satisfied that exceptional circumstances such as illness prevent you, the education authority or a witness from attending, or if certain of its own members are prevented from attending.

the committee decides to combine the appeal within another hearing.

The resumed hearing must take place not earlier than 14 days or not later than 28 days of the first hearing, unless you and the education authority agree otherwise. Any further information must be given to you, the authority and the committee at least seven days before the resumed hearing.

After the hearing

The appeal committee must now decide whether or not to confirm the education authority's decision to turn down your request for a choice of school. To confirm the education authority's decision, the committee must not only be satisfied that it was based on one or more of the legal grounds mentioned previously but also that it is appropriate to confirm the education authority's decision. The committee might conclude, for example, that although the education authority's refusal was based on proper legal grounds, your case was exceptional enough to justify your request being granted. If the committee decides not to confirm the education authority's decision, your request must be granted. The education authority cannot appeal against the committee's decision.

The appeal committee should give you its decision in writing within 14 days of the hearing. If your appeal was unsuccessful it must also tell you the reasons why. In this case, you must also be told about your right of appeal to the sheriff.

Appeal to the sheriff

If you disagree with the appeal committee's decision, or if you have not heard from the committee after 14 days, you have a further right of appeal to the sheriff court. You must appeal to the sheriff within 28 days of the decision, although if you have a genuine reason, for example if you are away from home at the time, you may be able to appeal to the sheriff after this time. Your appeal will be heard in private. To confirm the education authority's decision the sheriff must not only be satisfied that it was based on one or more of the legal grounds already mentioned. He must also be satisfied that "in all the circumstances" it is appropriate to confirm the education authority's decision, for example if your child's case is exceptional enough to justify your request being granted even though legal grounds for refusal exist. Otherwise he must refuse to confirm the decision. Your request must then be granted. The sheriff's decision is final — neither you nor the education authority may appeal to a higher court.

You should try to get legal advice and help before deciding whether to appeal to the sheriff.

Review of decisions

The education authority must reconsider all other current decisions to refuse choice of school requests if any of these are inconsistent with the decision of the appeal committee or the sheriff court. These decisions must, however, relate to requests to place a child at the same time, at the same school and at the same stage of education. All of the parents affected by them must be told the reasons for reconsidering them. So, if you have been refused a choice of school request, and the appeal committee or the sheriff court has decided that the appeal of another parent in circumstances similar to your own should be granted, the education authority may decide that your request should be granted after all. If, however, after reviewing the situation the education authority still refuses to offer you a place, then you can appeal to the appeal committee or the sheriff in the same way as you could have done when your request was originally refused.

See also
ADMISSION TO SCHOOL
ADVICE AND ASSISTANCE
CURRICULUM (WHAT IS TAUGHT)
DENOMINATIONAL SCHOOLS
EXCLUSION FROM SCHOOL
HOME EDUCATION
INDEPENDENT SCHOOLS
INFORMATION FOR PARENTS
INSPECTIONS AND INSPECTORS REPORTS
LEGAL ACTION
SCHOOL CLOSURES AND CHANGES
SCHOOL COUNCILS
SPECIAL EDUCATIONAL NEEDS
TRANSPORT

Where to find out more
1980, c.44, s.28; 1981, c.58, ss.1 and 2 and sch.1; SIs 1982/950, 1982/1733 and 1982/1736; C 1074.
Choosing a School: a guide for parents, Scottish education department (current edition).

Parental Choice of School in Scotland: summary of report. Parental choice project, Department of Education, University of Glasgow, 1986.
The Balancing Act of 1980: parents, politics and education, National Foundation for Educational Research, 1986.

The number of pupils who may be taught together in a classroom is worked out according to:

(a)   **the scheme drawn up between teachers and employers governing teachers' conditions of service.** This says that the maximum number of pupils to a classroom should not ordinarily exceed:

> **33 pupils** in primary schools and the first two years of secondary school (but with an *upper* permitted limit of 39 pupils)
>
> **30 pupils** in the third to sixth years of secondary school (but with an *upper* permitted limit of 34 pupils in the third and fourth years)
>
> **20 pupils** in secondary school practical classes, as in home economics and technical and science subjects, etc (the *upper* limit is the same).

Teachers are not normally expected to take classes above the ordinary limits but they may not refuse to do so without good reason. They could be asked to take larger classes to cover for staff absences, for example. However, they are entitled to refuse to take classes above the *upper* limit under any circumstances. Disputes between teachers and the education authority about class sizes can be referred by either side to an arbitration panel of teachers' and employers' representatives.

(b)   **School building regulations.** These lay down certain minimum space standards in schools.

(c)   **the maximum number of pupils the education authority must from time to time consider to be suitably accommodated in a classroom.** The authority must take into account the floor area of the classroom, the type of equipment there, the sort of instruction given and the health and safety of pupils. Records must be kept of the room sizes and the number of pupils each classroom can hold. You may ask to see these records, which are normally kept either in school or at your local education office.

When different groups are taught together

Pupils from more than one age group may sometimes be put into the same class, referred to as a composite class. This can happen in small country schools, in schools where numbers of pupils are falling or where the numbers of pupils in different age groups are very uneven. In each case, there may not be enough staff to justify the teaching of each age group in separate classes. A fall in the birth rate in recent years has resulted in an increase in the number of these sorts of classes. Official guidelines recommend, however, that composite classes should *not* where possible:

contain pupils at more than two consecutive stages of primary education. For example, a class which includes pupils in their fourth and fifth years of primary school is acceptable, but not one covering another year group as well.

be set up simply to suit the administration of school numbers; they should only be formed after full consideration of possible alternatives.

have been formed or regrouped once the school year has begun except for educational reasons.

Composite classes should also where possible be smaller in size than ordinary classes. The guidelines do not say how much smaller they should be, although the Educational Institute of Scotland advises its members that composite classes should not number more than 25 pupils.

School staffing

The number of teaching staff at a school is known as the basic staffing complement and is decided by the education authority, taking into account the numbers recommended by the Secretary of State. In primary schools, this currently ranges from one teacher for a school with 1-19 pupils, and 25 teachers for a school with 632-658 pupils. In secondary schools, the staff numbers are worked out according to the number of pupils taking different courses and subjects there, the number of teaching periods, "non-teaching" time, and other factors. This is sometimes referred to as the "Red Book". Education authorities can staff schools above these basic complements but may have to do so out of local rates without additional central government grants. However extra money, known as the flexibility allowance, may be payable by the government for schools —

which are difficult to run because of small or changing pupil numbers.

with a lot of pupils from socially disadvantaged areas who need extra tuition, for example, in learning to read.

at which staff are away at training courses or on non-classroom duties.

Additional government grant can also be provided to employ extra teachers at schools to help pupils with learning difficulties living in certain urban areas with a lot of social problems.

How well a school is staffed is sometimes expressed in terms of the school's "pupil teacher ratio", describing the average number of pupils per teacher. This ratio includes any teachers without classes of their own, such as headteachers and assistant headteachers, and so is not a proper reflection of class size. In September 1984, the average pupil-teacher ratio was 20.3 in primary schools and 13.7 in secondary schools. The education authority can transfer staff between schools. It may do so, for example, to meet changes in pupil numbers at a school.

See also
CHOICE OF SCHOOL
SCHOOL BUILDINGS
TEACHERS' CONDITIONS OF SERVICE

Where to find out more
1980, c.44, s.1; 1981, c.58, s.28A; SI
1975/1135; Cs 991 and 1072.
Scheme of Conditions of Service, Scottish Joint
Negotiating Committee for Teaching Staff in
School Education, current edition. (Clause
22 "Class size" and STC/19 "Composite
Class Guidelines".)
Secondary School Staffing ('Red Book'),
Scottish Education Department, HMSO,
1973.

What should children wear to school?

Your child cannot as a rule be made to wear certain clothes or shoes — or be banned from wearing them — as a condition of being allowed in school. This should only happen if the clothes or shoes worn:

are unsuitable or inadequate — for example, if a child is not warm enough, he or she will be unable to concentrate.

could be dangerous, if for instance something got in the way of machinery.

are forbidden by the school rules or upset school discipline in some other way.

In practice, schools vary considerably in the amount of freedom they give to pupils to wear different sorts of clothing. Some insist on shirts and ties being worn while others may allow more casual wear. Your child could face exclusion from school for being unsuitably dressed, although this is only likely to happen in very serious cases. It is very doubtful whether schools could use the threat of exclusion to:

make your child wear school uniform — you should certainly not be put under any pressure to buy one.

prevent small items of jewellery being worn, but expensive jewellery may not be allowed.

ban forms of dress like national or religious costumes, especially if racial or sex discrimination could result.

Schools would probably be justified, however, in not allowing lipstick, certain hairstyles, tattoos, and so on, if it can be shown that they upset school discipline. The school can insist that certain types of clothing should be worn for practical classes, such as gym kits, cookery aprons, laboratory coats, workshop overalls, etc. The school may supply these items itself.

In cases of hardship, you may be able to claim a means-tested clothing grant to help you to buy clothes needed by your child. The amount of grant is left to the education authority to decide on and depends on your income and other circumstances — you should get some financial help if you are on supplementary benefit or family income supplement. It is up to you to claim the grant. The grant should cover all or part of the cost of:

essential clothes and shoes to enable your child to attend school.

any special items of clothing like PE kit needed for games or gym, if these are not already provided by the school.

The education authority does not have to give you a grant to buy school uniform (although you could be given a grant if the authority has arranged for your child to go to an independent school at which uniforms are worn). You could be given a voucher instead of cash to buy items of clothing. You may still claim the grant if your child has not started school but has reached the age of five.

Education authorities must publish written information for parents saying what their policies are about what clothes or uniform should be worn at school. This must include details about clothing grants available and the costs of each item of uniform.

See also
EXCLUSION FROM SCHOOL
INDEPENDENT SCHOOLS
INFORMATION FOR PARENTS

RACIAL DISCRIMINATION
SEX DISCRIMINATION
SCHOOL RULES

Where to find out more
1980, c.44, ss.54-56; SIs 1975/1135 and 1982/950.

Complaints

What to do when something goes wrong

Parents are free to complain to various bodies or individuals when they are dissatisfied with something to do with their children's education. This should only happen after their first attempts to get a problem or difficulty sorted out have proved unsatisfactory. Many complaints may in fact be based on simple misunderstanding, prejudice, inaccurate information or be directed at the wrong people. By following the steps below you should at least be able to make sure that a problem or difficulty is presented in the right way to the right people.

Bear in mind, though, that the law provides only a limited number of safeguards such as appeals to see that a complaint is properly taken up. Much depends on the amount of goodwill between parents and school in making sure that complaints are dealt with sensibly. There are unlikely to be many complaints at schools which already have good relations with parents and who take care to explain or consult them about what they are doing. You should not, of course, wait until you have a complaint before approaching the school or education authority about anything — schools usually welcome visits by parents who simply want to talk about a problem before this turns into a "complaint". You may also want to visit or write to the schools to thank or praise staff for the work being done there!

Before making a complaint, you should first ask yourself:

is your complaint justified? Do you have reliable evidence to back up your claim or is it based on hearsay and second-hand accounts? Talk to everybody concerned to try to discover the true facts or take it to a higher level until you do so. Before complaining that your child is not getting enough homework, for example, find out if the school actually gives out homework and, if so, whether it is being brought home. You should be very wary about airing your complaints in public, especially to the press, unless you are absolutely sure of your facts, and even then only as a last resort — otherwise you could find yourself being sued for defamation!

who is the best person or body to complain to? Often this will be the headteacher or another senior member of staff at the school concerned, but there may be circumstances in which it is appropriate to take your complaint to:

a member of your school council or parents' group

the education authority
an elected representative
the local Ombudsman
the Secretary of State.

Certain official bodies also deal with complaints about:

professional conduct of teachers — General Teaching Council for
Scotland.

racial discrimination — Commission for Racial Equality.

sex discrimination — Equal Opportunities Commission.

See the relevant sections of this Guide for further details about these
sorts of complaints.

You should note, too, that certain legal procedures exist for hearing
appeals from parents against a choice of school or exclusion from school.
Some voluntary organisations may also agree to take up your complaint.
A list of these appears at the end of this Guide.

Next you should consider:

what should the complaint be about? This might seem an unnecessary
question to ask yourself, but there is no doubt, that many complaints
are made to the wrong people or hide underlying problems. You
might wish to complain about your child not getting enough
individual attention in class, for example, when the real cause for
complaint may be oversize classes or staff shortages.

how should your complaint be presented? The best way is probably
by talking to the people concerned, usually the headteacher or another
senior staff member. Complaints should be put down in writing if
personal approaches have proved unsatisfactory and several copies
should be kept for showing to other people such as local councillors or
MPs if necessary. Keep a cool head and avoid saying anything which
might be defamatory. Be polite, but insist on getting a satisfactory
answer, questioning anything which cannot be confirmed. You
should decide if you want somebody to represent you, such as a
friend, advice worker, representative from a parents' group, solicitor,
etc.

Complaints to the headteacher. It is advisable to take any complaints
you have about a school to the headteacher or another senior member of
staff to start with. Only if the outcome of this is unsatisfactory or you
find it difficult to deal with the headteacher should you consider

approaching any of the other individuals or bodies below. The headteacher is not under any legal obligation to deal with your complaint unless told to do so by his or her employer (usually the education authority). The headteacher may wish to make some enquiries into your complaint and you should allow some time for this in waiting for an answer.

Complaints to the school council. Any complaints you have about matters concerning school courses or discipline and not just those about your own child could be taken to your parents' representative on the school council, (the school or education authority will be able to tell you who this is). You could also complain about an individual matter as well if the approach to the headteacher was unsatisfactory. Of course, school councils are not legally obliged to deal with your complaint, although the parents' representative is honour-bound, if nothing else, to see that it gets some attention. School councils are also restricted in what they can do by the education authority; their powers tend to be rather limited at present, although they can recommend a course of action to be taken by the school in dealing with your complaint.

Complaints to parent-teacher or parents' associations (PTA/PAs). Complaints of a non-personal kind, for example about shortage of school textbooks may be worth making to your PTA or PA, if your school has one. The PTA or PA may be able to put some pressure on the school or education authority to see what can be done. As it has no legal standing, however, the PTA/PA can only hope to influence those in charge of the school by appealing to their sense of goodwill and co-operation in attending to your complaint. It is unlikely that PTA/PAs groups will want to take up complaints on behalf of individual parents, and these will usually be referred to the appropriate official or member of school staff. However the kind of complaints which come up frequently such as the lack of playground supervision may be used by a PTA/PA to mount a campaign of its own. Complaints about policy matters can be drawn to the attention of national parents' organisations such as the Scottish Parent Teacher Council, which might be interested in bringing them to the attention of central or local government.

Complaints to the education authority Complaints which the school is unable or unwilling to deal with satisfactorily should be addressed to the director of education or divisional education officer for your area. This official can do a number of things:

refer the matter back to the school for further action or investigation.

arrange for your complaint to be brought before the education committee or one of its sub-committees.

get another official to look into your complaint and possibly discuss this with you.

refer you to another body, such as the school council, or to your local councillor or Member of Parliament.

take no further action. In this case you should insist on a proper explanation being given.

As the education authority may have to make enquiries of its own it may be some time before your letter is answered in any detail.

Complaints to elected representatives. You can write to or arrange to see your regional/islands councillor or local MP to take up a complaint about a school or education services in general. The best time to do this is probably after you have already complained to the school, school council or education authority without a satisfactory outcome. It may be worth checking on and reminding your elected representative of any election pledges made by his or her political party about education which relate to your complaint (ask for a copy of the party's election manifesto or policy statements on education). Your elected representative is not legally obliged to deal with your complaint, but it is likely that he or she may agree to:

follow it up by contacting the relevant officials or arranging for other enquiries to be carried out.

bring it to the attention of other elected representatives, including the chairman of the education committee, government ministers, and so on.

refer you to an individual or agency in a better position to deal with your complaint, such as an education authority official or citizens' advice bureau.

direct your complaint to the local Ombudsman if bad administration is suspected. (see below)

If your councillor or MP decides to do nothing, you could take your complaint to a higher level, for example by writing to the leader or spokesman on education from his or her local or national political party. You could also contact elected representatives from other political parties, who may be able to exert pressures of their own. Keep copies of all correspondence and be prepared to write to or see elected representatives more than once, repeating the details of the case.

Complaints to the Secretary of State. You can make a complaint to the Secretary of State if you think that an education authority has failed to carry out some legal duty. You can complain in writing to the Secretary of State yourself, giving a full account of your complaint and mentioning which part of the law you think is not being observed properly. You could also do this through your local MP or other representative. You should try to get advice before doing so.

The Secretary of State can conduct a local enquiry into your complaint, but does not have to. He must give the education authority the opportunity to reply to your complaint. If he is satisfied that the authority is at fault, he can order the authority to carry out its duty or take whatever measures he considers necessary. If the authority refuses to act within the time limit laid down, the Secretary of State or the Lord Advocate can refer the matter to the Court of Session to force the authority to carry out its legal duty. Even if the Secretary of State decides not to take any action, you may still be able to take legal action of your own in the Court of Session.

Complaints to the local Ombudsman. You can complain to the Local Ombudsman (Commissioner for Local Administration in Scotland) if you believe that you have been unjustly treated by the education authority as a result of bad administration. The Ombudsman will if necessary look into your complaint and issue a report saying whether or not there has been incompetence and if so what should be done. Although his recommendations are not legally binding, in the great majority of cases local authorities accept and act upon his findings. Maladministration may occur where:

a rule has been unfairly or inefficiently applied or where the rule itself has caused the problem and could be improved.

a procedure has not been correctly followed.

unreasonable delay or inefficiency has occurred in dealing with something.

misleading or incorrect advice or information has been given, whether verbally or in writing.

there has been a failure to keep somebody properly informed about a decision or proposal.

somebody has been treated with lack of proper consideration or respect.

The Ombudsman is not allowed to question a law or policy under which a decision or procedure was carried out, although he can report to parliament any changes in the law he thinks are needed to make administration more efficient. In education there are only a limited number of matters the Ombudsman is allowed to investigate. He cannot deal with complaints to do with what is taught, school discipline and rules and other matters connected with the internal running of the school. He can, however, take up complaints to do with the way the education authority has handled such matters as providing boarding accommodation, grants and other financial help, choice of school, information for parents, school meals, school closures and transport. In 1984-5, for example, the Ombudsman received 14 complaints to do with education, although none of these were subsequently accepted for formal investigation. Your complaint may normally only reach the Ombudsman through your district, islands or regional councillor.*

You should complain to the Ombudsman within 12 months of the matter in question, although you may still do so later than this in exceptional cases.

You must, however, have already made your complaint known to the local authority, which must also have been given a reasonable amount of time to investigate and reply to you. You must also have made sure that the matter cannot be dealt with by a body like a local appeal committee, court of law or the Secretary of State. Otherwise the Ombudsman cannot take up your complaint, except if he thinks it unreasonable to expect you to have done any of the above things.

The Ombudsman is free to decide whether or not to investigate a complaint and must let you know whether he proposes to do so. He must also give you reasons for a decision not to investigate. His investigations are carried out informally and in private. He will arrange for his staff to interview you, as well as local authority officials and anyone else concerned. He can ask for relevant documents, such as letters and reports, obtaining these through a court order if necessary. A friend, solicitor, or advice worker can represent you if you wish. Any out-of-pocket expenses or loss of earnings while attending interviews can be claimed.

It may take some time — possibly a few months — before the results of the Ombudsman's investigations are ready. The Ombudsman will then issue a report saying whether your complaint is justified and recommending what action, if any, should be taken by the local authority. You and the local authority must be given a chance to check any statements in the report before it is published. The Ombudsman

*In his 1984-5 report, the local Ombudsman remarked that it was "fundamentally wrong" that people should have to make a complaint through their local councillor, since many may be wary about doing so if the councillor is thought to have had some involvement in the matter complained about.

might recommend that a decision or procedure should be changed or that you should be compensated for any costs or inconvenience suffered as a result of bad administration. If the local authority refuses to act on his recommendations after a reasonable time — this does not happen very often — the Ombudsman can issue a second report, impressing on the authority what should be done, but the local authority still does not have to take any action.

A copy of the Ombudsman's report must be issued to you and copies must be available at the local authority's offices for any member of the public to look at. You cannot dispute anything in his report once it has been published, although there is nothing to stop you from criticising the Ombudsman's decision in public. You can get further advice and information about making a complaint in this way from the office of the Local Ombudsman at 5 Shandwick Place, Edinburgh EH2 4RS.

See also
ADVICE AND ASSISTANCE
INFORMATION FOR PARENTS
LEGAL ACTION
PARENT-TEACHER/PARENTS' ASSOCIATIONS
SCHOOL COUNCILS

Where to find out more
1868, s.91; 1973, c.65, s.211 and pt.II and
sch.5; 1980, c.44, s.70
Report of the Commissioner (Ombudsman) for
Local Administration in Scotland,
Commissioner for Local Administration in
Scotland, (current edition)
Which? Way to Complain, Consumers'
Association, 1983

Curriculum

What is taught at school

The law gives education authorities and schools discretion to decide what is taught and how children are taught. The only things which must be provided by law are:

    i.   religious education — but you have certain rights to withdraw your child from this.

    ii. Gaelic teaching in Gaelic-speaking areas — see under bilingual education.

    iii. adequate facilities for physical education, social and recreational activities.

The law otherwise uses very general terms when referring to what sort of education should be provided. It says that education must be "adequate and efficient" and that it must be according to the age, ability and aptitude of children benefiting from it. This would suggest that education authorities should provide education of an acceptable standard, but the law does not go into further detail. Although the curriculum is not laid down centrally, the authority probably is under some obligation to offer a broad curriculum. The authority and individual headteachers have considerable freedom to decide what courses should be available at particular schools. Schools are nevertheless expected to follow certain guiding principles recommended by the Secretary of State.

Primary education

In **primary** school (ages 5-12 approx), the curriculum normally consists of:

Language arts — reading, writing, discussion.

Mathematics — number work.

Expressive arts — art, craft, music, movement, drama.

Environmental studies — geography, history, nature study, science, and so on.

Physical education — including games and swimming.

Religious Education — including social and moral education.

73

Your child will usually be taught by one teacher most of the time but change teachers as he or she moves up the school. Special visiting teachers may provide extra tuition in things like learning to play a musical instrument. Teachers will usually work to some sort of timetable but with freedom to organise their own school day. Classes nearly always contain pupils of "mixed" abilities. They may be split up into smaller work groups within the classroom.

Secondary education

In **Secondary** school (ages 12-18 approx), subject areas normally covered include:

English — language and literature.

Mathematics — arithmetic, algebra, geometry, etc.

Expressive arts — art, drama, music, etc.

Science and technical subjects — biology, chemistry, physics, computing, home economics, engineering, etc.

Home economics — food and nutrition, health and hygiene, fabrics and fashion, consumer education.

Social subjects — geography, history, modern studies, social and vocational skills, with subjects like economics and business studies covered later on.

Languages — usually French and German but possibly Gaelic, Italian, Latin, Russian or Spanish as well later on.

Physical education — including games and sports.

Religious and moral education.

Your child is normally taught by different teachers for different subjects, often working to a school timetable divided into periods of at least 35-40 minutes, with longer periods for many activities. In the first two years, pupils will usually all take the same or very similar subjects, giving them a chance to find out what subjects they are good at and where their interests lie. From the end of the second year, your child will be allowed to choose different subjects within broad groups to study, keeping in mind the aim of achieving a balanced education. These will lead to national examinations (e.g. Scottish Certificate of Education) in most subjects by the end of the fourth year. Your child can stay on at school beyond leaving age (age 16 approx.) to take courses leading to further national examinations in the fifth and sixth years.

Information for parents

You are entitled to receive written information from the school giving you details of:

a statement of the school's educational aims.

the school's policies on what is taught and what courses are provided and

courses and subjects taught at the school for pupils in different age groups, including nursery classes.

subject options and choices available in secondary school and arrangements for consulting you and giving you guidance about these choices.

the out-of-school activities, such as clubs, societies, sports teams, and so on.

Details need not be given about the actual topics (syllabus) covered by particular subjects, but you may find that the school will put this information in its handbook or give it to you if you ask for it. If your child is preparing for a public examination, you can look at the topics covered in exam subjects in the syllabuses published by the examining body concerned. You should also be able to find out what is taught and how your child is taught at school by studying the school reports on your child's progress and any inspectors' reports published for your school.

Parental involvement

Parents have certain rights to see that their children are properly educated. The education authority must pay attention to the principle that children are to be educated according to your wishes, as long as the instruction you want is suitable for your child and unreasonable public expenditure is not involved. It may therefore be argued — in the absence of any court rulings on the matter — that you should have some say in what your child is taught at school.

Schools may in practice, involve you in what is taught by:

explaining to you what is taught, how and why, when discussing your child's progress with you.

holding parents' meetings to bring you up-to-date with new developments, such as Standard Grade exams.

consulting you and your child and offering guidance about choosing different subjects, usually before the third year of secondary school.

arranging for educational issues to be brought up at meetings of your school council, parent-teacher or parents' association.

encouraging you to take an interest in your child's schoolwork and perhaps arranging for you to see your child at work in class. Some schools may also encourage you to provide practical help, for example helping your child to learn to read. Secondary schools in some areas have now opened their doors to the whole community, allowing adults to learn alongside pupils in classes.

You have no clear rights to insist on certain subjects being taught (or not taught) to your child, except religious education. You can, however, complain to the school, school council, the education authority, your local MP, and so on, to see what can be done. In serious cases, you could make a complaint to the Secretary of State if you believe that the education authority is failing to provide proper education. You could also make another choice of school, or make private arrangements for your child to be given tuition in various subjects.

Curriculum Development

New approaches to teaching and learning and what is taught in school are always taking place through various curriculum development programmes supported by central and local government. The most notable of these are the "Primary Education Development Project", the "Standard Grade Programme" for 14-16 year olds and the "Action Plan" for those aged 16 and over (see the publications listed below for more details). New curricula for 10-14 year olds and for pupils staying on to do 'Highers' at 16+ are also under consideration. Various guidelines and reports on curricular matters are published by the Scottish Education Department (through bodies like the Consultative Committee on the Curriculum) and education authorities.

See also
BI-LINGUAL EDUCATION
COMPLAINTS
EXAMINATIONS AND ASSESSMENT
GUIDANCE
INFORMATION FOR PARENTS
INSPECTIONS AND INSPECTORS' REPORTS
PARENTS' RESPONSIBILITIES AND RIGHTS
RELIGIOUS EDUCATION AND OBSERVANCE
SCHOOL COUNCILS

Where to find out more
1980, c.44, ss.1, 28 and 30; C1090, C1093,
C1107 and C1112.

Scottish Education Department:

Primary Education in Scotland, HMSO 1965.
The Structure of the Curriculum in the third and fourth years of the Scottish Secondary School (the Munn report), HMSO, 1977.
Learning and Teaching in Primary 4 and Primary 7, HMSO, 1980.
Learning and Teaching in the First Two Years of the Scottish Secondary School, HMSO, 1986.
Primary Education in the Eighties: Consultative Committee on the Curriculum, 1983.
Education 10-14, in Scotland Consultative Committee on the Curriculum, 1986.

Scottish Information Office:

Scottish Education, Factsheet 15.
Consultative Committee on the Curriculum, Factsheet 21.
Scottish Secondary Education 'Standard' Grade, Factsheet 29.
The 16 + Development Programme, Factsheet 31.

Scottish Examination Board, *Scottish Certificate of Education Examination: conditions and arrangements* (current edition), Robert Gibson & Sons, Glasgow. This publication includes the syllabuses of SCE exam subjects.

Denominational schools

About one fifth of all pupils in Scotland go to schools associated with a religious denomination. These are nearly all Roman Catholic schools, managed by the education authority.* Although intended mainly for children from the denomination concerned, they are also open to children not belonging to the denomination; non-Catholic children may attend Roman Catholic schools, for example. Any church or other body, including non-Christian ones, acting on behalf of the parents of children belonging to it can ask the education authority to provide a denominational school. The authority is not obliged to provide schools for religious groups, however, and is only likely to do so if satisfied that there is enough demand for places at them. Nor need the authority provide your child with a place at such a school if this would lead to a significant increase in public expenditure, such as extending existing accommodation or, possibly, providing boarding accommodation.

How they are managed

Denominational schools have to be run according to nearly all the same legal requirements as other education authority schools, including those connected with the provision of religious education. But in addition, at these schools:

teachers appointed there, as well as being properly qualified, must have their religious beliefs and character approved by the church or body in whose interests the school is run.

the time set aside for religious education or services must not be any less than that which is customary for such a school. In Roman Catholic schools, this usually means not less than two hours a week.

the school must provide facilities for holding religious examinations.

an unpaid supervisor of religious instruction, such as a local priest, approved by the church or denomination, must report to the education authority on the efficiency of religious instruction provided. This supervisor is allowed to enter the school at any time set aside for religious instruction.

questions as to whether the school is properly observing these requirements may only be resolved by the Secretary of State and anyone may write to him about such matters.

*A very small number are Episcopalian schools, one is Jewish and another is Sikh.

The education authority is responsible for deciding what is taught in the school. At Roman Catholic schools, religious education is likely to be based on guidelines drawn up by the Catholic Education Commission for Scotland.

In all other respects, denominational schools are bound by the law on:

Admissions. Your child cannot be refused admission to a denominational school simply on the grounds that he or she does not belong to the appropriate church or body. These schools run by the education authority are open to all pupils from any or no denomination. Equally, children belonging to a particular church or group are not obliged to attend a school for that denomination. Roman Catholic children do not have to attend Roman Catholic schools, for example, although the Church may expect them to do so where these schools are available.

Religious education and observance. Whether you belong to the church or not, you are still entitled to withdraw your child from religious education and observance if you want to.

Information for parents. Denominational schools must provide you with the same range of information as other education authority schools, including details about their provision of religious education and observance and arrangements for withdrawing your child.

School councils. These must be provided for denominational schools in the same way as for other education authority schools.

School transport. Your child must be provided with free transport to school if offered a place at a denominational school beyond "statutory walking distance", but free transport need not be provided for children attending these schools as a result of parents making a choice of school.

Boarding accommodation. If your child is boarded away from home, he or she must be provided with opportunities for religious education and observance of the denomination belonged to, whether a denominational school is attended or not.

School closures and changes

Before it can close down or make certain other changes affecting denominational schools, the education authority must consult authorised representatives of the church or body concerned, as well as the individual parents of pupils affected (see also under school closures and other changes). The education authority must also ask for the Secretary of State's consent to any proposal which would result in any children not being able to receive education at a denominational school. Consent is, in addition, required where the Secretary of State, after receiving written representations from the Hierarchy of the Roman Catholic Church or other denominational body concerned, is satisfied that a proposal would result in significant reduction in the number of denominational places available compared with other education authority schools. This applies not only to school closures but also to:

the amalgamation and resiting of schools.

changes in school admissions arrangements, e.g. in ages or sexes of pupils admitted.

withdrawal of the special conditions under which denominational schools are managed by the education authority, as described above.

changing a denominational school into a non-denominational one.

The Hierarchy of the Catholic Church or other denomination concerned can only make written representations to the Secretary of State as to whether a serious loss in provision will result if it has already failed to reach agreement with the education authority about what should be done. The Secretary of State does not have to consider the views of individuals or members of the denomination about this, although he is likely to make additional enquiries of his own. In giving consent, the Secretary of State can lay down whatever conditions he thinks necessary for the religious education of pupils affected by the proposal. He may alter or withdraw these conditions at any time. The Secretary of State must take into consideration the education authority's own duties to provide religious education for these pupils and any views expressed by the Roman Catholic Hierarchy or other denominational body concerned. The Secretary of State must also decide whether or not a proposal is one which requires his consent and how the proposal, if he agrees with it, should be put into practice.

See also
ADMISSIONS
BOARDING ACCOMMODATION
INFORMATION FOR PARENTS
RELIGIOUS EDUCATION AND OBSERVANCE
SCHOOL CLOSURES AND CHANGES
SCHOOL COUNCILS
TRANSPORT

Where to find out more
1980, c.44, ss.8-10, 21 and 22, as amended by
1981, c.58, ss.6 and 7.

Discipline and punishment

Sparing the rod?

Schools are allowed to exercise a certain amount of control over the behaviour of pupils. Discipline may be used to promote:

good behaviour, conduct and habits among pupils.

the efficient and orderly running of the school.

certain standards of safety and welfare in the interests of pupils, school staff and others.

Mr JAMES 'FLOGGER' FINLAY HEADMASTER 1938 - 1965

When can discipline be used?

Schools may discipline pupils in order to:

care for children in the same way as a wise and sensible parent has to by law.

make sure that pupils are properly educated.

develop reasonable and responsible relationships among pupils, including a consideration for others, good manners and attitudes to work, initiative, self reliance and habits of personal hygiene and cleanliness.

There are limits to the circumstances in which punishment may be given however. Punishment must not:

be unreasonable or excessive, and it should not endanger the physical, or mental welfare of your child. It should result in the child knowing what is right and wrong.

be used simply because a child is unable to learn or perform well.

contradict any conditions or guidelines laid down by the education authority or whoever is in charge of school staff.

use methods involving unlawful treatment or discrimination (see also under children's rights, sex discrimination and racial discrimination).

interfere with any legal rights parents may have to do with the proper upbringing of their children.

An official code of practice encourages schools to create an atmosphere of "mutual respect towards adults and fellow pupils and responsible attitudes in their approach to discipline". This is done by schools making pupils feel secure there, providing courses relevant to pupils' needs, giving advice and involving pupils in school activities. Schools are also encouraged to discuss with parents any behaviour problems their children may be having.

What is the role of parents?

Parents are legally responsible for making sure that their children are properly cared for and educated. It may therefore be possible to argue that you have an interest in how your child is disciplined at school.

In providing education for your child, the education authority must have regard to your wishes. This could include paying attention to the way you want your child to be disciplined at school.

The education authority must issue written information for parents about its policies and practices on school discipline. Schools should include this information in their handbooks for parents.

What kind of punishment is allowed?

The law does not say what sorts of punishment may be given at school, but a number of court cases have established certain general principles. The punishment must take into account:

(i) how serious the offence is; minor offences should not be severely punished.

(ii) the extent to which the pupil is to blame.

(iii) the child's age, state of health and sex.

(iv) the duty of the authority to provide a proper school education.

How are children disciplined at school?

Actual practices vary from school to school, and even among individual teachers; but schools are likely to make use of all or most of the following punishments. Which ones are used depend on how serious the offence is and are subject to any official guidelines.

verbal reprimand by the class teacher or other members of staff.

additional or alternative schoolwork, done in or out of school time; "lines" may be given as long as they have some educational content or purpose.

loss or suspension of privileges like playtime, membership of school clubs or teams, joining in school outings or holidays, as long as no loss of school education is involved. Removal from positions of trust or responsibility such as prefects or monitors could also happen.

detention outside school hours, although it is very doubtful whether this can be done without your written permission (there have been no court rulings on this question). Your child should be given schoolwork to do during detention time, which normally lasts up to half an hour after pupils have been dismissed. Schools and education authorities may have rules or regulations of their own about how detentions should be conducted. The school must make reasonable arrangements for making sure children get home safely, taking into account their age and other relevant factors (e.g. disablement). Any free school transport home that children are entitled to must still be provided.

withdrawal from class or class activities to allow the education of other pupils to be carried on properly. Alternative arrangements must still be made for educating children withdrawn from ordinary class if they have not been lawfully excluded from school.

referral to the headteacher, guidance staff or an education authority official to decide what other action needs to be taken.

letter or report to parents, who may also be asked to visit the school for an interview or discussion.

exclusion from school — see the relevant section of this guide for further details.

Education authorities do not have to record details of any misconduct or punishment given. Any decision to exclude your child from school must be recorded, however, and it may be that your child's conduct will be mentioned in school reports and in references for employers or colleges.

With the possible exceptions of corporal punishment and detention, you have no rights of your own to insist on what sort of discipline or punishment should or should not be given to your child at school. But you should draw the school's or education authority's attention to any medical, social, emotional or other problems which may justify your child being excused from certain forms of punishment. The school must take notice of these and any failure to do so could be unlawful. Any special needs your child has must have already been taken into account before punishment is given.

Can corporal punishment be given?

Pupils at schools receiving public funds, including many independent schools, can no longer be given corporal punishment. In Scotland the traditional form of corporal punishment has been the "belt" or "tawse" Under a new law (expected to be passed by parliament at the time of writing) this is now made illegal in such schools. Corporal punishment has in fact been abolished by most education authorities in Scotland, and an earlier code of practice restricted its use. Unlawful corporal punishment covers any form of punishment involving physical assault on a pupil, except when the use of physical force is justified to stop pupils endangering or injuring themselves or others or causing damage. Even when physical force is justified, it must be reasonable force, not excessive or vindictive. Pupils cannot be refused admission to or excluded from school for refusal to accept corporal punishment.

Corporal punishment can still be given to pupils at independent schools which are not publicly funded in any way or to pupils who are being educated by other private means, for example by private tutors. But it is against the European Convention on Human Rights to give corporal punishment to children of parents who object to it. So that private schools which ignore parents' objections could still be breaking the law when giving corporal punishment or when refusing admission to or excluding pupils as a result of parents' objections.

What about pupils who make a nuisance of themselves?

Pupils who persistently disrupt classes may need special help for which ordinary school discipline may be inappropriate and possibly harmful. There are no set procedures for dealing with these pupils, but possible courses of action include:

referring children to school guidance teachers or education authority child guidance staff, doctors or social workers. The code of practice referred to above recommends early referral of children who frequently misbehave.

placing children in a special class or unit attached to the school or at another school to give them the attention and help they probably need so that they can eventually be returned to the ordinary class. A limited number of these units exist in Scotland, but an official report has recommended that they should become a regular feature of the school system.

referring children to the reporter of a children's hearing if child care and protection is thought to be necessary.

exclusion from school — but only if all other remedies have failed.

You should expect to be consulted about and become involved in all these decisions and it is likely that the school will make special efforts for this to be done. The school is legally entitled to transfer your child to another class or group of pupils but must continue to provide proper education. This means that your child cannot be moved down into a class doing less advanced work simply because of bad behaviour. Your child cannot be transferred to another school without the education authority first giving you the opportunity to ask for your own choice of school, when you can appeal against the authority's decision to transfer your child.

Can schools discipline pupils for misbehaviour outwith school hours?

Parents are responsible for the conduct and discipline of their children outside school hours, including lunchtimes if you have given permission for your child to be out of school then. Schools have, however, from time to time punished pupils for offences outside school hours, such as fighting or smoking on school buses, if it appears that they have broken the school rules or tarnished the school's good name in some way. In the absence of any Scottish court ruling on this question, the offence would probably have to be a serious one to justify punishment at school, as this could otherwise be unlawful.

When are the police brought in?

Schools are only likely to call in or report an incident to the police if they think that a child either has or is about to commit a criminal offence. The police are not likely to become involved with minor offences such as petty theft or damage done at school, as this will usually be dealt with by the school itself. The school may report an incident to the reporter of the children's hearing if a child is thought to be in need of child care and protection. The school should not normally involve the police or children's hearings without discussing this with parents first, except when urgent action has to be taken.

Assault and other offences?

If your child is assaulted or the victim of some other offence committed at school, whether by a member of staff, another pupil or a parent, you or your child are free to report the incident to the police or take legal action of your own. Assault might include not only physical injury but verbal abuse or threatening behaviour as well. Police or legal action would only be justified, however, if the assault or offence is a serious one or if the school or education authority had failed to take proper action of its own. The person concerned would not probably be guilty of assault or offence if:

(i) the injury, loss or damage was caused while he or she was acting in self-defence or defence of someone else, provided reasonable and not excessive force was used.

(ii) this was unintentional or happened accidentally. The person concerned would have to prove that his or her action was unintentional if you dispute this.

(iii) the action committed was lawful corporal punishment or necessary to enforce school discipline. You could take legal action against the school or member of staff for punishing your child for something he or she was not to blame for, except when the school can show that your child was genuinely mistaken for somebody else.

Your child is legally responsible for any injury or damage caused by his or her own deliberate wrongdoing or carelessness. This applies regardless of how old your child is, although in working out the degree of blame and how much compensation is payable, the court will consider the standard of conduct expected of children of similar age, intelligence and circumstances and not that of an ordinary adult. Parents are not automatically responsible for their child's actions but could be where any wrongdoing or carelessness was due to improper supervision on their part.

When parents and schools disagree

If you think that your child has been unfairly or wrongfully punished or you disagree with the school's policy or practice on discipline, you can:

    i.   make a complaint to the school, education authority or other body or person concerned, possibly including your school council if this deals with disciplinary matters as well.

    ii.   seek advice about whether you should take legal action.

    iii.   campaign with other parents or through your parents' group to get policies or practices changed.

See also

ADVICE AND ASSISTANCE
CHILDREN'S HEARINGS
CHILDREN'S EDUCATIONAL RIGHTS
CHOICE OF SCHOOL
COMPLAINTS
EXCLUSION FROM SCHOOL
GUIDANCE
INFORMATION FOR PARENTS
LEGAL ACTION
PARENT-TEACHER AND PARENTS' ASSOCIATIONS
RACIAL DISCRIMINATION
SEX DISCRIMINATION
SCHOOL COUNCILS
SCHOOL RULES
SPECIAL EDUCATIONAL NEEDS

Where to find out more
1980, c.44, ss.1, 28 and 30; 1981, c.58, s.1; SI
1975/1135; SI 1982/950; C1100; M 3/68.
Truancy and Indiscipline in Schools in Scotland
(the Pack report), Scottish Education
Department, HMSO, 1977.

Education authorities

What their duties are:

There are twelve education authorities in Scotland covering nine regional and three islands areas. Each has a legal duty to see that "adequate and efficient" school and further education is provided for its area. School education must be progressive and appropriate to the needs of pupils taking into account their age, ability and aptitude. This includes provision of compulsory education for children of school age (from age five up to age 16 approximately) and may, but need not, include provision of nursery schools and classes. With minor exceptions, school education must be provided free of charge.

Education authorities also have a duty to provide for school pupils adequate facilities for physical education and training and for social, cultural and other recreational activities, (e.g. sport and playing fields, outdoor centres and swimming pools); they may also provide these facilities for people not at school. The Secretary of State has power to make regulations which set standards and other conditions which education authorities must follow, such as regulations dealing with the day-to-day running of schools and school premises for example.

In particular, the education authority must:

allow parents to ask for a choice of school.

publish information for parents.

enforce attendance at school.

consult parents about school closures and certain other changes affecting their children.

arrange for parents to be represented on school councils.

provide the schools with adequate books, equipment and materials and maintain school buildings properly.

cater for any special educational needs which children may have.

keep progress records about each child at school.

offer boarding accommodation, clothing, grants and financial help, school meals and transport whenever children qualify for any of these.

safeguard children against sex or racial discrimination at school.

offer bilingual education in Gaelic-speaking areas.

ensure that children receive certain sorts of attention and proper safety and supervision while at school.

provide people over school age with further educational opportunities.

These and other topics are covered in detail in the relevant sections of the rest of this Guide.

Powers

Education authorities are only allowed to do things permitted by law. They can be taken to court and penalised for exceeding their powers, for example charging for school textbooks. In serious cases, such as unlawful use of public funds, the local authorities they come under can be taken over by special commissioners appointed by central government. Even so, the law gives education authorities very wide discretion to carry out various activities which are neither specified nor expressly forbidden by law, including matters to do with.

the curriculum (what is taught at school), examination and assessment of pupils, and the discipline of pupils.

teachers' conditions of service, subject to various national agreements.

school funding.

the running of school councils.

Education authorities, if they want to, may also provide:

nursery schools and other forms of pre-school education.

community and other education classes or activities for people no longer at school.

grants or assistance to community and voluntary organisations, including parents' groups whose aims or activities are educational, cultural or, recreational.

libraries and museums.

organised games, outings, and classes during school holidays or at other times.

Education authorities may also provide education in private homes, in hospitals, or in centres other than schools if they wish. Indeed they may be obliged to do so if children are prevented from attending school regularly due to illness, incapacity, or some other reasonable excuse.

Administration

Each authority must appoint its own:

(i) **Education committee** At least half the members of the committee must be regional or islands councillors belonging to the authority. The committee must also include at least two teachers employed by the authority and three people interested in the promotion of religious education.*

The education authority can, if it wants to, co-opt parents', pupils' or other representatives onto the committee. Committee meetings must be publicised in advance. You are entitled to attend meetings but not to take part in committee discussion unless specifically invited to do so. You can be ordered to leave when confidential agenda items are being discussed or for causing a public disturbance. The education authority can also appoint its own education sub-committees, to deal with specialist matters like school staffing, finance, school closures, etc.

(ii) **Director of Education** The education authority must appoint a Director of Education under whatever terms of service it thinks fit. The director, who is responsible to the authority, will usually head a number of education officers with special responsibilities. Larger authorities may be organised into territorial divisions headed by a divisional education officer. The authority usually appoints its own specialist advisers on the curriculum and other educational matters. It also employs child guidance specialists, school attendance staff, and organisers dealing with school meals, transport and so on. The authority is free to decide how schools will be staffed, subject to the requirements governing the size of classes.

(iii) **School councils** Education authorities must appoint school and college councils, to which they can delegate certain functions. Parents must be represented on these bodies.

Access to Information

All council, committee and sub-committee meetings must be open to the public and can only exclude the public when confidential and related matters, laid down by law, are being discussed. Copies of agenda and reports to be discussed in public at these meetings must be made available to you on request three clear days before the meeting. Minutes

---

*One of these must be a representative from the Church of Scotland, another must be from the Roman Catholic Church (except island authorities) and another from either of these churches or some other church or denomination (two such representatives in islands).

of meetings must also be made available for the public to see, together with any connected reports and background papers, except ones dealing with genuinely confidential matters, although you may be able to get a summary of minutes dealing with confidential items. For example, you should be entitled to see minutes, reports and background papers connected with educational expenditure or proposals to close down a school.

Complaints

If you think that the education authority is failing to carry out some duty or acting unlawfully, you can complain to the Ombudsman or Secretary of State. You can also take legal action of your own in the courts. Initially, though, you should complain directly to the authority or the school concerned before taking your complaint to a higher level. You should seek advice before making a complaint.

Where to find out more
1973, c.65, sch. 10; 1980, c 44, esp. ss. 1-2;
1985, c.43.

Employment of schoolchildren

Can schoolchildren take a job?

Children are not allowed to take up full-time employment until they have reached legal school leaving age (age 16 approx). Your child may be allowed, however, to take up a limited amount of part-time employment under conditions laid down either in local byelaws or government regulations. These conditions limit the hours and the amount and type of work children may do in the interests of their education, welfare, health or safety.

No child under 13 years of age may normally be employed at all, regardless of whether the work is paid or unpaid. Nor may any child who has not reached school leaving age work:

before 7 a.m. or after 7 p.m. *on any day*

for more than two hours on any *school day* or a *Sunday* (not more than one hour should be before school starting time)*.

during *school hours* or school lunch intervals.

You are responsible for making sure that your child arrives at school on time after doing an early morning job. You can also forbid your child to work during these hours if, for example, you believe this is interfering with his or her education, including homework.

Local byelaws may lay down special exceptions or restrictions concerning the employment of schoolchildren in your area; the education authority will be able to tell you what these are. Likely exceptions or restrictions could include:

allowing children of 10 and over but under 13 to be employed by their parents in light agricultural or horticultural work (e.g. fruit picking). At one time, children in farming areas were allowed up to a week off school in the autumn term to help with harvesting, but this practice was probably unlawful.

limiting Saturday or holiday work to four hours a day.

limiting work on milk delivery or newspaper rounds to one hour before school and one hour after school.

---

*These requirements, based on byelaws (under review) for Strathclyde, may be slightly different for other parts of Scotland.

The law and local byelaws forbid or restrict employment of children in certain industries and occupations, such as heavy manual work, window cleaning, etc. Contact you education offices for more details. You or employers can be required to give details at any time about employment your child is in, including hours worked — it is against the law to fail or refuse to do so or deliberately give wrong information. The education authority may allow your child to do certain work, for example in shops under 'licence', although this is not always necessary if you yourself are employing your child only at school holiday times. Compensation may be payable for any injuries or resulting from your child's employment.

Work experience

In their last year of compulsory schooling, that is in the 12 months up to legal school leaving age, children can be employed in work arranged or approved by the education authority as part of their education. Children are not paid for this work, but the education authority must meet the extra costs of any transport or meals. It is expected to make adequate arrangements for insurance cover against accident or injury, as employers' liability and industrial injury protection does not extend to pupils on work experience schemes, pupils not being under a contract of employment. In arranging work experience for your child, the education authority is expected to take into careful account the safety and type of work and how medically fit your child is. It should explain to the employer the educational purpose behind the work experience, the preparation that has been made for it at school, and the kinds of work activities pupils should take part in. You should expect to be given full details about the work your child will be doing, the hours and travel involved, and safety, health, insurance and other matters. You should expect the school to consult you before sending your child on a work experience course.

Public performances by children

Children who have not reached school leaving age can be allowed to take part in public performances or rehearsals (on the stage, television, films, etc) under a licence granted by the education authority. The licence covers any performances for which a charge is made, in licensed premises or clubs, or for use in a film, broadcast or other recording intended for the public. Detailed regulations lay down the conditions under which children can take part in public performances and rehearsals. A licence is not needed for children taking part in school or amateur performances.

Children over school age

Once school leaving age is reached, your child can take up full or part-time employment without waiting for any permission. This can be done even if your child is continuing with his or her education. Careers guidance must be provided for your child.

See also
LEAVING AGE

Where to find out more
1937, c.37, pt.III, as amended by 1963, c.37,
ss.37-39, and 1973, c.24; 1980, c.44, s.123; SI
1968/1728; C 95, C 895 and C 949.

Examinations and assessment

How is your child getting on at school?

Schools need to judge the progress which your child is making at school. This is called assessment. Assessing children can be a continuous process, with teachers recording progress in ordinary classwork. Children can also be assessed by sitting formal written, oral or practical exams although nowadays this does not normally happen until they have started secondary school. Exams may be run 'internally' by the school, or 'externally' by public examination or other outside bodies. Scotland has a separate public examination system from England and Wales, run by the *Scottish Examination Board*, although it is possible for children in Scotland to sit examinations of other bodies as well.

What is required by law?

Education authorities must:

keep a school record of the educational progress of each pupil every year and include in this the results of any psychological or diagnostic tests carried out.

give parents' written information about each school's arrangements for assessing pupils, although the law does not say what sorts of details should be given.

mention any opportunities you have for making a choice of course, including ones leading to examinations.

publish each year in the written information given to parents the results of Scottish Certificate of Education examinations taken by pupils at secondary schools (except special schools). Details must also be given about the school's policies for selecting pupils for public examinations. Results must be shown separately for each subject for the fourth, fifth and sixth years, with the number of pupils getting different grades being listed out of the total number of pupils in each year. The school does not have to say how many pupils sat each examination. The results of any other examinations taken (e.g. Certificate of Secondary Education, General Certificate of Education) may be published as well.

Schools may, but do not have to, enter any of this information on school reports issued to pupils and their parents. They may arrange for you (or you can ask) to meet staff to discuss your child's progress or examination results.

Is there any choice of exam subjects?

From about the end of the second year of secondary school, your child will usually be given the chance to decide which subjects he or she wants to study, with a view to taking exams in these subjects later on. Schools will usually insist that a minimum number of subjects are chosen from certain areas of the curriculum, including English and mathematics.

The choice of exam subjects or courses need not be granted, however, if this would result in:

your child receiving education unsuitable for his or her age, ability and aptitude.

unreasonable public expenditure, such as the employment of additional staff or provision of extra accommodation or facilities.

You have no legal right to insist on your child taking exams in any subjects, although you could, if you want to, arrange for your child to sit a public examination privately. You could make a complaint to the education authority if you think that your child has been prevented from taking an exam course without good reason. It is also possible for your child to be transferred from one exam course to another, depending on progress, or to switch to a different exam subject as your child develops new interests. Again, the decision will largely rest with the school after consulting you about the matter.

When are exams taken?

Though not under any legal duty to do so, nearly all secondary schools will enter pupils for school and public examinations. Education authorities and schools are left to decide on the timing of school exams, but the dates of external exams are normally fixed by the exam body concerned. Pupils may sit school exams sometime in their first two years of secondary education before deciding which subjects to specialise in later on.

What exams are taken in Scotland?

The main secondary school examination in Scotland is the Scottish Certificate of Education (SCE), which is offered in a wide range of subjects.

SCE exams can be taken at Ordinary Grade, usually from the end of the fourth year of secondary education, and at the Higher Grade, usually in the fifth and sixth years. From about the age of 16, short courses (called "modules") can be taken in a large number of technical, vocational and other special subjects leading to a National Certificate award by the Scottish Vocational Educational Council.

From 1986 a new Standard Grade exam is being introduced to replace the Ordinary Grade, which will continue to be in use, however, until the new exam has been properly established in different subjects. Unlike the Ordinary Grade, which was only meant for more academically able pupils, Standard Grade will cater for pupils of all abilities by offering courses of study at two or three overlapping levels in each subject. The new Standard Grade certificate will show your child's overall performance in the different courses taken. Performance in each course will be graded from 1 to 7, 1 being the highest level and 7 meaning "course completed". The certificate will also show how your child got on in particular aspects of each subject such as "talking", "reading", "writing" and "listening" in English. Resits are allowed. The publications listed at the end tell you more about the new exams.

The SCE Higher Grade exams (known as 'Highers') cover more advanced work, although it is possible for pupils of outstanding ability to sit Highers without having taken ordinary or standard grade exams. A certain number of Highers passes are needed to get into university and various professional courses. A Certificate of Sixth Year Studies gives pupils further opportunity to do more advanced work after sitting Highers.

It is possible for pupils in Scotland to take other secondary school exams besides the SCE. Some schools arrange for pupils to sit English exams, such as the General Certificate of Education and the Certificate of Secondary Education, which are now due to be replaced by a new Certificate of Secondary Education (GCSE).

How are SCE exams organised?

Education authorities are responsible for deciding how their own internal examinations are organised, but for SCE and other public examinations special conditions and arrangements are laid down by the examining body concerned. SCE exams take place in April and May each year, usually at the school your child is attending but possibly at another school or centre for more specialised subjects. Your child must normally have reached the fourth year of secondary school in order to sit the Standard or Ordinary Grade examination and the fifth year for the Higher Grade. A pupil may be allowed to sit an examination at an earlier stage of education, however, if he or she shows great promise. Your child can still sit SCE and other examinations after leaving school —

there is no upper age limit! — at a local college or through correspondence courses.

At SCE exams, candidates are supplied with essential writing equipment and materials. They are allowed to use their own calculators and coloured pencils for certain subjects but are not normally allowed to bring in other equipment or materials, including blotting paper. Non-native English speakers who have been living in the UK for less than a year before the exams may be allowed to use a dictionary in an exam, except when the subject of the exam is English or their own mother tongue.

Candidates are given 10 minutes to settle down before the exam starts. Late comers can be admitted to most exams, but in some cases only at certain points in the exam. They are not allowed to make up for lost time, regardless of the reason for their lateness. Candidates may not leave the room until at least half an hour after the beginning of the exam, except of course if they are taken ill or for some other exceptional cause. They can leave and return to the room only if accompanied. If they are found copying from somebody or using unauthorised books or notes, their examination in any or all subjects may after investigation be cancelled.

If your child is prevented from attending or finishing an exam owing to illness or other good reasons acceptable to the Scottish Examination Board, results may be based wholly or partly on ordinary school work instead, with supporting medical evidence where necessary. You should let the school know that your child will be unable to attend well beforehand if possible.

Special arrangements must be made for candidates with a disability which could handicap them in an examination, such as providing special reading, writing or listening aids and materials, with special provision for candidates with dyslexia (word blindness).

SCE results are posted to candidates and school at the end of July. An individual's results can also be shown to colleges, universities or employers asking to see them but not to anybody else.

Is there a chance to appeal?

It is possible to appeal against SCE exam results if your child has not done as well as expected. You cannot appeal to the exam board yourself, this has to be done by the school. Appeals must normally only be for pupils who were expected (and failed) to get a grade C in the Ordinary or Higher Grades (or Standard Grade equivalent).*

Appeals cannot be made for candidates who were absent from an exam, except when part of an exam was missed because of a clash of exam times. Appeals cannot be made for external candidates (i.e. sitting the exam privately).

The school or college must provide supporting evidence to back up its appeal such as examples of work done in the class or the pupil's place in the class "Order of Merit". Appeals may be submitted by 31 August following the exam, the outcome being announced by the end of September in time for candidates applying to college or university. Appeals can also be considered up to 1 October, with results announced a month later. If the appeal is successful, a revised examination certificate is issued to the candidate.

See also
COMPLAINTS
CURRICULUM (WHAT IS TAUGHT)
INFORMATION FOR PARENTS
SCHOOL RECORDS

Where to find out more
1980, c.44, s.28, 30, and 129; SIs 1975/1135
and 1982/950; C 758, C 1093 and C 1107.
Your Guide to the New Exams BBC Scotland
(free from Network, 74 Victoria Park
Crescent, Glasgow G12 9JN).
*Scottish Certificate of Education Examination:
conditions and arrangements,* Scottish
Examination Board, (published annually
and available from Robert Gibson and Sons,
17 Fitzroy Place, Glasgow G3 7SF).
The 16 + Development Programme, Factsheet
31, free from the Scottish Information Office.

---

*In 1986, because of the disruption in many schools during the teachers' pay dispute, appeals were also allowed for candidates who failed to get A or B grades.

Exclusion from school

When can your child be excluded from school?

The education authority is entitled to stop (or 'exclude') your child from attending school if in its view:

your child refuses to obey the school rules or accept school discipline or lawful punishment (or if you as parent have prevented your child from doing so).

your child's behaviour has had a serious effect on the order and discipline of the school or prevented other pupils from being properly educated.

Disciplinary reasons

Exclusion is most likely to happen if your child has caused serious disturbance at school. This should only happen after all other attempts to deal with your child have failed. But it could also arise as a result of:

your child committing a criminal offence at school

you preventing or discouraging your child from obeying some school rule or requirement which you disagree with or object to.

Your child will not normally be prevented from attending school for minor disobedience or breaking the school rules, such as not wearing school uniform. If at a school receiving public funds, including many independent schools, your child cannot be excluded for refusing corporal punishment, now that this is unlawful there. Even when this is not the case, a European court ruling suggests that exclusion is not justified if parents have made known their objection to corporal punishment.

Your child is not excused from being educated if he or she has been excluded for disciplinary reasons. You continue to be legally responsible for seeing that your child is educated and risk further action being taken against you for failure to do so. You must therefore decide whether you want to:

allow your child to obey the school's rules and discipline, or any conditions made in connection with your child being readmitted to school.

appeal against the decision to exclude your child from school (see below).

educate your child by other means, for example at an independent school or at home.

You should seek advice about the best course of action to take.

Medical and other reasons

Your child may also be prevented from going to school because he or she is considered to be too ill or puts at risk the health of other pupils. In this case, the child's condition could count as a reasonable excuse for non-attendance. The education authority must make suitable alternative educational arrangements elsewhere if necessary.

Children cannot be prevented from attending school for educational reasons, such as failure or inability to benefit from schooling or because they have special educational needs which can be catered for at school. The most the education authority can do is transfer your child to school more suited to your child's needs, but not without first giving you an opportunity to ask for your own choice of school.

What happens when your child is prevented from going to school?

The law does not lay down any set procedure which must be followed before a decision to exclude your child from school. But education authorities and schools are expected to take reasonable steps of their own to deal with a problem before it becomes necessary to take this course of action. Efforts should be made to warn you or your child that exclusion from school could result if your child continues to be disruptive, for example. It may not always be possible for the school to warn you in time, however, especially when the safety or welfare of others is immediately at risk. Once a decision to stop your child from attending school, has been made however, certain legal procedures must then be followed. You must be told, verbally or in writing, of a decision to exclude your child on the same day that the decision is made. You must also be given a time, date and place at which to discuss your child's exclusion with school or education authority staff. This date must be within seven days immediately following the date of the decision to exclude your child.

If your child has not been allowed to return to school within eight days of the decision to exclude, the authority must by that time have (in writing)

informed you of the reasons for its decision.

set out any conditions under which your child will be readmitted to school.

told you of your right of appeal against this decision and given you an address to write to.

given you any other information it thinks relevant, for example the name of somebody who can give you further advice.

The education authority may also do this as soon as a decision to exlude a child has been reached or at any time in the following eight days. There are no legal limits to the length of exclusion from school. Your child could be excluded for anything from a day upwards to several months or more. Actual practices vary between education authorities and schools, and you should write to your authority to find out what its practices are. The authority or school is entitled to use reasonable force or summon the police to prevent your child entering a school from which he or she has been excluded.

How to appeal against a decision

You can appeal against a decision to exclude your child from school at any time the decision is in force, but it is obviously in your child's interest to appeal as soon as possible. The appeal hearing should take place within 28 days of your appeal being received. The appeal committee must tell you whether your appeal has been successful within 14 days after the hearing, if you have not already been told at the end of the hearing. Appeal committee procedures are otherwise the same as for parents who want to choose a different school. While appealing, you are still under a legal obligation to see that your child is properly educated. You may be able to get round this difficulty while awaiting your appeal by for the time being:

arranging for your child to be readmitted to school if the education authority or school agrees to this.

getting your child admitted to another school.

educating your child privately at home.

Again, seek advice. Your appeal hearing can be called off or brought to a stop at any time you decide to agree to the education authority's conditions for letting your child go back to school. If your appeal is successful, your child must be readmitted to school immediately. The appeal committee may alter any of the conditions under which the authority will readmit your child. If your appeal is unsuccessful or you disagree with the conditions for your child's readmission, you have a further right of appeal to the sheriff. If it turns out that your child has been wrongfully excluded from school, you could ask the education authority to make up for the education your child has lost (e.g. by providing additional tuition), although it would appear that the education authority is not under any legal obligation to do so.

Removal from class

The school is entitled to keep your child out of the classroom in its everyday enforcement of discipline, but unless your child is excluded from school altogether, the school must make alternative arrangements to educate your child. This may be done by arranging for your child to work under supervision elsewhere until thought ready to rejoin normal class. If your child is denied education for too long, say for half a day or more, without being formally excluded, then this could amount to unlawful exclusion from school.

School records

Education authorities may include details of any decisions to exclude your child from school in their school records. You must be told as soon as possible whenever this has been done. The record must, in this case, also mention any appeal committee or sheriff court decisions. Although you are not legally entitled to inspect or amend the record itself, you must be told what information about your child's exclusion has been put there — this could be important if you decide to appeal.

Details from this part of the record may only be disclosed to people authorised by the education authority or the Secretary of State — this may not be done if you have appealed successfully against the exclusion of your child from school, however.*

Young persons

Once your child has reached school leaving age (approx. at age 16), the school or education authority will deal directly with your child without you as parent necessarily having to be informed or involved any longer in exclusion matters. You are still legally entitled to advise your child, however, and it may be possible for you to accompany or represent your child in discussions with staff or at appeals.

See also
ADMISSION TO SCHOOL
ADVICE AND ASSISTANCE
CHOICE OF SCHOOL
DISCIPLINE AND PUNISHMENT
HOME EDUCATION
INDEPENDENT SCHOOLS
LEAVING AGE
LEGAL ACTION
MEDICAL CARE
SCHOOL RECORDS
SCHOOL RULES
SPECIAL EDUCATIONAL NEEDS

Where to find out more
1980, c.44, s.35; 1981, c.58, ss.1-2 (28H); SI
1975/1135 as amended; C1087.

---

*Since the record is only for the use of people in charge of your child's education, information should not be disclosed to outsiders, such as the police or social workers, who have no educational grounds for wanting it.

Fees and charges

School education provided by the education authority must normally be free of charge. You cannot be charged for tuition and courses which are taught in the school or for things like books, materials and equipment or other articles which your child may need to take full advantage of school education. Fees and other payments may be charged, however, for:

school trips and special courses. Suitable alternative arrangements must be made by the school to educate your child if you cannot afford or refuse to send your children on a school trip or special course within school hours. The school may agree to waive or help with charges in needy cases. You could find out from your education authority or school whether you qualify for any financial help to allow your child to go on special study trips or courses.

additional tuition, provided that this is done out of school time and is not a substitute for ordinary lessons. You cannot, for example, be charged for being taught a musical instrument during ordinary music lessons; charges can only be made for tuition out of school hours. In practice, a lot of work may be done with pupils outside school hours free of charge (e.g. orchestra practice, sports coaching).

articles made in school lessons which pupils wish to keep, such as items of cookery or woodwork; but you cannot be charged for the materials used for for articles you do not want.

education other than school education. Charges can be made for further education classes and certain other kinds of education given after school leaving age, but education authorities are not allowed to charge for any nursery schooling they may provide.

social, cultural and recreational facilities, such as the use of youth and sports centres.

pupils from other areas. Education authorities can charge the "sending" education authorities concerned for any school places they offer to pupils of parents not ordinarily resident in their area. This could happen where the nearest suitable school for your child to attend belongs to another authority.

The education authority can arrange to pay for the cost of sending your child to an independent school or giving your child private tuition elsewhere. This could happen if the authority cannot provide suitable education at a school of its own. The education authority is entitled to charge fees at a limited number of schools of its own, as some authorities did up to the early 1970s, but only as long as this does not interfere with the adequate provision of free school education in its area.

You can complain or take legal action if you think that you have been wrongly charged for something to do with your child's school education. The Secretary of State and the courts have power to decide whether the education authority is entitled to charge for something.

See also
BOOKS, MATERIALS AND EQUIPMENT
CHOICE OF SCHOOL
COMPLAINTS
GRANTS AND FINANCIAL HELP
HOME EDUCATION
LEGAL ACTION
POST COMPULSORY EDUCATION

Where to find out more
1980, c.44, ss.3, 11, 14, 23, and 24, as
amended by 1981, c.58, sch.7 para.7.

Finance and funding

Who pays for children's education?

Public education is mostly paid for out of local rates and central government grants. The education authority is responsible for deciding how this money is spent on education, the largest item of local government expenditure. The education committee estimates how much needs to be spent in the forthcoming financial year (1 April to 31 March) before council approval is given. Most of the money goes on teachers' salaries, which are negotiated nationally, and interest payments, but some money also goes on school buildings, books and equipment and services like school transport. Independent schools get most of their income from tuition fees and other charges but may receive some public money through the Assisted Places scheme.

The school budget

Each school run by the education authority is given an annual sum of money (known as the capitation allowance) to spend on books, equipment and materials. This sum and the specific items it covers vary from one authority to another and may be higher for one type of school compared with another. In 1983-4, for example, money spent on books and equipment ranged from £6.40 to £19 per primary school pupil and from £9.66 to £35 per secondary school pupil among education authorities in Scotland. The headteacher of a school may be left to decide how to share out the money between different school departments and how much to spend on books compared with equipment and other materials. The education authority may, however, issue guidelines or directions of its own on how the allowance is to be spent within schools.

The school fund

The school fund is made up of voluntary contributions from parents and other well wishers, such as local firms, mainly to pay for additional items of school expenditure, such as extra equipment. The school fund should not normally be used to pay for books and materials which form an essential part of school education — these items must be paid for by the education authority in most cases. It is by no means clear, though, what sort of books, equipment or materials are essential. Education authorities which *depend* on voluntary contributions to pay for essential items are probably acting unlawfully, but not if they use this money to supplement public expenditure. The school fund may nonetheless be used to pay for essential items, say, to add to or replace existing stock.

The headteacher will usually decide what the money will be spent on, perhaps with the agreement of parents and staff concerned. Although you or other parents could insist on donations being spent on certain items only, the school need not accept these contributions where disagreements arise. The school is also free to accept gifts in kind. School funds are not taxable. Official permission is needed to carry out public collections or lotteries, but not if these are conducted privately among parents groups, for example, at school fund-raising events.

Leaving money to the school

You can bequeath in a will money or property to the education authority to administer on behalf of any school or other body you name. If it accepts your bequest the authority must honour your wishes and in such a way as to raise the standard of education or efficiency of the school(s) concerned. It may depart from the terms of your will if the Secretary of State agrees.

Money from other sources

Education can also be paid for out of educational endowments. These are donations of money or property mainly provided by private foundations and charities and used for charitable and other special purposes such as school scholarships, educational prizes, and school boarding accommodation. They are mainly used to finance independent schools but can be administered by education authorities as well; some date back hundreds of years. Details of these endowments must be kept in a register held by the Scottish Education Department and be open to public inspection. The law lays down in detail how educational endowments should be managed, but the Court of Session and education authorities have certain powers to reorganise or alter the terms of endowments which have outlived their original purpose, keeping in mind the spirit of the founder's intentions and the educational interests of those benefiting.

How can parents find out about what is spent on education?

Educational authorities and schools need not publish details of their expenditure when they give written information to parents but may agree to give you the details you ask for. You can find out about public spending on education by referring to:

documents published by the education authority giving estimates and breakdowns in expenditure (committee minutes, official reports). A code of practice recommends that local authorities should include in annual reports details of expenditure per pupil in nursery, primary and secondary schools, etc. You are normally entitled to see copies of reports and background papers dealt with by the education and other committees and sub-committees of your local council.

annual abstracts of accounts. Local authorities must publish these each year, allow you to take away your own copies (although you may be charged for them), and give you the opportunity to object to any item in the accounts. You may wish to object if you have good reason to believe that money has been unlawfully or negligently spent. You must send in written objections, with your reasons, to the auditor named in the accounts within 14 days of publication. Arrangements can also be made for your objections to be heard verbally. The Commission for Local Authority Accounts, a government appointed body, is responsible (through an official called the Controller of Audit) for drawing public attention to any unlawful expenditure or misuse of public funds by local authorities. After studying the Commission's report, the Secretary of State may order the local authority or the individuals concerned to put matters right, with any money wrongly spent being paid back into the relevant account.

financial statistics published by organisations like the Scottish branch of the Chartered Institute of Public Finance and Accountancy, whose annual *Rating Review* includes breakdowns of education authority spending per pupil and on school staffing, supplies, meals and milk, clothing grants, bursaries, boarding accommodation, transport, administration, and so on. The Educational Publishers' Council from time to time publishes information on school book and related expenditure. Answers to parliamentary questions on money spent on education can be found in reports like *Hansard*.

See also
ASSISTED PLACES
BOOKS, MATERIALS AND EQUIPMENT
INDEPENDENT SCHOOLS
INFORMATION FOR PARENTS
PARENT-TEACHER AND PARENTS' ASSOCIATIONS
TRANSPORT

Where to find out more

1973, c.65, Part VII, as amended by 1975, c.30; 1981, c.23 and 1982, c.43; 1980, c.44, ss.73-81 and 104-122, as amended by 1981, c.58, ss.5, 14, 15 and sch. 4-6; 1985, c.43 (whole act).
Rating Review (published annually), Chartered Institute for Public Finance and Accountancy, Scottish branch.
Annual Report Commission for Local Authority Accounts,

Schoolbook Spending in Scotland Educational Publishers' Council, (current edition).
Local Government Finance in Scotland, Scottish Office, Cmnd.6811, HMSO, 1977.
Publication of Financial and Other Information by Local Authorities: a code of practice for Scotland, Scottish Office Finance Division, HMSO, 1982.

Grants and financial help

Financial help with education

Depending on your income you or your child may be entitled to a bursary, grant or other assistance to cover all or part of the cost of:

taking part in certain school activities, or attending a fee-paying school — see under assistance with school education below.

attending part-time education classes after school leaving age — see under part-time bursaries, etc., below.

maintenance while staying on at school beyond school leaving age — see under higher school bursaries below.

attending full-time further education courses — see under further education bursaries below.

attending university or college — see under student allowances below.

Bursaries and grants are provided on condition that your child regularly attends the courses they cover and shows satisfactory conduct and progress. The bursary or grant should normally be paid to your child directly if 16 or over. Since your level of income may limit the amount given, you may be expected to contribute towards your child's maintenance costs and it is obviously in your child's best interests that you do so.* Education authorities must publish written information for parents on their general policies or practices for providing bursaries or maintenance allowances for school pupils.

Assistance with school education. The education authority can award grants, allowances or other payments to enable children to take full part, in various school activities without causing financial hardship to themselves or their parents. This could include assistance towards the cost of:

study trips, fieldwork and other special courses within or outside school hours.

educational visits abroad or elsewhere, for example, to learn a foreign language — but *not* school holiday trips.

---

*The National Union of Students in Scotland estimates that in 40 per cent of cases, parents fail to pay their proper contribution.

purchase of materials and equipment, such as musical instruments, which do not form an essential part of a school course.

The education authority can also pay for all or part of the cost of sending children to fee-paying schools; this is only likely to arise where the authority cannot provide suitable education in one of its own schools.

The education authority has complete discretion in most cases to decide how much financial help will be given. Help is only likely to be given if you are on a very low income or dependent on welfare benefits. It may be worth writing to the education authority to find out what sort of help is available.

Part-time bursaries, etc. The education authority can award bursaries, grants, scholarships or other assistance to allow anyone over school age to take advantage of part-time education at colleges or elsewhere, within or outside Scotland. This could include help towards the cost of:

part-time attendance at a further education or other college after school leaving age.

adult, community education, evening and other classes, whether run by the education authority or some other body.

correspondence courses, including Open University courses.

weekend, residential or other short courses, including ones abroad.

It is by no means clear how widespread this assistance is or what sort of part-time courses are covered. Your child probably has a better chance of getting assistance towards part-time education, however, if:

you or your child are on a very low income or dependent on welfare benefits.

the course leads to a qualification leading to a career and is not already being paid for by an employer or some other body.

your child is likely to benefit from or complete the course.

Education authorities are free to decide whether to offer part-time bursaries and how much assistance to give, but they are officially encouraged to be generous in dealing with applications. To be regarded as part-time, the course should not normally involve more than 21 hours of classes a week and last more than 30 weeks.

Higher school bursaries

Your child may be able to claim a bursary to cover his or her maintenance costs while attending school beyond school leaving age. Bursaries are also payable to pupils attending special schools, fee-paying schools and schools in other local authority areas beyond school leaving age. The education authority has discretion whether or not to award a bursary, but if it does so, payment must be based on a sliding scale laid down (and revised annually) in government regulations. The amount depends on length of course and the parent's income. In 1985-6, for example, the maximum annual amount payable was £565 for pupils of parents with incomes of £4060 and under, falling to "nil" for incomes of £5911 and over. Income includes the income of both parents, less allowances for any other dependents, mortgage interest, superannuation, life insurance and other payments currently qualifying for tax relief. Only half the bursary is payable if your child is in free boarding accommodation.

Further education bursaries. Your child may be able to claim a bursary to attend a full-time course* at a college of further education after leaving school. As with higher school bursaries, the education authority can decide whether or not to award a bursary, but if it does so, the amount must be in accordance with a scale laid down by government regulations and revised from year to year. There are two types of further education bursary: "category A" bursaries for students under 18 and "category B" bursaries for students aged 18 or over, with higher amounts payable for the latter. Additional allowances are also payable to students over 26.

tuition, examination and other course fees.

the purchase of books, equipment, materials, special clothing and other necessary items.

student union and other membership fees considered necessary for taking part in student life.

necessary travel expenses.

Weekly maintenance costs during term-time. In 1985-86, for example, the allowance for students living with their parents during term-time was £14.15 per week (for students under age 18) and £19.76 (for students over age 18). For those living in lodgings during term-time because the parental home was outwith daily travelling distance of college, the weekly rate was £32.56 (for students under and over age 18). "Home" students whose parents are on low incomes may also be

---

*Full-time courses are normally regarded as ones taking up at least 21 hours a week over 30 weeks a year.

entitled to the £32.56 rate. Where the student lives in a college hostel during term-time, the hostel rate is paid.

personal expenses (£10.61 a week in 1985-6) and **Christmas and Easter vacation expenses** (£26.35 a week in 1985-6) for students aged 18 and over. Term time and holiday earnings are disregarded.

maintenance of any dependents of the bursary holder. The education authority in this case is left to decide on the amount which is reasonable to pay, taking into account any income of dependents.

The education authority is entitled to deduct a "parental contribution" from the bursary according to a sliding scale of income (revised each year), taking into account the age and number of any dependent children and any mortgage, superannuation, and other payments currently qualifying for tax relief. The parental contribution scale for students under age 18 is different from that for those aged 18 and over. For example, in 1985-86 for students under 18, a deduction in grant of £15 is made for each £50 that net parent income is over £4,061. For students over age 18, variable deductions in grant of at least £20 are made for parental income over £8,100.

Student allowances ("grants")

Student allowances are payable by the Scottish Education Department (SED) to most people accepted for full-time degree, teacher training, and certain other comparable advanced (e.g. Higher National Diploma) courses at universities and colleges anywhere in the British Isles. Grants cannot be claimed from the SED for part-time degree courses, including Open University ones, or by students who already have a degree or its equivalent. The grant covers student maintenance (in 1985-6 this was £1365 for students living with their parents during term time, £1775 for those living away from home and £2210 for those studying in London). Extra allowances are payable to students whose courses last longer than 30 weeks a year, who have dependents to look after, who are disabled or who are aged 26 and over. A "parental contribution", based on a sliding scale of income, is deductable from the maximum grant payable. For married students, this contribution may be deducted from the spouse's income instead. Parental contributions are not deducted, however, for students aged 25 and over who have been self-supporting for at least three years. No deductions are made for students' term time and vacation earnings. Tuition fees are automatically paid by the Scottish Education Department to the institution attended, irrespective of parental income.

Students who have been ordinarily resident in Scotland up to the time their course starts may claim their grant from the awards branch of the

Scottish Education Department, whose *Guide to Student Allowances*, published annually, gives details about how and when to apply. Students coming from England and Wales must apply to their own local education authority for a grant. Students doing higher degree courses should ask the University or College concerned about whom to apply to for a post-graduate award.

Welfare benefits*

You continue to be entitled to claim child benefit for your child if he or she is still under 19 and in full-time school or further education. But this is not payable if your child is already on a bursary, claiming supplementary benefit/income support, being sponsored on a course by an employer or the Manpower Services Commission, or doing courses above Higher National Certificate level or equivalent. Any holiday earnings of your child, if above school age, may also result in child benefit not being paid while he or she is working.

If your child is not employed, he or she may be entitled to supplementary benefit/income support from the end of the school holiday following school leaving age. Benefit can still be claimed while your child is doing a part-time course, and during summer vacations for *all* courses. For non-advanced part-time courses, for benefit to be payable the classes must not total more than 12 hours a week (school leavers under 18) or 21 hours a week (18 and over).

For advanced part-time courses, the allowable hours of classes are less clear and are left to a local supplementary benefit "adjudication officer" to decide on. In either case, your child must have been receiving benefit for at least three months previously or have been on a Youth Training scheme. The benefit covers maintenance only and not course fees or purchase of books, etc. Most education authorities in fact waive fees for people on supplementary benefit. Your child is regarded as being available for employment while on supplementary benefit, and benefit may be stopped altogether if your child turns down a reasonable offer of a job.

Other financial help

Your child may be able to apply for a bursary or scholarship awarded by a school or college, to which you should write for details. Students who cannot get a bursary or grant may be able to get help from one of a

*At the time the Guide was being prepared, a number of proposed changes to the social security system were being considered by parliament, so you should check with your local DHSS office or advice centre about what welfare benefits can be claimed by full or part-time students.

number of educational trusts. For further information about these, write to the Scottish Education Department at Haymarket House, Clifton Terrace, Edinburgh EH12 5DT.

See also
BOARDING ACCOMMODATION
FEES AND CHARGES
INFORMATION FOR PARENTS
LEAVING AGE
POST-COMPULSORY EDUCATION

Where to find out more
1980, c.44, ss.49-50, 73-74; SI 1986/1227.
Guide to Students' Allowances (published annually), Scottish Education Department (Awards branch), Haymarket House, Clifton Terrace, Edinburgh EH12 5DT
Social Security, School Leavers and Students: what you pay and what you get (leaflet NP12), *Going to College or University: a pocket guide to social security* (leaflet FB23), obtainable from local DHSS offices, advice and information centres and many post offices.

Guidance

When guidance is needed

Children will from time to time need guidance from school or other staff in connection with:

their studies and which courses or subjects to choose.

any personal problems they may be having at school.

choosing a career or deciding what to do after leaving school.

Education authorities must issue written information for parents about their provision of curricular, personal and careers guidance at each of their secondary schools. Specialist staff are appointed at secondary schools to provide guidance. In primary schools the headteacher or other senior staff may be able to offer guidance as well. You should expect your child to receive guidance at any time it is asked for.

Educational guidance

Education authorities are not under any legal duty to provide guidance about what education is available, but most secondary schools will make some arrangements to advise and consult parents and children about decisions to do with:

what subjects to specialise in, mainly after the end of the second year.

what public examinations to sit.

educational opportunities after school leaving age.

Many secondary schools publish their own booklets on subject choice and most will invite you to interviews or parents evenings to discuss choices available. You should expect your child's past performance, interests, and wishes to be taken into proper consideration before any decisions are reached.

Personal guidance

Children should be given personal guidance to help them cope with any problems they are having, including ones to do with:

settling in when starting school or moving to secondary school.

discipline and punishment.

study problems, for example poor concentration.

trouble with fellow pupils, such as bullying and victimisation.

The school in certain cases may call in or refer your child to outside sources of specialist help, such as the child guidance service, doctor, social worker, or educational welfare officer. You should expect the school to involve you at the earliest opportunity in personal problems your child is having. Many secondary schools now also provide social education courses to help children deal with everyday problems and handle personal relationships.

Child guidance

The education authority must provide its own child guidance service, staffed by educational and child psychologists, trained to deal with any behavioural or learning difficulties. Child guidance staff have special responsibility for attending to any special educational needs your child might have, but they may also become involved if your child is having discipline or other problems in class. Your child may be referred to guidance staff by the school for clinical observation and assessment and you yourself can also ask for an assessment. Reasonable requests may not be turned down. You may or may not be allowed to be present while your child is being psychologically examined.

Careers guidance

Careers advice and information must be given to children before leaving school or further education to help them to choose a suitable career. This must take into account your child's capabilities and the training needed for particular career. Careers advice may continue to be given once your child has left school or further education, although it need not be given to people attending part-time evening classes only. It is against the law to give careers advice which results in racial or sex discrimination — such as discouraging a boy or girl from taking up certain occupations traditionally associated with the opposite sex. Records of vocational advice must be kept for your child.*

Education authorities must appoint their own careers officers to take charge of careers services. They are free to make their own detailed arrangements about how careers services are organised, but they must follow any guidance the Secretary of State may give. Arrangements will usually be made at your child's secondary school or college to:

> invite you and your child to a meeting or interview to discuss careers opportunities with careers officers and school guidance staff.

---

*Part of the law which would have entitled school leavers to a written summary of these has not been brought into force.

to provide careers literature in the school or college library. Schools may also provide their own booklets about making a choice of career.

visit places of employment or invite guest speakers from these places.

Schools may also run careers education, social education and other courses to prepare your child for selecting, obtaining, and settling down in a career or job. Your child may be given the chance to go on a "work experience" course before leaving school.

See also
EXAMINATIONS AND ASSESSMENTS
DISCIPLINE AND PUNISHMENT
INFORMATION FOR PARENTS
POST-COMPULSORY EDUCATION
RACIAL DISCRIMINATION
SEX DISCRIMINATION
SPECIAL EDUCATIONAL NEEDS

Where to find out more
1980, c.44, ss.4, 28, and 126-8; SI 1982/950.
More than Feelings of Concern: guidance and Scottish secondary schools, Consultative Committee on the Curriculum, 1986.

Holidays

Schools must normally stay open for 200 "school days" (excluding Saturdays and Sundays) in the school year. In Scotland, the school year normally runs from mid-August to late June or early July in the following year, with holiday breaks in the autumn and around Christmas and Easter, plus various "local" and "bank" holidays. School opening, closing and holiday dates are fixed by the education authority, and these must be set out in the written information for parents which the authority issues. Different holiday arrangements may exist for different areas or schools within the same authority. Authorities may allow school councils to fix holiday dates as well. The general pattern, however, is for the school year to be arranged as follows:

Autumn term	Mid-August to mid-October	9 weeks
Autumn holiday	*Mid-October*	*1 week*
Winter term	Mid-October to late December	9 weeks
Christmas holiday	*Late December to early January*	*2 weeks*
Spring term	Early January to late March	11/12 weeks
Easter holiday	*Late March to early April*	*2 weeks*
Summer term	Early April to late June	9/10 weeks
Summer holiday	*Late June to mid-August*	*6/7 weeks*

Education authorities are free to alter the dates of the school session and holidays at any time, but a government circular advises them to consult parents, employers and school staff before deciding whether to do so. This should include giving parents reasonable opportunity to express their views through meetings at schools. Independent schools are responsible for fixing their own opening and closing dates and are not bound to stay open for 200 school days and can also open on Saturdays if they want to.

For certain reasons schools may stay open for fewer than 200 days a year, for example, as a result of industrial action, fire damage, or other circumstances beyond the school's control. The Secretary of State may also approve a reduction in the number of school days to allow teachers to do special training.

As a parent, you have a legal duty to see that your child goes to school regularly, except when there is a reasonable excuse such as illness or if the education authority has agreed to alternative arrangements for the education of your child. There may be occasions, however, when you wish or need to take your child on holiday or away from school during term time. You should check the school's holiday dates before doing so. You should write to the headteacher for permission to do this and give reasons for your request. All such requests should normally be granted if the school (or the education authority, in the last resort) thinks they are reasonable ones, such as going away at times which are more convenient for employers, other relatives, etc. Normally requests for up to two weeks holiday will be granted automatically. Requests for holidays observed by the religious body you belong to should normally be granted as well. You will need to get special permission from the education authority to take longer holidays or leave of absence, otherwise action could be taken against you if your child does not go to school.

See also
ATTENDANCE
INDEPENDENT SCHOOLS
SCHOOL COUNCILS

Where to find out more
SI 1975/1135; SI 1982/950, sch.1 (pt.II); C879.

Home education

Education of your child at home

As parent you are legally responsible for seeing that your child is properly educated once he or she has reached school age (age 5 approx.). You normally do this by sending your child to school regularly but you need not do this at all — you can make arrangements for your child to be educated at home or elsewhere instead. You may want your child to be educated at home because:

your child may have medical problems or other difficulties which prevent regular attendance at school — the education authority may in certain cases agree to provide home tuition of its own, on a temporary or permanent basis.

you regard the nearest school as not suitable enough, too difficult to reach or as involving your child living away from home.

you prefer your child not to be educated at school at all — perhaps because of your philosophical or religious convictions.

If your child has not actually started school you do not need education authority permission for your child to be educated at home. Children who are already attending school can still be withdrawn at any time. The authority may not refuse permission without good reason. You do risk being served with a school attendance order, however, if you fail to satisfy the education authority that you are in fact providing your child with a proper education at home. The law says that the education provided must be efficient, although it does not say what this means other than that it should be education according to your child's age, ability and aptitude. The education authority is likely to be convinced that proper education is being provided if your child is following a suitable course of study, taking into account any special educational needs your child might have. It is therefore in the best interests of all concerned if you explain to the education authority how you propose to educate your child at home.

Once your child has started to be educated at home the authority can:

allow this to continue if satisfied that your child is receiving a proper education. The education authority may from time to time arrange for officials or specialist advisers to visit your home to see what sort of education is being provided, keeping this under continual review. You may be asked to produce examples of your child's work and your child may be interviewed. It is probably in your child's best interest to be as co-operative as possible. The education authority may wish to suggest certain improvements or modifications which should be made.

You do not have to have a teaching qualification to educate your child yourself. You can also get other people to educate your child, although you continue to be responsible for the education provided.

allow you to provide education at home only if certain requirements are met. The education authority may, for example, insist on a suitable course of study being provided for your child or certain educational methods being used before they are satisfied that your child is being adequately educated. You do not have to accept these requirements but you could face school attendance order proceedings if you fail or refuse to meet them.

order you to send your child to school. To do this, the education authority must serve you with a school attendance order, naming the school your child should go to. You must be given an opportunity to state your views before the attendance order is served. You can appeal against the attendance order to the sheriff court.

In reaching any decision, the education authority must pay attention to the general principle that children are to be educated according to their parents' wishes so long as suitable education is provided and unreasonable public expense is avoided.

For further advice and assistance, you should contact *Education Otherwise*, a voluntary organisation of parents, which may be able to put you in touch with other parents arranging for their children to be educated at home. The Advisory Centre for Education also publishes an *Alternative Schools Action Pack* for parents and other groups who wish to set up schools of their own.

See also
ATTENDANCE
CURRICULUM (WHAT IS TAUGHT)
SPECIAL EDUCATIONAL NEEDS

Where to find out more
1980, c.44, ss.1, 28, 30 and 35-44.
Schooling is not Compulsory: a guide to your rights, Education Otherwise, 1983 (mainly about the legal position in England and Wales, but most of the advice given is applicable to Scotland as well).

Homework

Homework can help children to get used to working on their own without formal supervision, to revise or catch up with work done at school, or to prepare for forthcoming lessons. Schools are not, however, under any legal obligation to give homework to your child, even if you ask for homework to be given. They must, however, publish information for parents about their policies on homework. Schools cannot force your child to do homework except possibly by making the proper completion of homework a school rule.

In practice, nearly all secondary schools and many primary schools will have some arrangements for giving your child homework, either as a matter of policy or if you ask for homework to be given. Schools are free to decide on the amount of homework given, but you would be entitled to object to your child not getting enough homework or getting too much in relation to his or her age and ability. The school should be able to tell you how many hours of homework a week your child should expect,

which school subjects and activities it is given for, and the amount of time (in days) allowed for handing homework in.

You can help and enourage your child to do homework by:

providing space to study and freedom from distractions such as television while homework is done.

checking that homework is properly completed and handed in on time — you may be asked to sign a homework completion book or slip provided by the school.

making sure that homework jotters, school books, etc are kept in a safe place.

dealing with any study difficulties your child is having and drawing these to the attention of the school if necessary.

discussing the homework with your child, praising him or her for work which appears to have been well done (your support should not, however, extend to providing your child with answers or doing the homework yourself!).

If you object to homework which is given or your child has not completed some homework, your best course of action is to write to or visit the school and explain why. The school may persuade you it is in your child's interests to do the work, alternatively it may agree to give your child a reduced amount of homework or none at all. You should draw the school's attention to any medical, social or other problem your child may be having which prevent homework being done properly. You can also object to particular sorts of homework your child is asked to do; the school may then arrange for your child to do something different to fit in with your religious, philosophical or other beliefs.

See also
DISCIPLINE AND PUNISHMENT
EXCLUSION FROM SCHOOL
INFORMATION FOR PARENTS
SCHOOL RULES

Where to find out more
1980, c.44, s.28; SI 1975/1135 and 1982/950.

Independent schools

How parents can send children to independent schools

Any parent is entitled to seek a place at an independent (or private) school for his or her child. You do not have to send your child to a school run by the education authority if you can satisfy the authority that you have made adequate alternative arrangements of your own for your child's education. You simply write to the independent school of your choice asking for an application form and information about the school and fees charged. Your child will probably have to attend an interview and may have to sit a school entrance examination or test before being offered a place. A number of independent secondary schools make use of the Common Entrance Examination at 13+ for children coming from preparatory schools or departments catering for 8-13 year olds.

If the school is a secondary school and your family income is below a certain level, your child may qualify for an Assisted Place. You should also ask if the school offers any bursaries or grants of its own. Schools will be able to advise you about any easy payment arrangements, capital transfer tax and insurance prepayment schemes. You can find out more about independent schools in Scotland, including fees charged, from a free booklet issued by the Independent Schools Information Service (Scotland).

Organisation and courses taught

Independent schools vary greatly in their character, and size and in the range of pupils admitted. Some are different in their educational approach from others or have special interests like creative arts. Some provide schooling from age 5 right through to school leaving age and beyond. Some take in boys or girls only, and some are mainly for boarders. A number cater for children with special educational needs, such as physically disabled or mentally handicapped children. Others cater specially for children with special abilities and aptitudes, for example in dance, drama and music. Most independent schools will offer a very similar range of courses and subjects as educational authority schools and enter pupils for the same public examinations, such as the Scottish Certificate of Education. Classes may be smaller than in education authority schools, however.

Registration of independent schools

It is possible for any person, group of persons or organisation, including parents and parents organisations to set up a school.* Any school, apart from an education authority school, which offers full-time education for five or more children of school age must be registered as an independent school. This must be done within one month of the school being set up. The school will be given provisional registration until inspected, after which it may be given full registration. The register, kept by the Scottish Education Department, may be seen by any member of the public. It gives the name, address, and proprietor of the school. The registrar must be notified of any changes in these and certain other particulars. Anyone found running an independent school which is not registered faces a fine of up to £500 or 3 months' imprisonment. Notes of guidance on how to register a school are obtainable from the Scottish Education Department.

Inspections

Independent schools like education authority ones are open to inspections at any time. Inspectors have to be satisfied that:

efficient and suitable education is being provided for pupils there, taking account of their ages and sex.

the school is owned and staffed by "suitable" persons.

the school's premises are suitable and accommodation adequate, taking account of the ages and sex of pupils there.

Failure to meet these requirements could result in removal of the school from the register.

Complaints

You may at any time make a complaint to the Secretary of State about an independent school. You may want to do this if, for example, you think the school is being badly managed. Get advice before doing so. If he accepts your complaint, the Secretary of State must give the school at least six months to put matters right or face removal from the register. The person(s) running the school are entitled to refer any complaints taken up by the Secretary of State to an Independent Schools Tribunal.

The Tribunal can, if it upholds the complaint,

order that the school be struck off the register.

---

*The law regards a school as any institution (including a privately-run one) which offers nursery, primary or secondary education.

give the school a certain date to put matters right (to the satisfaction of the Secretary of State).

disqualify the person(s) complained about from running or teaching in any private school.

disqualify the premises from being used as a school.

Special rules lay down the proceedings at tribunals.

See also
ADVICE AND ASSISTANCE
ASSISTED PLACES
GRANTS AND FINANCIAL HELP
INSPECTIONS AND INSPECTORS' REPORTS
SPECIAL ABILITIES AND APTITUDES
SPECIAL EDUCATIONAL NEEDS

Where to find out more
1980, c.44, ss.98-103, as amended by 1981, c.58, ss.9-11; SIs 1957/1058, 1975/1412, 1977/1261.
Which School (current edition), Independent Schools Information Service, Scotland.
Alternative Schools Information Pack, Advisory Centre for Education (for parents and voluntary groups wishing to set up their own school).

Information for parents

Getting to know about the school

As a parent you are entitled to receive written information about any school which is run by an education authority, whenever you ask for it or are offered a place at a school.* The type of information you are entitled to receive is laid down by regulations and falls into three broad kinds: "basic information", "school information", and "supplementary information".

Basic information, intended mainly for parents thinking of choosing an alternative school for their child other than the one normally serving their area. This must include information about how the education authority goes about:

offering school places to pupils, including priorities for the admission of pupils to schools at which there are more requests for places than places available.

arranging for the admission of pupils who have not reached school age, including details of school starting arrangements.

providing school meals, transport, and boarding accommodation, including provisions for pupils living in exceptional circumstances or attending schools which the parents have chosen.

For each school the basic information must cover its name, address, telephone number, approximate roll, stage(s) of education provided, denomination (if any) and the sex(es) of pupils admitted.

The information must also include addresses and telephone numbers of education and divisional education offices and contact points for parents who want supplementary information (see below) or who think that their child has special needs. Basic information need not include information about nursery schools or classes, although you are entitled to this information if you ask for it.

School information, intended for parents of children already attending or about to attend a particular school or who want to choose a school in another area. This information must cover:

---

*Independent schools offering assisted places must also provide written information for parents.

the name, address, and telephone number of the school, its present roll, stages of education provided, denomination (if any) and the sex(es) of pupils admitted.

the name of the headteacher and the number of teaching staff. Nursery schools or classes must also give the number of nursery nurses, and special schools must also give the number of specially qualified staff.

arrangements for parents to visit the school.

the school's educational aims.

details about the curriculum provided, including the school's policy on homework and the provision of religious education. Secondary schools must also mention the courses they provide, personal and careers guidance, and arrangements for parents to be consulted about school subject options and choices.

the school's arrangements for assessing pupils' progress and making pupil's progress reports available to parents.

out-of-school hours activities.

school sports and outdoor facilities.

the school's policy on uniform and clothes and the approximate cost of each item of required uniform.

the school's policy on discipline, school rules, and the enforcement of attendance.

arrangements for providing transport and help with travelling costs.

arrangements for providing meals, including entitlement to free school meals and where to apply for this, also facilities for eating packed lunches.

arrangements for medical care.

organisation of the school day, including arrival and dismissal times, school term dates, and holidays for the forthcoming session.

the name, address and telephone number of the school to which pupils will normally transfer when they go on to secondary education.

Secondary schools (other than special schools) must also:

say how pupils are grouped into classes by:

pupils of different ability being taught together (mixed ability).

pupils being separated into groups of different ability (streaming).

pupils from the same class being taught in separate groups for certain subjects (setting).

set out their policy on entering pupils for public examinations.

give the number of pupils passing exams conducted by the Scottish Examination Board, including the numbers awarded different grades in each subject and for each stage of education in the most recent school year.

give the corresponding numbers of pupils in the fourth, fifth, and sixth years of secondary education (S4, S5, S6) in the year to which the exam results refer.

Special schools must provide information about what particular children are catered for, and say what specialist services are available.

Supplementary information, intended for parents wanting additional information for a variety of reasons but which is not given out as a matter of course. Parents are entitled to receive on request supplementary information about:

School admission arrangements: school catchment areas; secondary schools to which primary school pupils are normally transferred; names of "feeder" primary schools normally sending pupils to a particular secondary school; primary or secondary schools receiving pupils from other primary or secondary schools which do not cover all stages of primary or secondary education.

choice of school: the right of parents to request an alternative school, the circumstances in which such requests can be refused, the rights of parents to refer their requests to an appeal committee and the sheriff court.

Any guidelines issued by the education authority for admitting pupils to schools or nursery classes at which there are more requests for places than places available.

School rolls: how the education authority goes about fixing the maximum number of pupils whom they consider should be educated in any school or at any stage of education in any school; the considerations taken into account by the authority in fixing the maximum number.

Rights of parents of children and young persons with special needs to appeal against certain decisions.

Right of parents of pupils facing exclusion from school to appeal against this.

Policies and practices of the education authority about:

what is taught, assessment and exams
pupils with special abilities
school meals
school clothing and uniform
bursaries, grants and other financial help
discipline and school rules
pupils with special needs.
school councils.

Names of nursery schools and nursery classes, with addresses, telephone numbers and approximate rolls.

Names of special schools not run by the education authority but to which they normally send pupils, including for each school the address and telephone number, current roll, stages of education covered, the special needs catered for, and specialist services provided.

Names of schools in which Gaelic is taught.

Education authorities and schools may, if they wish, provide information in addition to what is required by the regulations, which only cover the bare minimum. This could include information about what the education authority does concerning parents' groups, access to school records, provision of education after school leaving age and so on.

Where will you find this information?

Basic information. The education authority must let you see the basic information at any of its schools, main or divisional education offices and, if possible, public libraries in its area. This information only has to be about schools in the areas covered by these schools, offices or libraries, although you must be told that similar information about schools in other areas is obtainable and their addresses and telephone numbers must be given to you.

You are entitled to see this information if you live in the area of the education authority concerned, if the authority knows you are proposing to move into its area, if you are considering asking for a choice of school there, or if the authority is satisfied that you have a good reason for asking for it, for instance if you want your child to attend a denominational school in its area.

School information

The education authority must give you a copy of the information about a particular school as soon as your child is offered a place there or whenever you ask for the information yourself. This will often be in the form of a school handbook or prospectus. It must be given free of charge. The information must also be available for you to see at the school concerned (including nursery schools and classes) during school working days and times. You are entitled to receive information about any number of schools run by your education authority or by authorities in other areas.

Basic and school information

The education authority can publish the basic school information in booklets, leaflets, circulars, letters to you or in any other written form, together with any other information. The basic and school information must be brought up to date each year and say which school year it refers to. The basic and school information must also be published in Gaelic in Gaelic speaking areas or in other languages if necessary.

Supplementary information

The education authority must give you any supplementary information you ask for if you live or propose to live in its area or are considering asking for a choice of school there. This information can be given verbally or in writing, although it must be confirmed in writing if you want or if it is about your legal rights concerning choosing a school, exclusion from school, or special needs. You can ask to see a map showing the area from which a school normally takes pupils; this must be available at the school concerned and either at the head office of the education authority or at the divisional education office whose area covers the school.

Supplementary information must be available in places such as public libraries, but supplementary information about a particular school must be available at that school. The education authority can provide supplementary information in other languages it considers necessary.

Delivery of information

The education authority may if it wants to arrange for written information to be hand-delivered to you through your child. This will normally only happen if your child is of secondary school age or possibly an older primary school pupil, depending on the sort of information involved. Pupils at special schools are not allowed to do this. To guard against possible loss, educational authorities are advised to notify you about the delivery in advance and to arrange for you to acknowledge receipt.

See other relevant sections of the Guide for further details about the topics on which written information for parents must be provided.

Where to find out more
1981, c.58, s.28, SI 1982/950; C1080.

Inspections and inspectors' reports

What do inspectors do?

All nursery, primary, secondary, special, independent and other schools in Scotland — as well as further education and other colleges — are visited from time to time by Her Majesty's Inspectors of Schools. As their title indicates, inspectors are appointed by the Queen on the recommendations of the Secretary of State. They carry out a continuous programme of expert assessment and inspections of the quality of education and training provided in schools and colleges throughout Scotland, reporting to the Secretary of State from time to time on major aspects of education. They also provide advice and information on various educational matters to education authorities, individual schools and colleges and a wide range of other bodies.

The timing of inspections is decided by the inspectors through arrangement with the schools or colleges concerned. You do not have any right of direct access to school inspectors, but you can write to the Scottish Education Department at any time about some educational matter which is causing you concern.

Inspectors' reports

Apart from publishing reports of national interest on various aspects of education, the inspectorate also issues reports on individual schools. You are allowed to see copies of these. To get a free copy write to the education office in your area or to the Scottish Education Department. Your local library may also stock copies. Reports have now been published for a large number of schools and colleges, although you may have to wait for some years before one is published for the school or college you are interested in. The education authority will be able to tell you which schools have been covered — about 150-200 reports on different schools and colleges are published each year. When reading the report, you should note the date when the inspection took place, as important changes may have taken place since the report was published.

Each report usually contains detailed remarks about:

the school or college and its community

accommodation and resources (books, equipment, staffing, etc).

the management and policies of the school or college.

courses taught and teaching methods.

the assessment of pupils or students.

support for pupils or students with learning difficulties.

guidance and social education.

relationships with parents.

Reports will conclude with an overall appraisal and usually contain some suggestions or recommendations for making improvements or putting matters right, for example, replacement of outdated equipment, better planning of courses, or more contact with parents. Provided that education authorities are carrying out their legal duties, these recommendations cannot be legally enforced, but both the authorities and schools or colleges are expected to take any follow up action that is required and to inform the inspectorate and others concerned like the school council that they have done so.

Before the report is finalised, the inspection team will discuss their provisional findings and conclusions with the headteacher or college principal and the education authority. One week before publication, copies are sent in strict confidence to the Director of Education, who is expected to forward them to:

the chairman of the education committee.

regional or islands councillor in whose ward the school or college is situated.

the chairman of the school council (where this applies).

the headteacher or principal.

the appropriate denominational body (where this applies).

The Director of Education is invited to comment on the report, taking into account any reactions from the headteacher or principal and the school council. The education authority is expected to make copies of the published report available to the general public on request, place reference copies in the school or college concerned, and issue copies to any public libraries in the area. Copies will also be sent to the press. The education authority is left to decide on any other suitable publicity, for example in school newsletters, in bringing the reports to your attention.

Within a few months of publication, inspectors will discuss any action which has been taken on the report with the education authority and headteacher or principal concerned. You have the chance during this period to send in any comments of your own on the report, either to the education authority or the Scottish Education Department, possibly with the support of your school council representative. Each report is only valid for a limited period of time and may no longer be obtainable after three years. The Scottish Parent Teacher Council has published a guide for parents on inspectors' reports, with guidance on how to read and make most use of them.

See also
CURRICULUM (WHAT IS TAUGHT)
SCHOOL COUNCILS

Where to find out more
1980, c.44, s.66, as amended by 1981, c.58,
s.16; C 1095.
*HM Inspectors' Reports on Schools: a guide for
parents,* Scottish Parent Teacher Council,
1985.

Leaving age

When can children leave school

Your child can leave school as soon as he or she is no longer of "school age" (age 16 and over approximately). Depending on when your child's birthday is, school leaving age is reached on either:

31 May of the year your child is 16 if his or her birthday is between 1 March and 30 September inclusively (officially referred to as the "Summer leaving date").

or

the start of the Christmas holidays or, in other cases, 21 December if your child's sixteenth birthday falls between 1 October and the end of February (officially referred to as the "Winter leaving date").

This means that some pupils will have reached 16 before their summer or winter leaving date — they are not regarded as being over school age until then — while others will be entitled to leave school shortly before they have actually reached 16.*

Once your child is over school age, you are no longer legally responsible for your child's education, although you are still legally entitled to advise and, in some cases, represent your child. From school leaving age up to the age of 18, your child is a "young person" as far as the law is concerned. This means that young people can make their own decisions on matters like asking for a choice of school or education after school leaving age. If your child has special educational needs, however, you may continue to have certain parental rights if in the opinion of the education authority your child is not able to express views of his or her own.

Your child may continue to attend school beyond school age for as long as the school is prepared to admit him or her. Any free school boarding accommodation, meals and transport your child is eligible for must still be provided. Some financial assistance may be also payable. Your child can seek, register for and take up employment while attending school beyond school leaving age.

*In exceptional cases your child can be allowed to leave school after the age of 14 if exceptional hardship would otherwise result by staying on.

See also
CHOICE OF SCHOOL
GRANTS AND FINANCIAL HELP
PARENTS' RESPONSIBILITIES AND RIGHTS
POST-COMPULSORY EDUCATION
SPECIAL EDUCATIONAL NEEDS
TRANSPORT

Where to find out more
1980, c.44, ss.33-34; C956.

Legal action

Going to law

You may take legal action — or legal action may be taken against you — to enforce or protect certain parental rights and responsibilities you have. Legal action may be taken against both public and private bodies, such as education authorities and independent schools, and against individuals, including members of teaching staff. You may particularly want to take legal action in order to:

force the education authority to carry out one of its statutory duties, that is, a duty which by law it must perform. An example of this would be the authority's duty to provide "adequate and efficient" school education. You should first complain to the authority concerned if you think that it is failing to carry out some legal duty. Next you could take your complaint to the Secretary of State if the authority still fails to act. The Secretary of State can take legal action of his own to force the authority to act if necessary. You can also take advantage of an old law which allows you to take the authority to the Court of Session, which can order the authority to carry out a statutory duty.

appeal against decisions by the education authority refusing you your choice of school, excluding your child from school or recording of any special educational needs your child might have. You would first have to go to the appeal committee set up by the education authority. If you lose your appeal, you have a further right of appeal to the sheriff court. Appeals connected with special educational needs will be referred to the Secretary of State.

stop or prevent the education authority, school or whoever is in charge of your child doing something which you think is unlawful, for instance inflicting corporal punishment. In some cases, like assault, you could report the matter to the police or to the Reporter of the children's hearing for your area. In other cases, you might have to take the education authority or person legally responsible to court yourself. This could include taking your case to the European Court of Human Rights.

get compensation for loss, damage or injury, resulting from some action, negligence or breach of contract. For example, the school may have been negligent in taking reasonable care of your child. This would normally involve you taking the education authority or person concerned to court, although is may be possible for you to obtain an out-of-court settlement instead.

Before deciding whether to take legal action of any kind, you should first seek advice. You will almost certainly need someone legally experienced to represent you if you decide to go to court, such as a solicitor or legal advice worker. You should also seek legal advice whenever action is taken *against* you, for instance in school attendance cases or if your child is faced with exclusion from school.

What sort of difficulties may be met?

When thinking of taking legal action you should also keep in mind the following sorts of difficulties:

Some law to do with education is difficult to enforce or interpret properly because it is too general to apply to individual cases. An example of this is the general duty of the education authority to provide proper school and further education.

Many decisions made and actions carried out by education authorities and schools are not covered by the law at all but are discretionary, for example whether or not homework or nursery schooling is provided.

It is not easy to appeal against various educational matters — other than those mentioned above — through the courts. You cannot normally use the courts to appeal against the school's rules, for example, or your child being prevented from taking a particular course or exam. It is possible that education authorities or schools will have appeals procedures of their own for dealing with certain educational matters, and it is worth checking what these are. Special arrangements exist for appealing against SCE exam results.

Only a very limited number of cases to do with education have been brought before the courts in Scotland. Any rulings in the sheriff court are not, in any case, legally binding on other sheriff courts, although the sheriff will be influenced by the decisions of other courts and is bound by the rulings of higher courts.

The cost and effort involved in preparing your case and going to court may outweigh whatever you hope to gain by taking legal action, unless of course you can get free legal advice and aid.

European Court of Human Rights

In certain cases to do with human rights, including educational rights, you may be able to take legal action through the European Court of Human Rights, which meets in Strasbourg. Its decisions have to be implemented in the UK as it has signed the European Convention of Human Rights and Fundamental Freedoms. You may only take legal action at a European level if you have already taken all possible legal action in Scottish courts. You must write to the European Commission of Human Rights in Strasbourg saying which articles of the Convention you think have been broken, stating the facts of your case, referring to other laws which you think support your case, and explaining what steps you have already taken to get matters put right. Again, it is important that you get advice before writing to the Commission. The Commission may ask you to give evidence verbally and invite the government concerned to present its own views.

After it has examined your case, the Commission then reaches a provisional opinion with a view to negotiating a settlement between the two sides. If a settlement is reached, a report is published, setting out the facts of the case and the remedy agreed to by both sides. If a settlement is not reached, then the Commission reports whether there has been a breach of the Convention, mentioning any differences of viewpoint among members of the Commission. The Commission, or the government concerned (but *not* the individual bringing the case), may then refer the case, within three months of the report being published, to the Court of Human Rights at Strasbourg for a decision. Even if the case does not go to the court, the Commission's committee of ministers may still decide on a two-thirds vote that the convention has been breached and direct the government concerned to carry out appropriate measures.

If the ruling of the European Court goes against the member government concerned, then that government, under its treaty obligations, has to make the necessary changes in its domestic law to bring the ruling into proper force. Until that happens, the ruling is not, strictly speaking, legally binding as far as the legal systems in the UK are concerned, although the courts are certainly most likely to be influenced by the ruling.* A few years ago, a parent from Scotland successfully turned to the European Court to prevent her child receiving corporal punishment, for example.

See also
ADVICE AND ASSISTANCE
COMPLAINTS
EXCLUSION FROM SCHOOL
PARENTS' RESPONSIBILITIES AND RIGHTS

Where to find out more
1868, c.100, s.91.
Taking Your Own Case to Court or Tribunals, Consumers' Association, 1986.
The Council of Europe: a concise guide, Council of Europe, Strasbourg, 1982 (see section on "European Court of Human Rights").
Your Rights: A-Z guide to the law in Scotland, Readers Digest Association, 1984.
Scottish Courts, Scottish Information Office, Factsheet 16.

---

*At the time of writing, a private member's bill was introduced in the House of Lords to make the European Convention of Human Rights part of domestic law in the UK.

Meals and milk

Meals, milk and other refreshments may be provided for your child at school. Mid-day meals *must* however be provided, free of charge, for pupils of parents on supplementary benefit/income support claiming them. Families on family income supplement also qualify for free school meals, but will lose them after April 1988, when FIS is replaced by family credit. To compensate, however, parents on family credit are entitled to a free school meals cash benefit of £2.20 a week, payable throughout the year, including school holiday times. If you are on supplementary benefit/income support, it is up to you to claim free meals for your child, as the education authority will not automatically be told that you qualify. To avoid possible embarrassment, the authority is expected to take steps to minimise identification of pupils receiving free school meals.

Education authorities are free to decide how much to charge for meals and the sort of food to provide. No minimum nutritional standards are laid down. School meals and milk can also be provided for children who are chronically ill or disabled and are not able to attend school. Meals and milk do not have to be provided at holiday times or at weekends. Written information for parents must be issued about arrangements for providing meals and milk, including entitlement to free school meals.

The school is normally responsible for supervising pupils taking meals at school. Pupils continue to be bound by the school rules and discipline. The school is entitled to ban items like alcoholic drinks, chewing gum or cigarettes. Schools may run their own tuck shops — a method of raising school funds — but an official report recommended some years ago that they should not be open at school meal times and that only items which minimised tooth decay and other health risks should be sold.

If you have any complaints to do with school meals, the school may agree to refer the matter to the education authority's school meals service or to the medical/environmental health authorities, or you could contact these bodies yourself.

See also:
COMPLAINTS
DISCIPLINE AND PUNISHMENT
SAFETY AND SUPERVISION
SCHOOL RULES

Where to find out more
1980, c.44, s.53 as amended; c.1052.

Catering in Scottish Schools, Scottish
Education Department, HMSO, 1975.

Medical attention

The school doctor

While at school, your child must be given proper medical attention. This must include regular medical examinations covering things like eyesight, hearing, speech, teeth, cleanliness etc. These examinations are likely to take place when your child starts school, moves to secondary school, or is about to leave school, but inspections and other routine checks will take place at other times as well. Checks and treatment may be given at school or in clinics run by the school health service.

The education authority must issue information describing its medical care arrangements. You must be told beforehand about any medical checks due to take place. You are entitled to be present at these. You can be taken to court and fined for refusing or failing to let your child be examined. Your consent is needed for any medical treatment given, including vaccination. Relevant medical information about your child must be kept in pupils' school records.

Pupils must be encouraged to make use of the school medical service. Schools will have a doctor who visits them regularly and some larger schools may have a doctor or nurse of their own. You can also arrange for checks and treatment to be carried out by your own family doctor or dentist. The school must have its own medical room and it is expected to have arrangements for giving first aid. The school must keep a note of your name and address and the name and address of someone else such as a relative or friend for contacting in emergencies. If your child goes to hospital, even for only a few days, the education authority may arrange for education to be provided there by hospital or visiting teaching staff. Special hospital schools may be provided for children with chronic medical problems. Arrangements can also be made for your child to receive tuition at home during convalescence. Your child may even be allowed to sit examinations while in hospital or confined to home.

You should remind the school of any medical problems your child may have before school trips or visits abroad. You could be asked to fill in a consent form in case your child has to be given medical treatment while away from home. Staff who are responsible for the safety and supervision of pupils on school trips must give due consideration to your child's medical condition.

Your child may be encouraged to take an interest in his or her health through health education and other lessons at school. Education authorities and schools are expected to take special steps to combat drug misuse among pupils.

See also
INFORMATION FOR PARENTS
SAFETY AND SUPERVISION
SCHOOL BUILDINGS
SCHOOL RECORDS

Where to find out more
1980, c. 44, s. 1, 50 and 57-58; SI 1947/45;
SI 1975/1135; SI 1982/950; M57/48.

Scottish Education Department:
Health Education in Schools, Curriculum
Paper 14, HMSO, 1974
*Health Education in Primary, Secondary and
Special Schools in Scotland,* HMSO, 1979.

Education for Children in Hospital, National
Association for the Welfare of Children in
Hospital.

Migrant and other mobile children

Children from other areas

Because education authorities have to ensure that proper education is provided for *all* children of school age in their areas, this means that education should be provided not only for children permanently resident in the area but also for children of:

i.   migrants from EEC and other countries.

ii. mobile workers or parents whose jobs require them to travel.

iii. travelling people.

Parents of these children have the same rights and responsibilities as other parents to see that their children are properly educated. Education authorities will normally have to provide the same range of services as for children of permanent residents.

(a) *Children of migrant workers in EEC countries*

Free and compulsory education must normally be provided for school age children who are dependents of migrant workers and living in the country where their parents are working.

Children of workers from or moving to other EEC countries* are automatically entitled to the same range of educational services of children ordinarily resident in each member state. Each EEC country does of course have its own educational and legal system giving migrant parents different rights and responsibilities from those of their own country. Certain basic rights and obligations are, however, legally binding in all member countries although some countries may give parents more rights and responsibilities than others, such as the right to a choice of school**.

In addition, these children must be provided with free tuition in one of the official languages of the host country and other free tuition to help them to adapt. Member states must also promote teaching in the mother tongue and instruction about the culture of origin of these children.

---

*Currently Belgium, Denmark, Eire, France, Germany, Greece, Italy, Luxembourg, Netherlands, Portugal, Spain and the United Kingdom.
**For further details, see especially A. Macbeth, *The Child Between: a report on family-school relationships in the countries of the European Community,* Commission of the European Communities, 1984.

Tuition does not have to be provided in school time, education authorities being left to work out their own arrangements, for example through voluntary self-help schemes.

(b) *Other countries*

Children of workers who move to non-EEC countries are not automatically entitled to the educational services of the host country. The UK government has agreed to extend the provisions for children of EEC workers to children of migrant workers from non-EEC countries, although this arrangement does not necessarily apply the other way round. If moving to a non-EEC country you should contact the cultural attache at the Embassy or High Commission of the country concerned for further details about its country's arrangements for educating children from other countries.

Children of mobile workers, etc.

If your occupation or circumstances result in you having to spend a lot of time away from home or move from place to place, because of your job, the education authority may be able to arrange to:

   i. provide your child with boarding accommodation and education while you are away.

   ii. send your child to a school belonging to the education authority in the area where you are having to work or live, as long as this does not cause too many changes of school.

These special arrangements are not likely to be made if you are away on a temporary basis and the education authority thinks your child can be cared for by a relative or friend. Even when you are living away from your child, you continue to be legally responsible for your child's education.

Children of travelling people

Children of travelling people are just as entitled to education as children permanently resident in an area. Travelling people must make sure that their children go to school regularly or are educated in some other way as they move from place to place. Education authorities may appoint special teachers of their own to provide tuition at recognised camp sites. Classes in basic education, including learning to read, may be provided for the parents as well.

An official report has recommended that travelling children should be educated alongside children in local schools whenever possible. This report also suggested that education authorities should issue information sheets to travelling people, written in simple language, telling them what to do and who to see about getting their child educated each time they move from place to place.

See also
ATTENDANCE
BOARDING ACCOMMODATION
PARENTS' RESPONSIBILITIES AND RIGHTS

Where to find out more
1980, c.44, ss.1, 13-14, 23-24, 30 and 50;
C1071.
Travelling People: third report of the Secretary of State's Advisory Committee on Scotland's Travelling People, 1971-82, Scottish Office, HMSO, 1982.
The Education of Travellers' Children, Department of Education and Science, HMSO, 1985.

Parent-teacher and parents' associations

How can parents become involved?

Many schools now have their own parent-teacher (PTA) or parents' association (PA) giving parents the opportunity to keep in touch with what is happening at the school and in education generally.* Any parents and teachers can get together and form their own PTA or PA, but the school or education authority is not under any legal obligation to set one up for you if asked to do so. The school may agree to provide accommodation and other help for parent-school activities but it may refuse or withdraw co-operation at any time.

*The difference between a PTA and a PA is usually purely nominal, both sorts of bodies being open to parents and teachers, but some PAs may limit their membership to parents only.

About half of all schools in Scotland now have PTA or PAs. Some are more active than others and their aims and activities tend to vary from school to school. In certain schools they take an active interest in what is taught and in other educational matters, while in others they mainly exist to raise school funds. Schools may make special efforts to consult or involve PTA/PAs in the work of the school and in general try to encourage good home-school relations. Members of parents' groups may also help the school to run school outings or out-of-school activities and welcome new parents to school. Much will depend on the amount of goodwill which already exists between parents and staff. PTA and PAs may also have various links with the school council. You should be able to find out if your school has a PTA or PA and what it does from the school handbook. Parents of pupils at the school usually become members automatically.

Booklets published by the Scottish Parent Teacher Council (SPTC) tell you how to set up a PTA or PA and run it properly. These booklets include guidance on aims and activities, drawing up a constitution, running meetings, co-operating with school staff and parental involvement in school generally. The SPTC itself also tries to encourage the setting up of parents' organisations, and can put you in touch with local federations which exist in several parts of Scotland. The SPTC also represents parents on various national bodies and puts the parents view across to government. A European Parents' Federation has recently been set up to put forward parents' interests at an international level and exchange ideas and information among member organisations.

Schools without a PTA or PA

The headteacher is usually left to decide whether a PTA/PA should be set up, but education authorities may themselves encourage the setting up of PTA/PAs as well — you could write to the education authority to find out more about its policies or practices on this. If the school refuses to set up a PTA or PA, you could make a complaint to the authority to see what can be done. If you can show that enough demand for a PTA or PA exists, the school might be persuaded to change its mind. Alternatively, you and other parents could set up a PTA or PA of your own, and in such cases, the education authority may agree to let you meet on school premises — but you could be charged for room hire. You and other parents could also set up your own group to campaign about some special issue that is causing you concern — such as the closure of a local school. Again, you may be allowed to meet on school premises but should be prepared to meet elsewhere if necessary.

Schools with or without a PTA or PA may encourage parents to become involved in various other ways. For example, they may allow parents to take part in classroom activities, group discussions and other work of the school. It is also possible to have a parents' group for each class or year group, as happens in some other European countries. Schools will usually provide you with opportunities to meet your child's teachers at school "open days" and other times of the year. If the school does not already do so, you can ask to meet staff privately to discuss your child's progress or any other problems or difficulties your child might be having. It is probably best to make an appointment with the school first, but many schools will be willing to see you without an appointment. Parents are also formally represented on the school council.

See also
ADVICE AND ASSISTANCE
COMPLAINTS
INFORMATION FOR PARENTS
SCHOOL COUNCILS

Where to find out more
1980, c.44, ss.28 and 30
Why Have a PTA? *Setting Up a PTA,* and *Ideas for an Active PTA,* and other booklets published by the Scottish Parent Teacher Council.

Post-compulsory education

After leaving age

When pupils reach school leaving age (age 16 approx) they are free to decide whether to stay on at school, enter college, take up employment or join a scheme for unemployed school leavers.

Staying on at school

Pupils may stay on at school after the official leaving age at age 16 approx. for as long as the school is willing to keep them, normally up to the age of 18 but possibly longer. They need not be allowed to stay on if suitable education can be offered elsewhere, for example at a college of further education. It is doubtful whether they can be turned away from school if no alternative provision exists, however. The same standard of education must continue to be provided, including regard to any special educational needs pupils might have. Pupils may be given the opportunity to resit exams or take more advanced courses and exams. Arrangements may be made for pupils to attend some courses at other schools or colleges part of the time. Tuition continues to be free. It may also be possible for pupils to continue claiming for free school meals, milk, transport and boarding accommodation. Means-tested bursaries may be payable to cover maintenance.

Further education

The education authority must make "adequate and efficient" provision of further education in its area. This means that further education (although not necessarily particular courses) must be available at a college, school or other institution for anyone who wants it and is likely to benefit from it. The authority is entitled to turn down applications for places at a college of further education which is full up, but it is expected to provide further education elsewhere in its area when this happens. Alternatively the authority can arrange for attendance at a further education course at a college in another education authority area.

Further education includes:

any voluntary or part-time course* for people over school age.

---

*Part-time courses generally take place for not more than 21 hours a week and last for not more than 30 weeks a year.

social, cultural and recreational activities, physical education and training, whether as part of a formal course or organised voluntary leisure time activities (e.g. at community and sports centres).

Gaelic teaching in Gaelic speaking areas.

Part of the law which would have made further education compulsory up to the age of 18 has not been brought into force.

Further education may be provided at colleges, schools and other centres (e.g. youth clubs, community centres). It covers:

non-advanced courses up to SCE Highers grade, GCE A-level, OND (Ordinary National Diploma) including a wide range of short courses in technical, vocational and other subjects leading to the National Certificate awarded by the Scottish Vocational Education Council. Non-advanced courses are taught mainly at colleges of further education, including technical colleges, but also in some schools as well.

advanced courses at Degree, Higher National Certificate and Diploma levels and beyond. These are taken from about age 18 mainly at universities, central institutions, colleges of commerce, education, technology, etc.

non-vocational courses covering a whole range of leisure-time interests for people of all ages. These are taught part-time at evening, adult and community education classes in schools, colleges and community centres.

Fees are payable for further education but education authorities do not normally charge fees to 16-18 year-olds taking vocational courses or unemployed people studying part-time. Grants or other financial help may be obtainable for many non-advanced and nearly all advanced courses but not normally for evening, community education and similar classes. Pupils may be excused from attending school in order to take a course of further education which starts before they have reached school leaving age. Arrangements can also be made for pupils to attend part-time link courses at further education colleges while they are in their fourth and fifth years at secondary school.

Other educational opportunities after 16

Part-time day or block release training courses paid for by employers.

Training and education under the Youth Training Scheme for unemployed school leavers.

Adult education classes run by the education authority, university extra-mural departments, Workers' Educational Association, etc. Some schools have also opened up their classes to adults.

Correspondence and "open learning" courses run by bodies like the National Extension College the Open University, various professional bodies, and commercial concerns.

Young people can get advice about these and other opportunities from guidance and student advisory staff services at most schools and colleges of further education.

See also
ATTENDANCE
BOARDING ACCOMMODATION
GRANTS AND OTHER FINANCIAL HELP
FEES
GUIDANCE
LEAVING AGE
MEALS AND MILK
SPECIAL EDUCATIONAL NEEDS
TRANSPORT

Where to find out more
1980, c.44, ss.1, 45-48, 76 and sch.5; SI 1959/ 477, as amended; Cs 929, 948, 1021, 1085, 1090 and 1112.
16-18s in Scotland: the first two years of post compulsory education in Scotland, Scottish Education Department, HMSO, 1979.
16 + Development Programme, Factsheet 31, Scottish Information Office.

Pre-school education

Nurseries and playgroups

Children start learning from the minute they are born, and long before they go to school they are acquiring essential skills like recognising shapes, colours and sounds, communicating with others, making things, and so on. These early years are considered to be very important as far as their future development is concerned. Government reports have recommended that all children from 3-5 years old should be able to benefit from some kind of pre-school education. Children who live in housing areas where there are no proper play areas or have very limited contact with other children, for example children in high rise flats, are considered to have the highest priority for pre-school education.

Nursery or pre-school education is usually provided in:

nursery schools and classes.

playgroups.

day nurseries, family centres and child minding.

Spending time with your child, playing and talking, all help with your child's education and development as well.

When children suffer from a severe disability or mental handicap and therefore have special educational needs, the education authority is likely to make arrangements for them to be educated before reaching school age. This could mean attendance at a special school or receiving home visits from specialist staff.

Nursery schools and classes

Education authorities may, but are not legally obliged, to provide nursery schools and classes for children below compulsory school age. Provision varies from area to area. Children may start nursery from about the age of three. Your child may have to go on a waiting list before being allowed to start there, however. When applying for a place, you should mention any difficulties your child is having, such as speech problems, so that a place can be offered sooner if necessary. Health visitors and social workers are expected to inform nursery school headteachers of any children at risk who would particularly benefit from nursery education. Special arrangements may also be made for children with special educational needs, such as mentally or physically handicapped children, to attend nursery school.

Children often attend nursery school for mornings or afternoons only, but children with special needs or who are thought to be at risk may be allowed to attend all day. If you live in the country, your child might be asked to attend two or three full days a week instead to save journey time and expense. Nursery education is normally free, but you can be charged for any meals, milk, morning or afternoon snacks provided.

At nursery school or class your child will be given a wide range of things to do, such as painting, music making, games, listening to stories, looking at picture books, outdoor activities, etc. Reading, writing and arithmetic are not usually taught, but in a well-run nursery school the organised activities will help the children to learn in a more formal way later on. Education authorities are expected to encourage close links between home and nursery school, and parents may be allowed to join in nursery school activities. Nursery schools are responsible for the proper safety and supervision of your child in the same way as other schools.

Some nursery education is provided in classes attached to primary schools, making the move from nursery to primary school less abrupt. The first term or two at primary school may also be a continuation of the sorts of activities provided at nursery school.

Playgroups

Parents, community groups and voluntary organisations are free to organise their own pre-school playgroups and a large number of these have now been set up in Scotland (for the address of your nearest playgroup, contact SCOPE, the Scottish Pre-School Play Association, which can also advise you how to set one up). Playgroups are much the same as nursery schools, but because parents take part in the day-to-day activities of the playgroup, children there may get more adult attention, too. Playgroups meet in different places, such as private homes, community halls and hired premises. There is usually a charge to cover basic running costs; in many cases, local playgroups get financial or other help from the social work department.

Day nurseries, family centres, childminding

Day nurseries are run by social work departments to provide day care for children under five who are seriously at risk. Children may be admitted from six weeks after birth. Qualified teachers may be attached to nurseries and centres to provide learning through organised play activities. You should also expect registered child minders to provide some educational support for your child as well, through play and other activities.

See also
INFORMATION FOR PARENTS
SAFETY AND SUPERVISION
SPECIAL EDUCATIONAL NEEDS

Where to find out more
1968, c.49, ss.10 and 12; 1980, c.44, s.1 as
amended by 1981, s.28C; SI 1956/894, as
amended by 1975/1135; SI 1982/950; C861
and C1108.
*Before five: report of the working party on
nursery education,* Scottish Education
Department, HMSO 1971.

Property loss and damage

Who is responsible for taking care of pupils' personal belongings?

Children are responsible for taking reasonable care of personal belongings brought into school. These include items such as books, bicycles, schoolbags, clothing, footwear, dinner money, lunch boxes, personal valuables, etc. The amount of responsibility children bear depends on their age, capabilities and the particular circumstances of the case. Parents bear some responsibility for allowing their child to take personal belongings to school.

Equally, though, the school must take reasonable care of items left in its safekeeping, for example coats and hats left in cloakrooms, valuables entrusted with teachers during games. You should be able to claim compensation or reimbursement for property which has been lost or

damaged while being cared for by the school in this way. However, you are unlikely to be able to claim for loss or damage which was due to the neglect or carelessness of your child — such as leaving valuables lying around unattended — or where loss or damage was quite unforseeable, caused by, say, a school break-in. You can lessen the chance of this happening if you allow your child to take only essential items to school, if name tags or labels are put on belongings, and by making sure that any cash or other valuables taken to school are delivered and kept there safely by your child. You may also be able to insure against loss or damage to personal belongings under an "all risk" policy.

What are children allowed to take into school?

The school can say in its school rules what sort of personal property may or may not be brought into school or lessons. Pupils risk being disciplined for bringing in items which are not allowed in school. These could include cigarettes, contraceptives, drugs, knives, and so on. Schools may also forbid or confiscate articles like portable radios, toys and games, comics and magazines, jewellery, etc. which are deemed to interfere with schoolwork. Articles taken away from pupils should be left in safe keeping and eventually be handed back; the school could be guilty of theft for not doing so. The school may hand over to the police any illegal articles, such as dangerous weapons or drugs.

Can you claim for loss or damage?

You may be able to claim either against your own insurance for loss or damage to your child's personal property, or against the school, which will have its own insurance arrangements. If the school denies responsibility, you may have to make a claim against the individual member of staff if he/she is thought to be at fault. If a substantial sum of money is involved and the school or member of staff refuses to pay up, although at fault, you should get advice about taking legal action.

Can you be charged for damage to school property by your child?

Your child is expected to take reasonable care of school property, including school books, equipment, materials and furniture. The school could demand payment from you (or your child if old enough) for loss of or damage to school property caused by your child (or by any other members of your family if school items are brought home). Payment could not be demanded for damage which is simply the result of fair wear and tear: the damage must have been intentional or due to deliberate neglect, such as ignoring or disobeying instructions about the care of books or equipment. Schools will usually take a sympathetic view of damage or loss which they are convinced was genuinely accidental.

Wilful damage, destruction or theft of school property is of course a criminal offence, and in serious cases, the incident would be reported to the police.

See also
ADVICE AND ASSISTANCE
CLOTHING AND UNIFORM
DISCIPLINE AND PUNISHMENT
EXCLUSION FROM SCHOOL
SCHOOL RULES

Racial Discrimination

When children are treated differently

Racial discrimination can occur in two ways:

directly, by treating a person less favourably than others because of their race, colour or nationality. This could be done by refusing to offer a child a place at a school or putting children into separate classes because of their colour.

indirectly by applying a condition by which people are apparently treated equally but which —

actually results in a considerably smaller proportion of a particular racial group* being able to comply with this condition compared with the proportion of people not belonging to that group.

cannot be justified irrespective of the colour, race, or nationality of the person it is applied to.

is harmful to a person because he or she cannot comply with it.

Indirect discrimination might occur, for example, where a school only accepts pupils from certain localities which are associated with certain racial groups.

For a claim of discrimination to be proved the circumstances of the person discriminated against must be more or less the same as those of a person not belonging to the same racial group. It would be for the court to decide what the relevant circumstances are. For example, refusal to admit a black boy to a school would not be unlawful if the school actually only admits girls. Discrimination does not have to be intentional for it to be unlawful; unintended discrimination may be illegal as well.

By law local authorities have to get rid of unlawful racial discrimination and encourage equal opportunities and good relations between people from different races. This is meant to encourage local authorities to set a good example in their policies and practices to do with race relations. This could be done, for example, by education authorities getting schools to outlaw textbooks which stir up racial prejudice and by educating pupils in such a way that good relations are encouraged.

---

*The law defines a racial group as "a group of persons defined by reference to colour, race, nationality or ethnic or national origins".

Services like boarding accommodation, school meals and transport must also be provided without regard to race.

Admissions

Schools cannot refuse your child a place or entry to a course or examination because of race. Pupils should not be taught separately in classes according to race, even if this happens unintentionally. But schools are allowed to run special classes in English or other activities for racial groups to help them with their education. Admission to school, courses or classes can also be refused if this is based on age, ability and aptitude, rather than on race.

Books and materials

You should expect education authorities and schools, to discourage the use of books and other reading materials which show one race as being inferior or superior to another. However, it is not actually against the law to use such literature. Anyone who publishes or distributes literature likely to stir up racial hatred could face prosecution. You could complain to the Educational Publishers' Council if you come across any books which you think could upset race relations.

Clothing

Pupils can be made to wear suitable clothes in order to be admitted to school. It is very doubtful, though, that schools can prevent the wearing of national costume if this is against the beliefs of a particular race. In an English case, the House of Lords has ruled that a headmaster's refusal to admit a Sikh boy unless he removed his turban was unlawful discrimination.

Games and sports

It is not against the law to discriminate against people according to their nationality, place of birth or length of residence in an area when selecting them to represent their own country or area in competitive events. But it is illegal for schools to select pupils on this basis for events of their own.

Complaints

If you think that the education authority or school is unlawfully discriminating against your child because of their race, you can make a complaint to the Secretary of State, who can:

order the authority to carry out its legal duties, through a court order if necessary.

conduct an investigation or local enquiry of his own on the matter.

order an investigation to be carried out by the Commission for Racial Equality (CRE). The CRE must notify the Secretary of State of the results of this investigation, recommending any changes in the law or practice that are needed — although the Secretary of State does not have to act on this. Reports must normally be made public.

decide to take no action at all.

Before complaining to the Secretary of State you should write to the CRE for advice and information. The CRE should be able to tell you whether it is worth complaining to the Secretary of State or what other action to take. It can give you, or help you to draw up, a set of questions to ask the education authority or school to find out whether discrimination has taken place. These questions do not have to be answered but failure to do so without reasonable cause could allow a court to decide that unlawful discrimination has taken place.

If your child is at an independent school you can complain directly to the Commission for Racial Equality without necessarily having to write to the Secretary of State*. It may agree to investigate the case and if necessary order the discrimination to stop. The school must be given a chance to state its own case and may appeal to the court within six weeks against a "non-discrimination" notice. You can also take the school to court yourself, and the CRE may again agree to advise, assist or represent you. The CRE and the court also have certain powers to deal with persistent discrimination.

If — and only if — the Secretary of State decides to take no action, or if you have not heard from him after two months, you can take your case to the sheriff court. You must normally refer your case to the court within eight months** of the act of discrimination, notifying the CRE, that you have done so. The CRE may give you free legal advice and assistance. It may also offer to represent you in court but normally only if your case raises questions of principle or is very complex, or if you have language or other difficulties which prevent you presenting your case properly. The person making the complaint must prove the case. The court can order the discrimination to be stopped if it is continuing and pay compensation for damage or distress caused by the discrimination***. Either side can appeal to a higher court.

---

*The Secretary of State may nonetheless take up complaints about a private school, which he can order to end discrimination.

**This time may be longer if you have applied to the CRE for free legal advice and assistance.

***Compensation need not be payable for *indirect* discrimination if this can be shown to be unintentional.

See also
ADMISSION TO SCHOOL
CLOTHING
COMPLAINTS
INDEPENDENT SCHOOLS

Where to find out more
1976, c.74, ss.1-3, 17-19, 35, 39, 43-52 and 71;
1980, c.44, ss.67 and 70; C 979.
Ethnic Minorities in Scotland, Factsheet 30,
Scottish Information Office.

Religious education and observance

Religious education and observance (prayers, services, etc) must be provided at education authority schools where it has been the custom to do so. These practices may be discontinued only by a majority ballot among those on the electoral roll in the area covered by the education authority.* Religious education is the only subject which the law says must be taught at school, but you have a right to withdraw your child from religious education or observance. The law does not say how often either of these things must take place, so long as they are not less than is customary. Schools usually provide religious instruction at least once a week. The law is not concerned with what religion is taught or observed — it need not be a Christian one — so long as the school follows the accepted custom. You are entitled to receive written information from the school telling you about religious education and observance at the school and your right to withdraw your child from either of them.

Withdrawal from religious education and observance

The law allows you to withdraw your child from religious education and observance at any time. In law, this is known as a 'conscience clause'. You simply inform the school that you wish to do so and you do not have to give any reasons. You can also withdraw your child if the school is denominational. In practice, many schools now in fact provide religious education broad enough to satisfy nearly all religious beliefs, including non-Christian ones, making withdrawal of your child less necessary. A lot of schools also hold non-religious assemblies, with only a limited number of religious ones.

Children must continue to be educated while they are withdrawn from religious education; they must not be left at an educational disadvantage as a result. They might, for example, be allowed to join another class doing a non-religious subject or to do private study of their own. The school may also agree to provide classes in religious education suited to your particular beliefs.

Teaching of religious education

The teaching of religious education in school is influenced to a great extent by national and local guidelines, but with Roman Catholic schools working to separate guidelines of their own. Both Christian and

*So far as is known, no advantage has ever been taken of this legal provision.

non-Christian beliefs are covered. Pupils can take SCE examination in Religious Studies, and religious education is open to official inspection. Many schools now have courses in Moral and Social Education, although it would be unlawful for schools to allow these subjects to be taught instead of religious education. An increasing number of secondary school teachers hold a specialist qualification in religious education, and most schools have their own visiting minister or priest. School councils must include at least one member with a special interest in religious education.

Religious discrimination

All education authority schools (and independent schools belonging to the Assisted Places scheme) must be open to pupils from any denomination and religion and to believers and non-believers alike. The education authority must also normally allow you to send your child to a denominational school if you ask for one. Children in boarding accommodation must be given reasonable opportunities to go to church. Schools need not cater for special diets required by a particular religion but they may agree to do so if there is sufficient demand.

See also
BOARDING ACCOMMODATION
CURRICULUM (WHAT IS TAUGHT)
DENOMINATIONAL SCHOOLS
EXAMINATIONS AND ASSESSMENTS
INFORMATION FOR PARENTS
MEALS AND MILK

Where to find out more
1980, c.44 ss.8-10 and 66 as amended by
1981, c.58, s.16; SI 1982/950.
A Curricular Approach to Religious Education
and *Curriculum Guidelines for Religious
Education,* Bulletins 1 and 2 of the Scottish
Central Committee on Religious Education,
Consultative Committee on the Curriculum,
HMSO, 1981.
*Report of the Joint Committee on Syllabus and
Examinations in Religious Education,*
Consultative Committee on the Curriculum/
SCE Examination Board, 1982.
Conditions and Arrangements (published
annually) Scottish Examination Board.
Includes SCE exam syllabuses on religious
education.

Residential (former List D) schools

Children in difficulties

Residential schools, formerly known as List D schools*, provide special personal care for children with a wide range of emotional and social problems and behaviour difficulties — including persistent truancy — largely stemming from disadvantaged home circumstances. Such children are normally placed in these schools on the instructions of a children's hearing, but some may be there either under a court order, in more serious cases, or voluntarily without the children's hearing necessarily becoming involved.

At present (1986) there are 16 residential schools in Scotland catering for these children. Although most are residential, some admit day pupils as well. They are mainly for 11-16 year olds; rarely are children under 10 admitted. Most are single sex schools, admitting boys only, but some schools are starting to admit boys and girls.

They vary in character and size although the largest hold no more than 80 pupils. Children there normally continue to receive the sort of education they get at ordinary schools but they are taught in much smaller groups, with as few as six or seven pupils per teacher. Schools are also staffed by social workers, instructors, child care and night care staff.

The numbers of children at such schools have fallen in recent years as more efforts have gone into keeping children in their local area and as a result of approaches like "intermediate treatment".** Several residential schools continue to be full, however, and children may have to join a waiting list to get into one. Their case must be referred back to the children's hearing if the waiting time is over three weeks.

Which school will your child be sent to?

The residential school to be attended by your child is decided by the children's hearing in most cases***, usually on the recommendations of

---

*At the time of writing, no new name for these schools had been decided on; they are referred to in this Guide as residential (former list D) schools. Most of them are managed by church and voluntary organisations but get their funds from local authority social work departments. One social work department (Strathclyde region) also runs two schools of its own.

**See under "Educational and Legal terms explained" for an explanation of intermediate treatment.

***In court orders the Secretary of State names the school to be attended.

your child's social worker. In recommending a suitable school, the social work department must give first consideration to the need to look after the welfare of your child.

Consideration must also be given to your child's wishes and feelings and those of your family, such as a wish to be at a residential school closest to home. The social worker may arrange for you and your child to visit one or more schools before making any formal recommendations. Your child's age, sex and religion must be taken into account, as well as the ability of the school to meet your child's needs. Before a final decision is reached, your child may have to attend a residential "assessment centre", or "youth resource centre" (Strathclyde), for expert observation or take part in some kind of community assessment. Once admitted, your child can be transferred to another residential school, if this becomes necessary, but your child's case must be reviewed by a children's hearing within seven days of the transfer. You or your child have certain rights to appeal against or seek a review of a decision by the children's hearing to send your child to a residential school, but you cannot appeal against the actual school named in the supervision order.

How long will the child have to stay?

Your child may not attend a residential school for any longer than the children's hearing or court considers is necessary in his or her best interests. Except in court criminal cases*, no fixed period of attendance has to be laid down. The average length of stay is between six and eighteen months. The school must review your child's progress every three months, and the social work department must do so at least every 6 months. The school may arrange for your child to be discharged as soon as sufficient progress is shown**, allowing a return to ordinary school, if appropriate.

Your child can be called back to school if the need arises. The supervision order continues to be in force, however, and can only be brought to an end by a review decision of a children's hearing or when your child has reached 18. Attendance at the school may also be ended by the Secretary of State if he thinks that your child's interests and the circumstances of the case justify this.

---

*Children found guilty of a criminal offence can be sent to a residential school by the court for up to two years.
**The consent of the Secretary of State is needed for early discharge of children under court orders.

Children who run away from school or overstay leave can be arrested without warrant and be brought back to school by anyone, usually by a social worker or member of school staff, who is likely to deal with each case as sympathetically as possible. Children who run away repeatedly, who are likely to injure themselves or others, or who in some way put at risk their own physical, mental or moral welfare or that of others can be held in secure accommodation*. Schools will have various safeguards to lessen the chances of either of these things happening. The law places limits on how long children can be held in this way and gives parents and children rights of appeal to the children's hearing. A code of practice lays down the standard of care and treatment to be provided in such accommodation, which is not intended as a punishment. Education should continue to be provided for children held in secure accommodation as far as possible.

Pupils are entitled to annual holiday leave and are usually allowed home at weekends and on public holidays. Leave may be withdrawn for misbehaviour or because of difficulties at home. Extended leave (of up to 28 days in Strathclyde for example) can be given, but the Secretary of State's consent is needed for children under court orders.

What is taught at residential schools?

Like ordinary schools, residential schools can decide on the courses of study they want to provide. They will usually provide a range of academic and practical subjects, with some schools also giving emphasis to vocational work, like learning a trade, as a child gets older. Your child can be entered for SCE and other public examinations. Arrangements can also be made for your child to attend a local day school to take courses not provided at the residential school. Schools are expected to keep up with new educational changes and are open to inspection.

Looking after pupils' welfare

A lot of effort goes into building up confidence among pupils, many of whom arrive with a deep sense of failure, frustration and rejection. Much work is done in very small groups or individually, with most teachers holding child care as well as ordinary teaching qualifications. Children may also be encouraged to take part in various community, outdoor and recreational activities.

---

*Children, whether already attending a residential school or not, may also be put in secure accommodation under a "place of safety" order of a court or children's hearing. Schools with secure accommodation are open to inspection and approval by the Secretary of State.

Schools must keep records of children in their care, including details of their home circumstances; these need not be shown to pupils or their parents but often are. Pupils must be given a medical examination as soon as they have been admitted and shortly before they are due to leave. The social work department is responsible for providing adequate after-care arrangements. Schools are likely to be in regular contact with child and careers guidance services.

What discipline is given?

Residential schools are free to draw up their own rules and discipline, but the amount and type of punishment given must depend not only on the seriousness of the offence but on the age, temperament and physical condition of your child. Corporal punishment is no longer permitted.

Can parents be involved?

You will usually continue to have the same parental rights and responsibilities while your child is at a residential school, except when these have been completely taken over by the social work department — even then you may still be allowed to see your child and be encouraged to stay involved. The school will often make very special efforts to keep you involved through school and home visits and when reviewing your child's progress.

The social work department may meet your travel and other costs on school visits and you may be allowed to take your child out somewhere during a visit. In some circumstances access to your child may be denied but usually only if the child's welfare would otherwise be at risk. You can be asked to pay a contribution towards your child's maintenance, but this rarely happens. Unlike ordinary schools, residential schools do not have to give parents written information, but increasing numbers are now doing so.

Management

Special residential schools must be registered either as social work establishments with the social work department of the local authority funding them or as independent schools with the Secretary of State (or both). Their management, maintenance, equipment and standards of treatment including education and training are open to inspection by the Secretary of State. The headteacher is in charge of the day-to-day running of the school but is normally answerable to the school's board of management. There are no school councils for residential schools.

Schools will usually have some arrangements for dealing with complaints from parents or pupils.

See also
COMPLAINTS
CHILDREN'S HEARINGS
CHILDREN IN CARE
DISCIPLINE
GUIDANCE
PARENTS' RESPONSIBILITIES AND RIGHTS
SCHOOL COUNCILS
SCHOOL RULES

Where to find out more
1968, c.49, ss.32, 43-44, 42-52, 59-71, as
amended by 1975, c.72, ss.7-8; SI 1961/2243
as amended (under review).

Taking care of schoolchildren

Schools must take reasonable care of children at school and look after their safety. When protecting children, the school has to take precautions according to their age and the activity they are taking part in. The law does not assume that your child will behave in the same way as a responsible adult.

Safety and supervision in the classroom

School staff, including non-teaching auxiliary and technical staff, are expected to:

provide safe and healthy working conditions for pupils in their care.

supervise the children and keep control in a responsible adult manner.

Special care is required when there is a greater risk of injury, such as during science lessons or sports activities. Staff cannot be held responsible for accidents or injuries which they could not reasonably have foreseen or prevented. The school will probably be free from blame if it can show that injuries were directly due to wilful disobedience or ignoring an instruction or warning. It is less clear where the school stands if a child's injury is caused by another pupil. A great deal would depend on the amount of control and supervision the school could be expected to have over pupils, according to their age and whatever activity was concerned.

Playground and lunchtime supervision

The headteacher is usually made responsible by the education authority for the safe and efficient running of the school throughout the school day, including playtime and lunch intervals. Staff supervision need not be provided in the playground itself, however. It is only necessary for there to be a responsible person on the school premises whom pupils can turn to for help, if for instance an accident or bullying occurs in the playground. Any playground or lunchtime duties done by teachers are done on a voluntary basis and do not form part of the teachers' conditions of employment. Schools take the view, and the courts are likely to agree, that parents allow their children at home to play outside without adult supervision and that schools are therefore in the same position. A parent was unsuccessful some years ago, for example, in claiming damages for an accident to his son while playing shinty in an unsupervised playground. The education authority or school, on the other hand, must take reasonable steps to prevent foreseeable accidents in the playground likely to be caused by things like scaffolding or moving vehicles.

If your child stays at school over lunchtime, whether for school meals or not, the school continues to be responsible for his or her safety and supervision. Reasonable steps must be taken to ensure that children do not leave the school premises without parents' permission. You are responsible for safety and supervision if you have allowed your child to leave school at lunchtime.

Supervision outside school hours

Parents are normally responsible for the safety and supervision of children outside school hours. It is up to you to make sure that your child gets to and returns from school safely.* However, the school must make

*or to and from any arranged pick-up point, such as a school bus stop.

suitable arrangements for receiving your child in the morning and dismissing your child at the end of the day. It may do this by making sure that there are staff on the school premises shortly before school starting times and after dismissal times. Patrolled crossings around the school may also be provided. You should expect to be given at least a day's notice about early school closing times so that you can make any necessary arrangements for your child to be collected from school.

Schools are not expected to supervise pupils who arrive at school very early or leave long after school has finished, except when special arrangements have been made for your child to do so. The education authority or school is probably to a certain extent responsible for the safety and supervision of pupils taking part in out-of-school activities such as sporting fixtures — but only as long as they have been officially authorised.

School trips

The education authority or school must also take proper care of pupils on school outings and field courses and any other place outside the school. Your permission is needed before your child can go on outings and field courses, regardless of whether these are during or outside school hours. You should expect the school to tell you what supervision arrangements are being made. You should tell or remind the school about any medical problems your child has which need extra care. The school will normally be responsible for arranging proper insurance cover for pupils on school trips, including trips abroad.

Safety of buildings, fire risks, etc

The education authority or school must make sure that the school buildings and equipment meet current safety requirements. This means that the school should have well sign-posted exit routes so that people can leave the building quickly in emergency, such as fire. In large or multi-storey buildings, corridors, doorways, staircases and other escape routes should be completely enclosed by fire resistant materials. Schools must carry out regular fire drills, especially after each new intake of pupils. The school should also take other measures to prevent the risk of injury from unattended machinery, building defects, faulty equipment, workmen's tools, etc.

Legal action

You may be able to claim compensation for accidents or injuries to your child, even if your child was partly to blame. In some cases, blame may rest with the education authority, in other cases an individual member of staff or a third party, such as an outside contractor. You will need to get legal advice about whether to go to court and whom you should claim against. In a successful case, you would be entitled to claim all of your legal, medical and other costs as well.

See also
ADVICE AND ASSISTANCE
SCHOOL BUILDINGS
TEACHERS' CONDITIONS OF SERVICE

Where to find out more
1974, c.37 ss.2 and 7; C 848 and C 917; M 22/70.
A Guide to Fire Safety in Schools, Scottish Education Department, HMSO 1979.

School buildings

Standards for schools

School buildings, like any other public buildings, must be built according to certain standards and requirements, including health and safety. The sort of buildings provided are determined by:

Building standards and regulations laid down by the Secretary of State. Planning permission must also be given by the district or islands council before a school can be built or altered. Building standards cover things like the resistance of building materials to fire, access and escape routes, structural stability of the building, accommodation, drainage and supply of services (water, gas, electricity). Any extensions or improvements must also meet the latest building standards.

Health and safety requirements. Education authorities have to maintain and equip their schools in such a way that any occupants or visitors to the school premises are in healthy surroundings. They must obey any directions from the Secretary of State for this purpose. People occupying or in charge of school premises must take reasonable care to make sure that anyone entering or using the building will not suffer damage or injury which may arise because of the condition of the building. This might, for example, involve keeping pupils out of classrooms while repairs are being done. The Secretary of State can make rules about the use of dangerous materials or apparatus in schools.

Special regulations for school premises Apart from the normal building and health and safety regulations education authorities must in addition provide school premises and sites that meet other requirements.

These requirements cover the following matters:

School sites and playing fields The minimum size of school sites and playing fields is worked out according to a legally prescribed sliding scale based on pupil numbers. For example, a secondary school with 751-1,000 pupils must cover a site of at least 2.4 hectares. Nursery schools and classes must have a garden or playing space nearby; minimum standards are also laid down for the amount of playroom accommodation there. The Secretary of State can relax or modify these requirements if he considers them unreasonable or impracticable for particular schools, however.

School meals accommodation Adequate and suitable accommodation must be provided for serving school meals and for washing up, even if the meals are cooked outside the school premises.

Washrooms A sliding scale, based on pupil numbers, lays down the number of WCs, etc. In nursery schools and classes, for example, there must be 1 WC for every 10 pupils. Except in nursery schools and classes, each WC should be lockable and partitioned to ensure privacy. Disposal facilities for sanitary towels must be provided in schools with girls beyond primary 4 classes.

Medical rooms Every school must have a room or other suitable place for carrying out medical inspections, except when the Secretary of State allows inspections to take place elsewhere. The medical room must have a WC and a wash basin with hot and cold water. A rest room with adjacent WC and hot and cold water supply, must be provided in every secondary school.

Storage and drying accommodation Cloakrooms and lockers must be provided for storing pupils' belongings and for hanging and drying their outdoor clothing. Every school must have sufficient storage space, for books and materials, furniture, and fuel.

Outdoor areas Playgrounds or other outdoor areas must be provided right beside the school building and be properly laid out and surfaced.

Lighting Both natural and artificial lighting must be provided. There are technical specifications which give the minimum amount of light which must reach desk tops and other working surfaces. Light fittings must be positioned in order to prevent excessive contrast or glare in normal working conditions. There must also be protection against glare from the sky and sun.

Heating, ventilation and acoustics Detailed specifications are laid down about room temperatures and ventilation in school buildings. For example, classrooms must have a minmum of 17°C, based on readings taken three feet from the floor, and be well enough ventilated, having regard to the use they are designed for. Classrooms and other parts of the school must be suitably insulated against noise and other disturbances.

Water supply Proper drinking water must be supplied and there must be warm water for washing in. Warm showers must have a temperature of at least 30°C but no more than 44°C.

See also
BOOKS, MATERIALS AND EQUIPMENT
MEALS AND MILK
SAFETY AND SUPERVISION

Where to find out more
1960, c.30; 1974, c.37, ss.2-4; 1980, c.44, ss.1
and 19; 1984, c.6; SI 1967/1199 as amended;
C654 and C863.

Can education authorities close down or make other changes to schools?

An education authority has considerable power to close down or make certain other changes to schools, for example, making them co-educational or moving them to another place. Before making a decision, however, the authority must give parents and bodies such as school councils a chance to say whether they agree with or object to a proposed closure of change. There are special legal procedures which must be followed when this is done. In certain cases such as rural or denominational schools, the authority may have to get government permission to close down a school or move it to another site.

The authority must explain to parents of children affected its proposals to close down a school or make certain other changes. The most likely reason for closing a school is that there are not enough pupils to justify keeping it open. The authority may have its own policies or guidelines for deciding whether a school should be closed down, and you could ask to see a copy of these.

Do parents and others have any say in the matter?

The education authority must seek the views of various groups of people before deciding whether to close a school down or make certain other changes:

Group 1   the parents of every pupil attending any school affected by the proposed closure or change.

Group 2   the parents of every child expected to attend the school concerned within two years of the date of the proposal to close a school or make other changes.

Group 3   the school council responsible for any school affected by the closure or change.

Group 4   any person authorised by the church or denominational body whose interests are affected by the closure or change.

It is also possible for anybody else to write to the education authority about any proposed changes.

When a school is closed down or affected by other changes, it is not only the parents of the children attending that school who must be consulted, but also parents of children at other schools affected by the proposal. School councils must also be consulted.

The education authority is also expected to seek the views of other people and organisations affected by proposed changes, not just those mentioned by the law, such as school staff, local employers, and (where applicable) the Highlands and Islands Development Board.

What sort of changes must the Education Authority seek views on?

The views of most or all of the people or bodies mentioned above must be considered whenever an authority wants to:

close down a school or stop providing a stage of education for example a nursery class or sixth year (groups 1-4).

provide a new school (groups 1-4).

move the school to another place (groups 1-4).

alter or create a school catchment area, that is the area from which the school normally draws pupils (groups 1-4).

change the secondary school to which primary school pupils will normally transfer (groups 1-4, including parents of secondary pupils who might be asked to transfer to another secondary school).

provide an additional stage of education at a primary or secondary school (groups 1-4).

provide or alter a special class for pupils for instance with special needs at a school other than a special school (groups 3 and 4 and parents of pupils who might be asked to change schools as a result).

make changes in the arrangements for the selection of pupils to be admitted to a school according to their ability or aptitude or the likelihood that they will benefit from a course of secondary education at that school. This includes special classes attached to ordinary schools (groups 1, 3 and 4).

change a single-sex school into one admitting pupils from both sexes or the opposite sex only, or change a coeducational school into a single sex school (groups 1, 3 and 4).

change the age or timing of transferring pupils from primary to secondary education (groups 3 and 4).

increase or decrease the number of school starting dates for admissions of pupils to primary school (groups 3 and 4).

draw up or change any guidelines for admitting pupils to particular schools or any schools where there are more requests for places than places available as a result of parents asking for a choice of school (groups 3 and 4).

fix or change the maximum number of pupils to be educated at a school or stage of education (groups 3 and 4).

withdraw transport or assistance with travel costs for children attending denominational schools (group 4). The education authority does not have to consult anybody about changes in its transport policies generally, however, as long as they do not discriminate against pupils attending denominational schools.

convert a denominational school into a non-denominational one (group 4).

Although the education authority does not have to consult parents and other bodies about changes in the day to-day running of schools, a government circular does recommend that there are many matters about which parents views should be considered. Those mentioned include changes to school:

school opening and closing times.

arrangements for providing meals, transport, boarding accommodation etc.

policy on discipline, wearing of uniform, etc.

exam arrangements.

provision of out-of-school activities.

How should parents be consulted?

If your child is affected by the closure of a school or any of the other changes listed above, then the education authority must write to each parent concerned giving:

brief details of the proposed closure or change, or those parts which affect parents.

an address from which you can get full details. These details should normally include:

a full explanation of the reasons for wanting to close the school down or make other changes.

the date(s) by which the school is expected to close down or other changes take place.

proposed alterations to transport and other arrangements affected by the change.

Either or **both**

an address to which you can write saying why you agree or disagree with what is proposed. You must be given at least 28 days in which to do this.

the date, time, and place of a meeting at which representatives from the education authority will be present to explain the proposals and answer questions. The meeting must take place no earlier than 14 days after you have been officially notified; it must also be held outside normal working hours and be convenient for parents to reach.

If your child is attending the school concerned, the education authority may arrange for him/her to deliver this notice to you by hand.

For the benefit of parents of children who have not yet started school, the education authority may simply advertise in the press, telling them whom to contact for more information or to give their views.

Certain proposed changes must also be announced in the local press: changes in the age or timing of transfer of pupils to a secondary school; changes in the starting date for primary school admissions; and changes to general guidelines for deciding which children will be offered places at schools which have become popular or oversubscribed as a result of parents asking for a choice of school. The announcement must say where you can get more details and invite those affected to send in their views by a certain date. This date must be at least 28 days after the announcement first appeared.

You may find that it is the school council of the school concerned which is responsible for dealing with your views about a school closure or other changes. Even if the school council does not make the final decision itself, it must make sure that the views of parents, as well as the views of its own members, are reported to the education authority in time.

You must be given 28 days in which to send in your views to the education authority and it must give you full details if you ask for them. These details should be available at the education offices at the school(s) affected, and in public libraries in the area. The education authority does not have to hold a public meeting to hear parents' views, although it is likely to do so if a lot of written objections have been received.

The authority does not have to inform you about, or publish reasons for its decision, although it is likely that it will do so by an announcement in the local press, by sending a circular to parents, at an education committee meeting or in the school council minutes. You are normally legally entitled to see committee or sub-committee minutes to do with the education authority's decision, including any background reports or other documents related to the minutes, for example papers prepared for education committee members by officials.

Are special schools affected?

The education authority consults parents and other bodies in the same way if it wants to close down a special school or make other changes to it. These consultations must also be carried out if the authority wants to attach a special class to an ordinary school or close it down; it does not have to consult parents of pupils not attending the special class, but a government circular recommends that it should do so.

How can parents make their views known?

If a school in your area faces closure or the education authority wants to make certain other changes, as listed above, you will be given a chance to state your views either in writing or at a public meeting, or both. There are a number of things you can say and do to make sure your views get a proper hearing.

You should say whether or not you agree with what the education authority wants to do, and if not, why not. For example, if you object to your school being closed down, you may wish to argue that closure would mean:

your child having to make longer or unsafe journeys to a school further away.

your child getting less attention at a different school with larger classes.

inconvenience to you personally.

the loss of a focal point of community life.

A lot would depend on local circumstances in deciding what arguments you wish to put forward for or against a school closure or other changes.

You could examine the reasons which the education authority gives for its actions. For instance would the proposed changes save money or result in a better education for your child? It would be helpful to get together with other parents to find out the answers to these questions.

You, or better still, a group of parents, could put forward alternative proposals of your own to avoid a school having to close down. Could there be more sharing of equipment or staff between different schools to save any of them having to close down, as already happens in some areas of Britain? Could parents be more involved in the running of the school to cut down certain costs? Could the school be used for other activities such as an adult education centre, a creche, health clinic, or advice centre?

The closure of schools is a complicated issue, however, beyond the scope of this guide, and you must seek further advice whenever possible.

Is the education authority's decision final?

In most cases it is. Having consulted parents and other bodies the authority can then decide to close down or make changes to a school. However, there are certain exceptions to this. The education authority must obtain permission from the Secretary of State to carry out changes which would result in:

a child at primary school having to attend a different school *five* or more miles away, by the *nearest available route,* from the school to be closed.

a child at a secondary school having to attend a different school *ten* or more miles away, by the *nearest available route,* from the school to be closed.

a child at a denominational school having to attend a non-denominational school. The government must consider what alternative arrangements are proposed and may impose special conditions of its own for offering denominational instruction before allowing a denominational school to close down.

significant deterioration in the distribution and provision of denominational schooling compared with other schools managed by the education authority, so long as the denominational body concerned has made such an objection to the Secretary of State.

In all other cases, the education authority's decision is final. You have no right of appeal to the Secretary of State or to the courts, but you may be able to take legal action if you think that the authority has failed to carry out its legal duties properly. You may be able to make a complaint to the Ombudsman that you were not properly consulted as a result of bad administration, but the Ombudsman's verdict is not legally enforceable. It may be worth lobbying your local MP, local councillors, etc to get the education authority to reverse its decision, and there is some evidence that pressure of this kind can sometimes result in a school being saved from closure, for example.

See also
ADVICE AND ASSISTANCE
EXAMINATIONS AND ASSESSMENTS
BOARDING ACCOMMODATION
CHOICE OF SCHOOL
DENOMINATIONAL SCHOOLS
SCHOOL COUNCILS
SPECIAL EDUCATIONAL NEEDS
TRANSPORT

Where to find out more
1981, c.58, ss.6-8; SI 1981/1558; C 1074.
Schools Under Threat: a handbook on closures,
Advisory Centre for Education, 1979.
Making the Case for Rural Schools, Rural
Forum Scotland, 1986.

School councils

What do school councils do?

School councils* are intended to act as a link between home and school and to allow communication between education authorities and local communities. They are appointed by the education authority, which decides what functions they should have. These functions are set out in the constitution of each school council and vary from one authority to another. In most areas, school councils will have some responsibilities to do with school attendance and may also cover such matters as the use and maintenance of school premises, the fixing of school holiday dates, the appointment of staff and whatever other functions the authority thinks are appropriate. School councils may also be involved in various education matters, such as new curriculum developments, although research has shown that school council involvement in such matters has so far been rather limited. School councils must be formally consulted about school closures and certain other changes.

The law also lets education authorities decide how many school councils to set up. The normal practice is to have one school council for each secondary school and its "feeder" primary schools, but in some areas there is one school council for a whole group of secondary schools and its feeder primary schools, while in a few (mainly rural) areas there is one school council for a single school only. As a result school councils vary greatly in size. A Glasgow University research team recommended that there should be one school council per school instead, bringing Scotland into line with most other western European countries, including England and Wales, where each school has its own governing body.

Who sits on school councils?

Each school council must include among its members:

parents representatives — probably at least one from each school, but possibly to represent more than one school, say, in rural areas.

---

*Similar bodies, known as "college councils" must be set up for further education and other colleges run by the education authority. Each college council is expected to give guidance to the work of the college, encourage close co-operation with local industry and with other colleges, recommend the range of courses which are offered and be involved in certain other matters, such as staffing, expenditure, and health and safety at work. Members must include representatives from college staff, industry or commerce, and other local interests. Students representation is also officially encouraged, and local headteachers and education authority representatives may be invited to join.

at least one teacher or other member of educational staff from each
school, but possibly to represent more than one school, say, in rural
areas.

one person interested in the promotion of religious education.

The education authority will normally arrange for parents' and teachers'
representatives to be nominated by election from among their own
numbers, although many school council elections go uncontested.
Headteachers are usually appointed to school councils as well (often as
non-voting "assessors") and some authorities allow pupil
representatives to sit on them. The authority is free to appoint other
sorts of representatives, for instance from industry and commerce,
community councils and other local interests. The appointment of local
councillors is also allowed. Non-parent or non-teacher representatives
may or may not be allowed to vote at meetings. The education authority
may arrange for meetings to be staffed by a paid clerk or other official
and provide school councils with their own budgets.

How can you find out more about your school council?

The education authority must issue written information for parents
saying what its policies or practices are about the running of school
councils, including details about what its school councils do and who
sits on them for particular schools. You should be able to get this
information from your local education offices or school.

The press and public are normally entitled to attend school council
meetings but can be excluded when confidential matters are being
discussed. The education authority is free to decide when and where
school councils should meet. You should check school, education office
or library noticeboards for dates and times of meetings.

The conduct of meetings should be laid down in the school council's
constitution. School councils are usually allowed to appoint their own
sub-committees, for example on school attendance. Minutes of
meetings (if kept) may be shown to you, except ones on confidential
items. Your school library will probably keep copies of the minutes.
Some school councils also publish their own newsletters.

School councils may be able to advise or help you if you have a complaint
about something to do with your child's school, but the most they may
be able to do is recommend some form of action to the education
authority or school staff — they cannot as a rule order something to be
done. They may also be able to give help or support to parent-teacher
and parents' associations. They should be able to inform you about any

educational and other major changes affecting your child's school and make your views known to the education authority. At the time of writing, the future of school councils and whether they need to be changed in any way was still under consideration by the government.

See also
ADVICE AND ASSISTANCE
COMPLAINTS
CURRICULUM (WHAT IS TAUGHT)
DISCIPLINE
INFORMATION FOR PARENTS
PARENT-TEACHER AND PARENTS' ASSOCIATIONS
SCHOOL CLOSURES AND CHANGES

Where to find out more
1973, c.65, ss.44-46 and 125-6, as amended by 1975, c.80, sch.16 and 1978, c.4, s.6; M 14/74.
Scottish School Councils: policy making, participation or irrelevance? by Alastair Macbeth, Malcolm MacKenzie and Ian Breckenbridge, HMSO, 1980.
Consultative Paper on School Councils, Scottish Parent Teacher Council, 1984.

School records and reports

What do school records contain?

Progress records must be kept for individual pupils at education authority schools*.

The record must give:

the pupil's full name and address, date of birth, position in his family, the parent's name and address, occupation, and where appropriate, place of work.

the name and address of any person, other than the parent, who may be notified in an emergency.

schools attended by the pupil (including independent schools), with the dates of admission and leaving and the name of the class left.

the results, with dates, of any psychological or aptitude tests given to the pupil.

*A progress record must also be kept for pupils who have Assisted Places at independent schools.

a note of any reasons why the pupil may have learning difficulties.

the pupil's health record.

information, where appropriate, about relationships with fellow pupils or teachers, attitudes and behaviour.

dates and details of any exclusions from school, including any appeal committee or sheriff court decisions.

the pupil's yearly educational progress.

information about any positions of responsibility held, such as school prefect, if the pupil is at secondary school.

This information must be used only in connection with your child's progress at school and for giving your child advice, for example in selecting suitable courses or exams. This means that the record should not be shown to people like employers, social workers or the police except on educational grounds.* Information may on the other hand be sought from doctors, social workers and other professional workers in putting together the progress record. The record, which usually comes in a folder containing additional information, must be checked and brought up to date at least once a year or before your child moves to another school. It must be retained for at least five years after your child has left school. The record may be seen by school inspectors.

Another record, called a Record of Needs, may be kept for children with special educational needs. This forms part of the ordinary progress record. Unlike ordinary school records, you are legally entitled to have a copy of this and appeal against statements in it.

Schools keep various other records of their own which do not appear in the progress record. These are mainly to do with the day-to-day running of the school and include things like notes on or marks awarded for work done by pupils.

Can parents see their children's records?

You are not legally entitled to see the progress record for your child but the education authority can give the school permission to let you or others see all or part of it**. You may want to see the record if your child

---

*Part of the record referring to exclusion from school may not be shown to outsiders if the exclusion was successfully appealed against.

**While the Guide was going to press, it was disclosed that the government would be introducing regulations to allow pupils, students and parents to see school and college records kept on them, subject to various safeguards. It is not clear, at the time of writing, whether these would apply to Scotland as well as to England and Wales.

faces exclusion from school, for example, or if you think it contains misleading or inaccurate statements. You may ask for the record to be corrected, if necessary, but the education authority is not normally obliged to do so. You may also ask for your own copy of the record, but if this is refused, you may still be allowed to take down your own notes from it. You could ask the school or authority to explain why you have not been allowed to see your child's record, and in serious cases you could write to the Secretary of State, who may order the record to be shown to you.

School reports

At least once a year schools will normally give to you a report describing your child's educational progress. The education authority will usually decide what sort of information goes into the report and how it is presented. The report usually contains remarks by teacher(s) on your child's performance in different subjects and attitudes to schoolwork, behaviour, relationships with others, etc. It may also include exam marks. The school will usually let you keep your own copy and may give you an opportunity to discuss the report with members of staff. The school must describe its arrangements for reporting on pupils progress to parents in its written information for parents.

Computerised records

The law now gives you the right to inspect and receive copies of personal information, including examination marks, intended for use on a computer. This could include information, including printed material, about your child kept on a computer at an education authority office, school or college. The information must be kept up to date and for no longer than necessary; you can ask for it to be corrected. The information must normally be shown to you within 40 days of you asking to see it and in a form you can understand. You may have to give proof of your identity before this information will be shown to you. The education authority will be able to tell you how the records are kept at your child's school. If the progress records are kept on a card file, it is unlikely that they would be put into a computer, in which case you would not be entitled to see them. Computerised information used only for research or statistical purposes, such as test marks, need not be shown to you. You would, however, be entitled to see this information if it is used for administrative purposes, such as selecting your child for a particular course. If damage or distress is caused to your child by inaccurate or misleading information contained in the records or by unauthorised disclosure, it may be possible to go to court and claim compensation.

See also
ASSISTED PLACES
EXCLUSION FROM SCHOOL
INFORMATION FOR PARENTS
SPECIAL EDUCATIONAL NEEDS

Where to find out more
1984, c.35; SI 1975/1135 as amended by SI
1982/1735.
Lucy Hodges, *Out into the Open: the school
records debate*. Readers' and Writers, 1982.
Where reports 148, 155, 156, 177, 194
Advisory centre for education.
National Consumer Council, *Consuming
Secrets*, Burnett Books, 1982 (see chapter 5 on
"Education").
*The Data Protection Act, 1984: an introduction
and guide to the Act*, Data Protection
Registrar, 1985.

School rules

Obeying the rules

Each school has its own set of rules which children are expected to obey. These rules, which vary from school to school, are meant to bring about the smooth running of the school and pupils' good conduct. Children risk being excluded from school if they do not obey the school's rules or if their parents prevent them from doing so. This is only likely to happen in more serious cases or if repeated warnings have been given. In the written information given to parents a statement of the school rules must be included, although these rules need not be written out in full. The headteacher will usually be responsible for drawing up the school rules. The school is entitled to use reasonable discipline to enforce its rules.

The education authority has to make sure that each school develops in pupils reasonable and responsible relationships, consideration for others, good manners and attitudes to work, initiative and self reliance and habits of personal hygiene and cleanliness. These requirements will usually be reflected in the school's rules as well as the school's day-to-day dealings with pupils. The school may also lay down rules about the conduct of pupils out of school hours or when they are outside the school, such as rules forbidding rowdy behaviour in public. The English courts have held that schools can also punish pupils caught breaking a rule in their own free time, such as smoking in the street, although there have been no court decisions on this question in Scotland.

If you object to a school rule or think it has been unfairly applied, you could arrange to discuss the matter with school staff. If no agreement is reached, you could make a complaint to your education authority, giving reasons for your objections. It may also be possible for you to have the matter brought up by your school council.

See also
COMPLAINTS
DISCIPLINE AND PUNISHMENT
EXCLUSION FROM SCHOOL
INFORMATION FOR PARENTS
SCHOOL COUNCILS

Where to find out more
1980, c.44, s.35(2); SI 1975/1135, as amended;
SI 1982/950.

Scottish Education Department

Who is responsible for school education in Scotland?

The Scottish Education Department (SED) is the administrative part of the Scottish Office, which looks after the provision of all education, except university education, in Scotland. The Scottish Office which is a central government department, is headed by the Secretary of State for Scotland, a member of the cabinet, who is responsible for helping to carry out government policies of the day. This includes steering government legislation through parliament. His educational functions are carried out on a day-to-day basis by a junior non-cabinet minister, currently the Minister of State for Education, Agriculture and Fisheries. The Secretary of State for Scotland is expected to pay close attention to Scotland's separate educational system in carrying out government policies. There is a separate Secretary of State for Education and Science, but in Scotland he is only concerned with university education.

The Secretary of State for Scotland

The law gives the Secretary of State a wide range of powers to:

issue regulations, directives, schemes and guidelines (or alter existing ones). The regulations have to be approved by parliament, which can either accept or reject them but not amend them. Much of the law on education is also found in regulations arising from acts of parliament, for example regulations about choice of school appeals procedures. There is a full list of regulations concerned with education at the end of the Guide.

help to make sure that education authorities carry out their duties under any law to do with education. This could arise from complaints to the Secretary of State, who can take action through the courts if necessary.

order inspections and local enquiries to do with the running of education. This includes ordering the medical examination of pupils and arbitrating in disputes between education authorities.

consider appeals from parents of children with special educational needs. The Secretary of State cannot deal with ordinary choice of school appeals.

give or withhold consent to certain school closures, for instance closure of certain denominational schools and some rural schools.

set up advisory councils on education matters. Two thirds of members must be qualified to represent the views of various bodies interested in education such as education authorities and colleges of education. For example, the Consultative Committee on the Curriculum advises the Secretary of State on what should be taught. Any advice given need only be taken into consideration by the Secretary of State: he is not obliged to accept it.

control standards of entry into teacher training and teaching.

give grants to education authorities and other bodies or individuals providing education or carrying out educational research. Parent's organisations could be awarded grants, for example.

award industrial scholarships or other payments to people in higher education courses leading to a career in industry.

The Secretary of State for Scotland may promote education through government publications, conferences, research, and grants to various bodies, but he is not obliged to by law.

The actual day-to-day running of education is largely in the hands of each education authority, not the Scottish Education Department. The SED is mainly concerned with matters like the overall planning and financing of education, supporting educational research, training and supply of teachers, providing inspections and inspector's reports, running the Assisted Places scheme, oversight of community and adult education, funding a number of youth and voluntary organisations, and students' grants.

The Scottish Education Department also promotes new educational developments, such as changes in courses and examinations. The SED cannot normally use the law to force changes on education authorities, but will often issue circulars and other guidance on various matters to help educational authorities to put new legislation and other changes into practice. (A number of these circulars are listed at the end of this Guide.)

See also
ASSISTED PLACES
CHOICE OF SCHOOL
COMPLAINTS
CURRICULUM (WHAT IS TAUGHT)
DENOMINATIONAL SCHOOLS
EDUCATION AUTHORITIES
EXAMINATIONS AND ASSESSMENT

INDEPENDENT SCHOOLS
INFORMATION FOR PARENTS
INSPECTIONS AND INSPECTOR'S REPORTS
SCHOOL CLOSURES AND CHANGES
SPECIAL EDUCATIONAL NEEDS

Where to find out more
1980, c.44, ss.66-76, as amended by 1981,
c.58, ss.7, 8, and 17.

Scottish Information Office:
Scottish Education, Factsheet 15.
Scottish Office, Factsheet 20.

Sex discrimination

Treating boys and girls alike

It is possible to discriminate between boys and girls at school in two different ways:

Directly, by treating boys more favourably than girls, or the reverse, for example by preventing girls from studying technical subjects taken by boys and not allowing boys to study home economics.

Indirectly, by laying down a condition which appears to treat boys and girls equally but which:

result in a much smaller number of boys compared with girls, or vice versa, being able to meet that condition.

cannot be justified regardless of sex.

is harmful to a boy or girl because he or she cannot comply with it.

Indirect discrimination might occur, for example, when fewer boys than girls, or vice versa, take certain subjects because of the way the school timetable is organised.

Either sort of discrimination, even if it is unintentional, is unlawful and the education authority or the school risks being taken to court. For a claim of discrimination to be proved, however, it is necessary to show that boys and girls were basically in similar circumstances. It would be for the court to decide what these relevant circumstances are. For example, letting more boys than girls take certain courses would not be against the law if it can be shown that more boys were academically qualified to take them.

Admissions

Schools which normally admit boys and girls are breaking the law if they refuse to admit pupils because of their sex, or say, have an entrance exam which favours one sex only. Pupils need not, however, be admitted to schools which cater mainly or wholly for the opposite sex. Schools admitting both sexes can educate boys and girls in separate classes, as long as this does not result in unequal treatment and access to school facilities. In a recent English case, a school which kept three girls back a year because there were not enough places in the year above, was found by the court to be breaking the law, since no boys had been kept back as well. Compensation was awarded to the parents for private tuition and other costs. In another English case, the court said it was unlawful to close down a boys-only school while keeping girls-only schools open.

Books and materials

Schools must provide books, and materials without discriminating against either sex. It is not against the law to use textbooks which show male and females in ways which would encourage sex discrimination or stereotyping but this would be contrary to the spirit of the law. Examples could include books with men or boys in dominant, adventurous roles and women or girls in passive or obedient, ones. Some publishers now produce their own non-sexist books or reading lists. One way of dealing with books and materials which you think are sexist is to write to the publisher concerned making your objections known.

School courses

Boys and girls must be given equal access to all the courses taught at school. Timetabling and staffing, etc. must not result in girls being denied opportunities offered to boys, or vice versa. Timetabling which prevents boys from taking a subject like home economics or girls from taking engineering or technical subjects is illegal. School must not only provide equal educational opportunities but are also expected to encourage boys and girls to take up subjects traditionally associated with the opposite sex. To prevent direct discrimination, boys and girls in co-educational classes should receive equal amounts of attention from teachers, although research has shown that boys still continue to get much more attention than girls.

Careers Guidance

Schools may not withhold careers guidance from boys or girls on the grounds that it is suitable for one sex rather than the other. They are expected to make boys and girls aware of all career opportunities including those traditionally associated with one sex, like engineering, nursing or secretarial work. This could be done, for example, by arranging for male nurses or female engineers to talk about their work to pupils.

Boarding accommodation

Schools with boarding accommodation for boys and girls are not allowed to refuse accommodation for reasons of sex, but schools with boarding accommodation for one sex only may do so, even where they provide education for both sexes. Accommodation at mixed residences can be refused, however, if this would mean a pupil having to share sleeping, washing and other facilities with the opposite sex. Mixed accommodation must still be run in a way which makes sure that boys and girls living there are treated equally.

Clothing and uniform

Schools have certain rights to insist that suitable clothes are worn but it is by no means clear whether boys can be required to wear different sorts of clothing or uniform from girls. You might be able to argue that certain practices, such as not allowing girls to wear trousers, reinforce sexist attitudes, but no such cases have so far been brought before the courts.

Physical education and recreation

Schools must provide boys and girls with equal amounts of time in physical education and sport and equal access to facilities such as playing fields, swimming pools, sports halls, outdoor centres, and so on. But schools can limit participation in competitive activities to one sex only if a woman does not have an equal amount of physical strength and would be at a disadvantage. This does not of course excuse schools from running, say, their own football or rugby teams for girls if there is a demand for them.

Complaints

If you think that the education authority or school is discriminating against your child because of his or her sex, you can make a complaint to the Secretary of State. The Secretary of State can:

aim to end the discrimination by ordering the authority to carry out its legal duties, through a court order if necessary.

conduct an investigation or local enquiry on his own on the matter.

order a special investigation to be carried out by the Equal Opportunities Commission (EOC) — the EOC must notify him of the results of its investigations, recommending any changes in the law or practice that are needed, although the Secretary of State does not have to act on these. Reports must be made public.

decide to take no action at all.

Before complaining to the Secretary of State you should write to the EOC for advice and information. The EOC should be able to tell you whether it is worth complaining to the Secretary of State or what other action to take. The EOC can give you or help you to draw up a set of questions to put to the education authority or school to establish whether discrimination has taken place. The authority does not have to answer these questions but failure to do so without reasonable cause could allow a court to conclude that unlawful discrimination had taken place.

If the Secretary of State decides to take no action, or if you have not heard from him after two months, you can take your case to the sheriff court. You must normally refer your case to the court within eight months* of the act of discrimination you have complained about, notifying the EOC, that you have done so.

The EOC may give you free legal advice and assistance. It may also offer to represent you in court but normally only if your case raises questions of principle or is very complex. The person making the complaint must provide the evidence. The court can order the discrimination to be stopped if it is continuing and pay compensation for damage or distress caused by the discrimination. Either side can appeal to a higher court.

If your child is at an independent school you can complain directly to the EOC without having to write to the Secretary of State**. The EOC as well as investigating your case, can order the discrimination to stop. The school must be given a chance to state its own case and may appeal to the court within six weeks against a "non-discrimination" notice. You can also take the school to court yourself, and the EOC may again agree to advise, assist or represent you. The EOC and the court also have certain powers to deal with persistent discrimination.

See also
BOARDING ACCOMMODATION
BOOKS, MATERIALS AND EQUIPMENT
CLOTHING AND UNIFORM
COMPLAINTS
CURRICULUM (WHAT IS TAUGHT)
EXAMS AND ASSESSMENTS
GUIDANCE
INDEPENDENT SCHOOLS

Where to find out more
1975, c.65, ss.22-28, 57-61 and 66; C 947.
Sex Discrimination: a guide to the Sex Discrimination Act 1975, Central Office of Information, 1978. (Available from the Equal Opportunities Commission.)
Sex Discrimination in Schools: how to fight it, National Council for Civil Liberties, 1978.

---

*This time may be longer if you have applied to the EOC for free legal advice and assistance.
**The Secretary of State may nonetheless deal with complaints about independent schools, which can be ordered to end the discrimination.

Special abilities and aptitudes

Children who have special talents or aptitudes in subjects such as art, music, maths, and technical subjects must be given every opportunity to develop them. This can be done by:

you yourself giving a lot of support and attention at home, through books, hobbies, conversation, etc and generally taking an interest in your child's activities.

the school providing your child with more challenging and demanding work to do in class or giving extra tuition or homework.

the education authority in exceptional cases arranging for your child to attend a school catering for children with special aptitudes (e.g. in music).

Responsibility for children's education rests primarily with parents, but the education authority must provide all children with suitable educational opportunities according to their age, abilities and aptitudes. The authority must publish written information for parents describing its policies and practices for educating children with special talents. When discussing your child's progress with teachers and reading school reports, you should expect the school to draw attention to any special talents your child has and how it is looking after them. You could also ask what efforts schools make to identify such children at an early stage.

If your child is gifted in subjects like art, music or drama, the education authority might arrange for the children to attend a national centre or school providing specialist tuition. This could be at an ordinary school running special classes of its own, possibly drawing pupils from a very wide area of Scotland. In some cases, the education authority may arrange for your child to get private tuition, for example at an independent school which specialises in music and drama. The authority may pay for the costs of any board and accommodation, travel and private tuition. If exceptional progress is made, special arrangements could be made for your child to sit public examinations at an earlier age. You can, of course, provide your child with special tuition, but you will probably have to pay for this yourself. An official report published some years ago recommended that pupils with special talents should continue to be educated alongside other pupils at ordinary schools as much as possible and not set apart from them. While they should spend as much time as possible developing their particular talents, they should receive a broad education as well.

Even if your child does not attend a school catering for pupils with exceptional talents, opportunities may be available for tuition from visiting specialists, special courses, and other activities, such as school concerts and plays. Some of these things may be provided outside normal school hours without charge, but you may have to meet some costs such as incidental travel, purchase of materials or course fees.

If you think that your child's abilities and aptitudes are not being adequately catered for, you should get advice from the school or education authority to see what can be done. In serious cases you could make a complaint to the Secretary of State, claiming that the education authority is failing to provide proper school education. You can get advice, information and support from some voluntary organisations. The National Association for Gifted Children may be able to put you in touch with parents living near you who share your concern (see list of Useful Addresses at the end of the Guide).

See also
ADVICE AND ASSISTANCE
COMPLAINTS
INFORMATION FOR PARENTS

Where to find out more
1980, c.44, ss. 1, 24, 28, 30 and 50; SI 1982/950
*Helping Children of High Intelligence: a
handbook for parents*, Gifted Children's
Information Centre.
*Gifted Young Musicians and Dancers: report of
a working group set up to consider their general
and specialised education*, Scottish Education
Department, HMSO, 1976.

Special educational needs

Children who need extra help with their education are said to have "special educational needs". They need not only be physically disabled or mentally handicapped to get special help. They may have less obvious difficulties or problems which may prevent them from coping with their schooling, such as behaviour or emotional problems. It is estimated that at least one in every five schoolchildren has special needs calling for some sort of special help — adaptations, therapy, special tuition — with their education.

As children's special needs vary so much, this part of the Guide can deal only fairly briefly with the special help your child may be given. The law is also very complex and it is only possible to give a summary of what parents' legal rights are in this area. Parents should therefore get as much advice and information as they can from the sources referred to below and in other parts of this Guide. This part of the Guide provides answers to the following sorts of questions parents are likely to ask:

What are special educational needs?

What does the law say about special educational needs?

Who decides whether children have special educational needs?

How are special needs assessed?

What happens after the assesment?

What is a 'Record of Needs'?

How is the Record of Needs kept up-to-date?

Who is allowed to see the Record?

What advice and help can you get?

How are your child's special needs kept watch over?

Can you appeal against any decisions made about your child?

What happens when your child is ready to leave school?

Because parents of children with special needs are likely to be faced with complicated situations which are not easy to understand, the law provides opportunities for getting advice and information. Education authorities must appoint people to advise parents at two different stages. Firstly, the authority must give parents the name of an official who can give advice and information at the assessment stage. Secondly, if the authority decides to open a "Record of Needs" for your child (see below), another adviser called the "Named Person" must be appointed to advise you. You may be unhappy about or disagree with decisions made about your child. When this happens, you have certain rights of appeal, explained below.

What are special educational needs?

Some time ago the government appointed the Warnock committee to make a number of important recommendations which altered our way of thinking about special education and resulted in changes in the law based on the concept of "special educational needs". The Committee took a much broader view by recommending that the old categories of "handicap" and the distinction between "ordinary" and "special education" should be abolished. It suggested that children's special needs were very widely based and could be catered for in ways ranging from short-term help to special courses and facilities being provided all the time in ordinary and special schools.

The idea of "special educational need" was seen as applying not just to children with physical disabilities and mental handicaps, affecting about two per cent of children but also to:

children whose difficulties were mainly emotional or social or who could be awkward or disruptive in class.

children in "remedial" classes whose difficulties stemmed from a variety of factors but who all too often were treated alike.

children whose difficulties were temporary or short-term from frequent changes of or absences from school for example.

children whose difficulties resulted from the language in which they were taught being different from the language they spoke at home.

When these children are added to those with the more obvious disabilities and handicaps, some 20 per cent of all children or more are in need of special help with their education. Special help could include any of the following:

adaptations to school premises or equipment.

provision of special learning aids, for example, to help pupils to write or read.

specialist tuition in special classes or units attached to ordinary schools.

part or full-time attendance at a special school.

Although these changes were not all spelt out in law, certain education authorities in Scotland are gradually beginning to introduce some of them, such as having special classes in ordinary schools. This means that parents will find varying arrangements made for children with special needs in different parts of the country.

What does the law say?

The law now states that children have special educational needs if they:

have much greater difficulty in learning than most other children of their own age.

suffer from a disability or handicap which prevents them being educated with their own age group.

are under five years old and belong to either of these groups.

The law does not cover children who have problems with learning because they are taught in a language which is not the language they speak at home.

The education authority is responsible for:

finding out whether your child has any special needs either before starting school or early on in schooldays.

assessing exactly what your child's special needs are and how best to cater for them. The authority is expected to involve you as much as possible in the assessment.

opening a special file, called a Record of Needs, if your child's difficulties are serious. You must be allowed to comment on the Record beforehand and be given your own copy.

appointing a 'Named Person' to give you help and advice for as long as your child has a Record of Needs.

giving you the opportunity to choose a different school for your child.

The education authority is also responsible for:

making arrangements for you to appeal if you think that your child should not have a Record of Needs, or against details in the Record you disagree with.

keeping a watch over your child's education and reviewing the situation when necessary.

carrying out an assessment about what sort of education or training would be most suitable for your child on leaving school.

discontinuing the Record of Needs as a result of an appeal or review, or if asked to do so after school leaving age has been reached.

Later on you might want your child to change schools, for example from a special to an ordinary school. You are entitled to ask for a transfer. You are also entitled to get information to help you choose a school, and you can ask for help from the person in the education department who is appointed to advise you while your child is being assessed.

The education authority can turn down a request for a different school on any of the legally permitted grounds laid down but must consider your child's special needs very carefully first. It must also give reasons for a refusal, such as having to spend too much money on altering the school building, and tell you that you have the right to appeal against its decision. You will find more information about appeals below.

Who decides whether your child has special needs?

Your doctor, health visitor or social worker will most probably tell you about any hearing, sight, speech or learning difficulties your child may have, especially those which are only obvious to an expert eye. With your agreement, these people can arrange for any necessary treatment, and put you in touch with the education authority if special help is needed, even if your child has not yet reached school age. The education authority will arrange for your child to be expertly assessed to find out whether your child does have special needs, how serious they may be and what to do about them.

The authority is responsible for publishing the importance of finding out if children have special needs either before they go to school or early on in their schooling. They must also publicise their arrangements for assessing children.

How are special needs assessed?

To find out whether your child has special educational needs or not, what these needs are and what special help should be given, an assessment of your child must first be carried out. The assessment includes a medical and a psychological examination of your child, but interviews or discussions with you or your child may be involved as well. Other professional staff, such as teachers and social workers, may be asked to provide their own expert assessments, too. The aim is to get as broad a picture as possible about what your child's special needs are and what special help should be given with your child's education.

The education authority must arrange for your child to be assessed as soon as he or she has reached school age (age five) if it has reason to believe that your child has special needs which are serious enough to call for a decision to "record" your child (see below). The authority may also assess your child before the age of five and in many cases will do so. You can also ask for your child to be assessed yourself; you can do this at any time, before or after your child has started school. Your request may not be refused without good reason.

At the assessment stage, the education authority must:

explain the purpose of the assessment to you in writing. The assessment must include a medical and a psychological examination and result in the issue of an education report on your child.

tell you when and where the assessment is taking place.

inform you of your right to be present at the medical examination of your child. Under *statute* law you need not be allowed to attend the psychological examination, but the authority may agree to let you be present.* You risk being taken to court and fined for failing or refusing to have your child assessed without good reason, but only if your child is of school age.

arrange for the medical and educational assessments to be done at the same time if your child is under five.

Education authorities are expected to encourage parents to take an active part in the assessment of their child. You should be told what is happening at your child's assessment, given an opportunity to meet those assessing your child and be encouraged to state your own views about what you think your child's special needs are and what should be done to help your child. You should be regarded as an "equal partner" with other members of the assessment team. You should also hear their views, their conclusions and the advice which will be passed on to the education authority. You could also ask to see copies of any background reports on your child prepared by those doing the assessment, although these need not be shown to you. (This could be important should you decide to appeal — see below.)

Before your child is due to be assessed:

you will get a letter from the education authority saying that your child is to be assessed.

---

*Some lawyers disagree with this interpretation and claim that the right to be present at the psychological examination of your child is supported by *common* law, although this right has not so far been tested in the courts.

you will be given the name of somebody in the education department who can give you more information and advice. This person is responsible for making sure that your wishes concerning the school you want your child to go to are passed on to the education authority.

you will be given at least 21 days in which to send in your own views, which will be considered during the assessment.

Young people (aged 16-17 approx) can also ask for an assessment at any time as long as they are still receiving school education. They cannot be assessed against their will, however. In some cases they may not be able to express themselves at all, and parents are entitled to ask for an assessment instead. In any event, you are still in a position to advise your child and make your views known to the education authority, no matter what the young person's state of mind may be. The authority is allowed to decide what sort of assessment to carry out, but otherwise the procedures are as for children of school age.

What happens after the assessment?

After the assessment, the education authority will have to decide whether your child:

has very serious needs which call for special help: for example, physical disabilities, requiring, say, physiotherapy or special adaptations to school buildings.

has not quite such serious special needs but which may still require special help, for example individual tuition for children with emotional difficulties.

has no special needs at all other than minor adjustments to his/her education.

The education authority will then have to decide whether or not to "record" your child. This means deciding whether to draw up an official document called a Record of Needs stating what your child's needs are and what special help should be given. It can only do this after your child has been assessed. However before coming to a decision the authority must consider:

all the reports from the assessment team and from any schools attended.

your own views about your child's special needs and the school you would like your child to attend. You could also submit reports of any assessments you have had carried out privately.

whether the school the authority wants your child to attend is suitable enough, for example for wheelchair access.

After this the education authority must:

let you know in writing whether it has decided to draw up a Record of Needs for your child and give the reasons why.

allow you 14 days to comment on this decision.

give you the name of somebody who can advise and help you (called the "Named Person").

after considering your views, give you a final version of the Record of Needs.

tell you about your right to appeal against the decision to record your child and against certain parts of the Record.

What exactly is a Record of Needs?

The Record of Needs is an official document describing what your child's special needs are, what special help is needed by your child, and how the education authority proposes to deal with those needs, whether in an ordinary or special school. This record can only be opened if the circumstances are serious enought to justify your child's needs being watched over regularly. The record has nine parts and includes information about your child's abilities and disabilities, what is required for his/her education, what the education authority proposes to do, your own views and details about reviewing the situation. It should contain:

Parts 1 and 2

Your child's name, address, sex and date of birth.
Your own name and address.
Name and address of the "Named Person" who can advise you.

Part 3

a. a description of your child. This covers your child's health, ability, interests, emotional development, and how well your child can talk, see and hear. This is called an "assessment profile". *You cannot appeal against this part of the Record.*

b. a description of your child's particular disabilities and the sort of specialist help needed. This is called a "summary of impairments". It should be written in plain language, avoiding technical terms which parents cannot be expected to understand.

Part 4

This part contains in more detail what your child would require, although not necessarily what can be provided. This could include requirements such as wheelchair access, special teaching and equipment, specially trained teaching or nursing staff, or special schooling, including hospital schooling.

Part 5

This section tells you how the education authority intends to help your child, for example by providing special transport, equipment, therapy, auxiliary help and so on. *This is the other part of the Record you cannot appeal against.*

Part 6

The name of the school to be attended. A school will not be named if, of course, your child is too young to go to school or is to be educated at home.

Part 7

The views of the "responsible party" — this will usually be yourself as parent but could refer to your child's guardian or to a young person (aged 16-18). In this part of the record you can disagree with any part of the Record, for example about the sort of help the authority intends to provide. Expressing your disagreement here does not initiate an appeal — this has to be done separately (see below).

Part 8

This section contains details of any re-assessments carried out, decisions about whether to continue the Record after review, and about any changes to the contents of the Record. You must be given the chance to comment on any changes before they are entered in the Record.

Part 9

This contains the names of people who have seen the Record, either in a copy of the complete document or extracts. It gives the names of officials who have let others see it, and the dates when the information was given out, returned or destroyed.

You must be told about any changes that are made to the Record, and your own copy must be brought up-to-date. If you move to another area, your child's Record must be transferred to the education authority in that area — this authority then becomes responsible for your child's special needs. If your child is being educated in England, Wales or Northern Ireland, your permission is needed before a copy of the Record can be sent there, however.

Who is allowed to see the Record of Needs?

The education authority keeps the original document and has to give you a copy. Another copy is kept at your child's school (if applicable).

The Record is a confidential document and can only be shown to:

the person appointed to advise you (the Named Person).

the government official dealing with your case, should your appeal go to the Secretary of State.

the Reporter, should your child be referred to a children's hearing.

These people must be supplied with a copy if they ask for one. The authority *may* also show the Record (except part 7 with your comments) to teachers, psychologists, medical staff and social workers dealing with your child. These people must have good reasons for wanting to see it. The Record cannot normally be shown to anyone else except with your written permission.

What advice and help can you get?

The importance of advice cannot be emphasised too much. The person from the education department who is appointed to give information and help while your child is being assessed has already been mentioned.

Once a decision to keep a record of your child has been made, the education authority must appoint another adviser called a "Named Person" who can give you and your family advice and help about your child's special needs. The law does not say who this person should be but it should be somebody you can talk to in confidence. He or she should be able to guide and support you in your dealings with the education authority. The Named Person might be:

someone already involved with your child, such as a health visitor, social worker or family doctor.

someone belonging to a voluntary organisation concerned with your child's special needs.

a friend, neighbour or relative whom you can trust and depend on.

Although you are not legally entitled to choose this person yourself, you could suggest the name of somebody who the education authority may agree is suitable. You should expect the appointment of a suitable Named Person to be discussed with you as soon as it becomes likely that a Record of Needs will be opened for your child. This person does not have to be appointed until your child's Record of Needs has been made final, but it may well be possible for you to get advice and information before the appointment becomes official. It is also possible to have a change of Named Person, who need not be the same person throughout your child's schooling. This change must be discussed with you. The Named Person does not have to have any special training, but the education authority is expected to provide some (or provide advice and information) if he or she does not already have some professional knowledge or professional involvement with your child.

Once appointed, the Named Person is expected to be readily available at reasonable times to discuss your child's special needs. It is possible to make contact by letter, 'phone or personal visit to fix a suitable time and place to meet. The Named Person should tell you about opportunities and arrangements for you to appeal if necessary. He or she may also agree to speak on your behalf at an appeal but should not be regarded as your legal representative — you may want to use a solicitor or someone else to represent you at the hearing. Try to get further advice at this stage.

What school will your child go to?

Children who need special help with their education may either go to ordinary schools in the normal way or attend special schools, depending on what their needs are. You can find out what the arrangements are in your area asking the education authority for written information about its policies and practices on special educational needs.

You have the same rights as any other parents to ask for a choice of school. If your child has special needs for which a 'Record of Needs' is kept, you still have the right to say which school you want your child to go to. You will be given the opportunity to state your preference when your child is being assessed (see above); the assessment must be at least two months before your child is due to start or transfer school. You can ask for an ordinary or a special school and you can name a specific one of either kind.

You can also ask for a place at an independent school; this is likely to be an independent special school catering for your child's particular needs, such as a private school for blind children. If your child has a Record of

Needs, the education authority may agree to pay for the costs of sending your child there. The authority need not do this if it can show, should you appeal, that it can provide suitable education more cheaply at one of its own schools and if it has offered to provide your child with a place there. But it must arrange for your child to attend an independent school if ordered to by an appeal committee.

If the authority will not let you send your child to the school of your choice, you can appeal in the same way as other parents wanting their own choice of school. It is possible, however, that your appeal may be linked with an appeal against a decision to open a Record of Needs for your child. In this case, you may have to wait for a decision from the Secretary of State before the committee you appeal to can decide whether to grant you the school of your choice. Appeals against a decision to record are described below.

Once a child has a Record of Needs, how are his or her special needs kept watch over?

Throughout the time that your child has a Record of Needs, which could be from starting to leaving school,

the education authority must keep your child's special needs under close watch or continuing review.

the school is expected to keep your child's special needs under review and report to you every year on your child's progress.

the authority must, whenever it thinks necessary, conduct a formal review of its own to find out whether it is necessary to continue keeping a Record of Needs and whether your child's needs have changed in any way.

you can ask the education authority yourself to bring your child's case under review; the authority must normally agree to this being done, unless there has already been a review in the previous 12 months.

If a review is to take place, your child must be assessed again. In this case:

you must be told how your child will be assessed.

you must be given 21 days to give your point of view.

you must be asked if you want additional assessments carried out; the authority must normally arrange to have these done.

The education authority will ask you (or may order you) to bring your child along for assessment. As before it must consider all reports and recommendations made by people involved in the case. It must also consider your views about what should be done and when.

Before reaching a *final* decision, the education authority must tell you about:

    its decision to continue to keep a record of your child and the reasons for doing so.

    any *proposed* changes to the content of the Record of Needs.

    your right to ask for a choice of school if the school named in the Record of Needs is to be changed.

The authority must give you *14 days* in which to give your views, which it must consider before reaching a final decision about any changes proposed. If it decides that your child should continue to have a Record of Needs or alters the Record in some way, you must be told about your right of appeal.

Can you appeal against a recording decision?

If you disagree with a decision to 'record' your child or with something in the Record, it is possible to have things changed by making an appeal. The diagram on page 216 explains what you can appeal against and how your appeal is dealt with. It is very important to be very clear in your own mind what it is you are appealing against to save time and possible frustration later on. Your Named Person should help you with this. The appeal committee can only decide which school should be attended; all other matters — what your child's needs are, and what should be done about them — call for a decision by the Secretary of State.

You must be given 28 days in which to lodge your appeal*. You cannot appeal against a decision *not* to record your child**.

You can ask for your child's case to be reviewed 12 months after the Recording decision (see above). You can appeal simply by writing to the address which the education authority will have given to you. You can still appeal after 28 days if you can show "good cause" (such as being away from home or too ill to write during this time). Your letter must be acknowledged within five days of receiving it.

---

*You are assumed to have been notified on the day after the authority's letter to you was posted, weekends excepted.
**At the time of writing, it was understood that the law may be amended to allow appeals against decisions *not* to record.

SPECIAL EDUCATIONAL NEEDS: APPEALS

You can appeal against:

a decision to record your child

statements in the Record of Needs, except parts 3a and 5

a review decision to continue recording your child

alterations to the record, except parts 3a and 5

The school to be attended, provided that a placing request has already been made. You cannot appeal again about this within 12 months

Your appeal goes to:

THE APPEAL COMMITTEE

The committee can only decide on the school to be attended. All other matters must be referred to the Secretary of State for a decision.

You must be given 28 days in which to appeal.

You can attend the Appeal in person, appeal in writing or do both. You can bring up to three other people with you.

At least one of the Appeal Committee members should be a parents' representative.

You cannot appeal against a decision *not* to record.

SHERIFF COURT

You have a further right of appeal to the Court against a decision by the Appeal Committee about the school to be attended. The Court must, however, refer your appeal to the Secretary of State if it thinks that a decision by him is also involved.

SECRETARY OF STATE

Secretary of State's decision is final and must be referred back to the Appeal Committee (or Sheriff Court), which must then decide on the school to be attended in the light of that decision.

The following examples suggest when and how you might want to appeal:

If, for example, you do not think your child has special needs calling for a Record of Needs, then you would simply appeal against the decision to keep a record. You might consider that your child's difficulties are not serious enough to prevent your child coping properly at school in the ordinary way.

If, on the other hand, you think that your child has special needs but disagree with the assessment team about what they are or what should be done about them, you would appeal against statements in parts 3b or 4 (or both) in the Record of Needs. You might argue, for example, that your child needs special tuition in addition to what is proposed.

Alternatively, you may agree with the education authority about what your child's special needs are and what sort of special help is needed but want your child to attend an ordinary instead of a special school, or the other way round. You may then want to appeal against the school named in part 6 of the Record of Needs, arguing that the help your child requires can or should be provided in the school of your choice. This need not arise, however, if you simply want your child to attend another school, whether a special or an ordinary one, which can provide the same sort of special help as the school selected for you. In this case, it may be possible to consider your appeal without referring the matter to the Secretary of State, who would only be involved if it was questionable whether specialist help could in fact be provided at the school you want.

You cannot appeal against part 5 of the Record, describing the practical measures proposed by the authority to help your child. You can express your disagreement with these in part 7 of the Record. By appealing successfully against other parts of the Record, however, it may be possible to get the authority to change its proposals in part 5.

When your appeal is in the hands of the Secretary of State

Any appeal to do with the recording of your child must be referred to the Secretary of State for a decision, including any "choice of school" appeals should the appeal committee or sheriff court consider that such a decision is called for. The Secretary of State, with the help of special advisers, then has to decide whether your child should be recorded and/or what special help your child requires.

These advisers will look at all the information and reports about your child's assessment, including any written statements or reports you make yourself. They will arrange to meet you and give you a chance to explain why you do not want a Record of Needs for your child or disagree with something in the Record. Your "Named Person" need not be present at this meeting but could be invited to come along. You could also arrange for anyone else who could give you expert advice or personal support to come to this meeting. You are of course free to give your views in writing as well.

The Secretary of State's advisers will probably want to see and talk to your child as well as listen to your own views. They will be anxious to find out what is the best way to help your child with his or her education. Anything you tell them should be treated in confidence and they will want to understand your point of view and pass on your views to the Secretary of State, who must take them into account. There is not time limit within which the Secretary of State must reach his decision. The Secretary of State can order the education authority to:

stop keeping your child's Record of Needs. The authority must then arrange for your child to attend a suitable school, taking account of your wishes.

alter something in parts 3 or 4 of the Record of Needs to do with your child's difficulties. This could result in the education authority having to alter parts 5 (measures proposed) and 6 (school to be attended) in the Record of Needs as well.

The Secretary of State's decision is final. The Committee dealing with your appeal must be notified of his decision and in the light of that decision decide which school your child should attend.

What happens if your appeal is unsuccessful?

If your appeal is referred to the Secretary of State for a decision, then that decision is final. But you can ask the education authority to review its decision to record your child (or review the content of the Record) 12 months after that decision.

If you disagree with the appeal committee's decision about the school your child should attend, you can take your appeal to the sheriff court. You normally have 28 days in which to do this. You should have already made a formal 'placing request' for a choice of school before the case can go to the sheriff. Your case will be heard in private.

Should you appeal to the sheriff, the court must take any decision by the Secretary of State into account before deciding whether to grant you the school of your choice. If the court considers that a decision by the Secretary of State is required and this has not been done, then the sheriff must refer your appeal to the Secretary of State; only after the

Secretary of State's decision can the court then deal with your appeal. The sheriff's decision is final.

What happens when your child is approaching school leaving age?

Before your child reaches school leaving age, about age 16, the education authority must carry out what is called a "future needs assessment". This is to find out what educational and training opportunities your child would benefit from such as courses at a college of further education. When your child is about 14 or 15, the authority must prepare a report saying whether your child:

  would benefit from staying on at school beyond the school leaving age, as he or she is entitled to do.

  should continue to have a record kept if staying on at school.

In drawing up this report, the education authority may carry out any medical, psychological or other examinations which they or you think are necessary. It may also make use of reports or advice from school teachers, careers, or guidance staff, training agencies, the health board, social work departments or voluntary bodies.

The education authority must give you at least 21 days to state your own views — and those of your child — about your child's future needs. Before finalising its report it must carefully consider your views and any reports you may present. It is expected to discuss the contents of the report with both you and your child. You may be asked to comment on it and a copy will be sent to you, usually six months or so before your child is allowed to leave school. Copies may also be sent to the health board, social work department or, with your permission, to another body, such as a voluntary organisation involved with your child.

You must be told about your right to have the Record of Needs discontinued once your child has reached school leaving age.

When is a Record of Needs discontinued?

A record must be "discontinued" by the education authority as a result of:

  an appeal or review decision to discontinue it.

  your child leaving school.

  your child asking for it to be discontinued if he or she is over school leaving age (age 16 approx).

The education authority must normally keep the "discontinued" Record for another five years. The Record must then be destroyed and you — or your child if over school age — must be told when this has been done. If the Record has been discontinued as a result of a decision by the Secretary of State, the authority must destroy it straightaway except when you ask it not to do so. You must be given 21 days after being told that the Record has been discontinued to say that you want the Record preserved. If you do this, the Record will be kept for another five years, otherwise it will be destroyed.

See also
CHOICE OF SCHOOL
INFORMATION FOR PARENTS

Where to find out more
1981, c.58, ss.3-4, sch.2 (part I); SIs
1982/1222. 1982/1733, 1982/1734 and
1982/ 1736; Cs 1074, 1080, 1083 and 1087.
*Committee of Enquiry into the Education of
Handicapped Children and Young People*
(Warnock report), Cmnd. 7212, HMSO,
1978.
*The Education of Pupils with learning
difficulties in primary and secondary schools in
Scotland,* Scottish Education Department,
HMSO, 1978.
Scots Law and the Mentally Handicapped,
Scottish Society for the Mentally
Handicapped, 1984.
The Educational Implications of Disability,
Royal Association for Disability and
Rehabilitation, 1985.
Portage: the importance for parents, ed. Brian
Daly, NFER-Melson, 1983 (help for parents
with handicapped or disabled children).

Teachers' terms of employment

The conditions under which teachers are employed are mainly governed by a national scheme negotiated between the teaching profession and education authorities. This arrangement covers matters like teachers' working hours and how much class teaching is done, grievance procedures, absences and other matters. Teachers are also bound by the contract of service with their employer, usually the education authority. They are under a common law duty to obey all reasonable directions from or on behalf of their employer, so long as this does not involve breaking the law or put health and safety at risk. What count as reasonable directions would in the last resort be for the courts to decide on.

Teachers' qualifications

These are normally the qualifications which teachers are required to have:

Primary teachers —	normally a degree in education from a college of education or university or a Post Graduate Certificate in Education.
Secondary teachers —	normally a university degree and a Post Graduate Certificate in Education.

Once qualified, both primary and secondary teachers must be registered with the General Teaching Council for Scotland before they are allowed to teach in a school. They are registered provisionally, to start with, while completing a two-year probationary period, which can be extended if necessary. At any stage in a teacher's career, registration may be withdrawn for serious misconduct.

Working hours

Normal working hours are 32½ hours a week, excluding lunch and playtime intervals. Primary school teachers should not spend more than 25 hours per week actually teaching classes. Secondary teachers must be allowed to spend at least 200 minutes per week (normally equivalent to five teaching periods) in non-teaching duties. This non-teaching time is spent in activities like preparing lessons and correcting work. Teachers

*At the time of writing, Scottish teachers' pay and conditions of service were under review by a special committee of enquiry set up by the government.

are entitled to extra pay for officially authorised "twilight" teaching duties between the end of the school day and 6.30 p.m.

Teachers are not under any legal obligation to take part in activities outside school time, such as school clubs, sports fixtures and parents' meetings. They may nonetheless do so, regarding these activities as an important part of their professional task, although they do not get paid for taking part in them.

How teachers carry out their duties

All teachers must perform their day-to-day duties in a reasonable and responsible manner. They are often given a considerable amount of discretion about what to teach, how to conduct lessons and how to discipline pupils, subject to directions or guidelines they may be given by their employer. They are responsible for the day-to-day safety and supervision of pupils officially in their care, including pupils on school outings and trips. Teachers can be asked to carry out various non-teaching duties, but they cannot be required to do so if these duties fall outwith their working hours, for example lunchtime supervision.

When teachers take industrial action

Teachers and other staff have the same rights as other employees in an industrial dispute. They are rarely dismissed for breach of contract if they are on strike officially. During an industrial dispute, the education authority is still under a legal obligation to take whatever reasonable steps are necessary to keep services running, although it need not keep schools open if prevented from doing so by circumstances beyond its control. If you think that the authority is not doing all that it could to provide an efficient level of service during a dispute, you could make a complaint to the Secretary of State or take legal action yourself in the courts. The Secretary of State or the court would then have to decide whether the authority was doing all that could reasonably be expected to maintain efficient running of services or whether circumstances made this impossible.

The school must tell parents about any industrial action which will affect attendance at school at least a day before the action is due to take place. Parents can make their own alternative arrangements for children to be educated while a dispute lasts, for example by arranging for their children to be educated at home. In some cases, where not all teachers are on strike, the education authority may arrange for the school to be kept partly open to receive some pupils.

Complaints

You may make a complaint about a teacher or headteacher normally by taking up the matter with the employers, such as the director of education, or the managing or governing body of an independent school. You can do this in writing and ask for an interview. If your complaint appears to be justified, the employer may take whatever disciplinary action is considered necessary. Certain procedures are laid down under the teachers' conditions of service for doing this. The education authority may suspend a teacher on full pay during this time. Serious misconduct or indiscipline may result in a teacher being dismissed, but for teachers employed by the authority, a two-thirds vote by members of the education committee is needed before this can happen, and even then only after due warnings have been given. You can also complain about serious professional misconduct to the General Teaching Council for Scotland, which can conduct disciplinary proceedings of its own and withdraw registration if necessary. Special procedures exist for complaints about racial or sex discrimination. You may need to take legal action in the courts when seeking compensation for damage or injury caused by a teachers' action or inaction. You should seek legal advice about whether it is the individual teacher or the employing authority who is wholly or mainly at fault, as this could affect your success in taking the case to court. It is often difficult to prove allegations about teachers being incompetent or adopting offensive behaviour, and you risk being sued for defamation if your allegations turn out to be false. Disciplinary action is only likely to be taken where professional misconduct is plainly obvious, such as leaving pupils unattended for too long or criminally assaulting pupils.

See also
ADVICE AND ASSISTANCE
COMPLAINTS
LEGAL ACTION
RACIAL DISCRIMINATION
SAFETY AND SUPERVISION
SEX DISCRIMINATION

Where to find out more
1980, c.44, ss.87-97, as amended by 1981, c.58, s.14.
Scheme of Conditions of Service (current edition), Scottish Joint Negotiating Committee for Teaching Staff in School Education.
General Teaching Council for Scotland Handbook, current edition.
Report into the Pay and Conditions of Service of School Teachers in Scotland (Main report), Cmnd. 9893, HMSO, 1986.

Transport

The school bus

Education authorities must when necessary arrange transport for pupils to get to school and back. Transport may be provided on school buses owned and run by the education authority or on public service or private buses. Private cars, taxis, ferries, aircraft, etc may also be used. Even bicycles can be provided. Education authorities may help to pay for all or some of pupils' reasonable travel costs. Written information for parents must be issued about transport arrangements, including entitlement to free school transport.

Transport must be provided for children living beyond a certain distance away from the school, except when boarding accommodation is offered instead. It should also be provided for children who because of some disability or handicap cannot travel unaided. Lack of suitable transport for getting to school normally counts as a reasonable excuse for your child not to go to school in these circumstances.

Free school transport

Free transport to and from school must normally be provided for:

   i.   children under eight living two or more miles away from school.

   ii. children aged eight and over living three or more miles away from school.

These children are said to be living beyond 'Statutory walking distance' of school. Free transport need not be provided for these children, however, if they are attending a school of their parents' choice, i.e. a school other than the one proposed by the authority.

The distance is based on the walking journey to and from school by the shortest available route, although there is no legal guidance on how this is actually measured. It is not clear whether the distance is measured only as far as the school gate or whether it extends to the school door, for example. A difference of only a few yards could be crucial in deciding whether your child is eligible for free transport. The route on which the distance is based need not be the safest one.

The education authority may still provide free school transport, or help with travel costs, to pupils living *within* statutory walking distance of school if appropriate to do so, for example, if there are medical or road safety reasons. Any spare seats available on school buses must in any case be offered free of charge to pupils who are otherwise not entitled to free school transport. There are legal limits to the number of seated and standing passengers buses may normally carry, but the law allows three children under 15 to occupy two seats.

Education authorities may also agree to pay all or part of your child's travelling expenses to attend exams and interviews at other schools and colleges. Help with transport costs may in certain cases be payable for pupils with Assisted Places at independent schools.

Safety and supervision

The safety and supervision of pupils on transport to and from school is the responsibility of whoever is providing the transport. This is likely to be the education authority for transport it provides itself. But in other cases, outside contractors (bus companies, taxi firms) may be responsible. If you bring your child to school yourself, for example, by private car, you yourself are responsible for your child's safety. You should find out from the education authority what its arrangements are for the safety and supervision of pupils using school buses and other forms of transport. Passengers can be ordered off buses by drivers, conductors or the police for misconduct and have their name and address taken.

See also
ASSISTED PLACES
ATTENDANCE
BOARDING ACCOMMODATION
DENOMINATIONAL SCHOOLS
INFORMATION FOR PARENTS
SAFETY AND SUPERVISION

Where to find out more
1980, c.44, ss.42, 50 and 51, as amended by
1981, c.58, s.2; SIs 1936/619 and 1984/1406 as
amended.

Acts of Parliament, Government Regulations and Circulars

ACTS OF PARLIAMENT, as in force, 1986*

Date	Chapter	Title
1868	c. 100	*Court of Session Act 1868*
1937	c. 37	*Children and Young Persons (S) Act 1937*
1960	c. 30	*Occupiers Liability (S) Act 1960*
1963	c. 37	*Children and Young Persons Act 1963*
1965	c. 19	*Teaching Council (S) Act 1965*
1966	c. 51	*Local Government (S) Act 1966*
1968	c. 49	*Social Work (S) Act 1968*
1973	c. 24	*Employment of Children Act 1973*
1973	c. 65	*Local Government (S) Act 1973*
1974	c. 37	*Health and Safety at Work Act 1974*
1975	c. 30	*Local Government (S) Act 1975*
1975	c. 65	*Sex Discrimination Act 1975*
1975	c. 72	*Children's Act 1975*
1976	c. 74	*Race Relations Act 1976*
1978	c. 4	*Local Government (S) Act 1978*
1980	c. 44	*Education (S) Act 1980*
1981	c. 23	*Local Government (Miscellaneous Provision) (S) Act 1981*
1981	c. 58	*Education (S) Act 1981*
1982	c. 43	*Local Government and Planning (S) Act 1982*
1983	c. 40	*Education (Fees and Awards) (S) Act 1982*
1983	c. 41	*Health and Social Services and Social Security Adjudications Act 1983*
1984	c. 6	*Education (Amendment) (S) Act 1984*
1984	c. 35	*Data Protection Act 1984*
1985	c. 43	*Local Government (Access to Information) Act 1985*
1986	c. 50	*Social Security Act 1986*

*For list of acts, with amendments, still in force, see the current edition of *Chronological Table of the Statutes,* part II, published by HMSO.

GOVERNMENT REGULATIONS, as in force 1986*.

Statutory instrument Date/Serial No.	Title
SI 1936/619	*Public Service Vehicles (Conduct of Drivers, Conductors and Passengers) Regs.* as amended by SIs 1975/461 and 1980/915.
SI 1946/1267	*Educational Development, Research and Services (S) Grant Regs.* as amended by SI 1959/476
SI 1947/415	*School Health Service (S) Regs.*
SI 1956/894	*The School (S) Code,* largely replaced by SI 1975/1135
SI 1957/1058	*Registration of Independent School (S) Regs. 1957,* as amended by 1975/1412
SI 1959/477	*Further Education (S) Regs. 1959,* as amended by SIs 1968/1849 and 1979/1185
SI 1967/1162	*Teachers (Education, Training and Recognition) (S) Regs. 1967,* as amended by SIs 1971/903 and 1973/864
SI 1961/2243	*Approved School (S) Rules* as amended by SIs 1963/1756 and 1983/1912 (under review)
SI 1967/1199	*School Premises (General Requirements and Standards) (S) Regs.* as amended by SIs 1973/322 and 1979/1186
SI 1968/1728	*Children (Performance) Regs.*
SI 1971/492	*Children's Hearings (S) Rules,* as amended by SIs 1983/1424 and 1984/100
SI 1975/1135	*School General (S) Regs.* as amended by SIs 1982/56 and 1982/1735
SI 1977/1261	*Independent Schools Tribunal (S) Rules*
SI 1981/1562	*Scottish Examination Board Regs.*
SI 1981/1558	*Education (Publication and Consultation Etc) (S) Regs.*
SI 1982†950	*Education (School and Placing Information) (S) Regs.*
SI 1982/1222	*Education (Record of Needs) (S) Regs.*
SI 1982/1733	*Education (Placing in Schools Etc — Deemed Decisions) (S) Regs.*
SI 1982/1734	*Education (Modification of Enactments) (S) Regs.*
SI 1982/1736	*Education (Appeal Committee Procedures) (S) Regs.*
SI 1983/973	*Education (Fees and Awards) Regs,* as amended by SIs 1984/1201 and 1984/1361
SI 1983/1912	*Secure Accommodation (S) Regs.*

*For list of regulations, as amended, still in force, see the current edition of *Table of Government Orders,* published by HMSO.

SI 1984/668	*Dangerous Materials and Apparatus (Educational Establishments) (S) Regs.*	
SI 1984/1406	*Public Service Vehicles (Carrying Capacity) Regs.*	
SI 1986/1104	*Education Assisted Places (S) Regs.*	
SI 1986/1227	*Education Authority Bursaries (S) Regs.*	

SCOTTISH EDUCATION DEPARTMENT CIRCULARS AND MEMORANDA*

(a) CIRCULARS

Circular No.	Title	Date
C95	Children and Young Persons (Scotland) Act 1937: Employment of Children — Byelaws.	1947
C364	Registration of Independent Schools.	1957
C614	Transfer of Pupils from Primary to Secondary Education.	1966
C654	School Premises (General Requirements and Standards) (Scotland) Regulations 1967 and Revised School Building Code.	1967
C661	Administration of the School Meals Service.	1961
C698	Commencement of Part II of the Children and Young Persons Act 1963 — the Children (Performance) Regulations.	1968
C758	Ordinary Grade of the Scottish Certificate of Education — Presentation of School Candidates.	1970
C781	Children in need of care. Co-operation between the Youth and Community Service, the Social Work Department and Children's Hearings.	1971
C794	Introduction of Children's Hearings on Points Affecting Education Authorities.	1971
C814	Report on the Working Party on Nursery Education.	1971
C816	Truancy.	1971
C820	Moral and Religious Education in Scottish Schools.	1972
C821	Independent Schools: use by Education Authorities.	1982
C838	Employment of Children and Performance by Children: effects of raising the school leaving age.	1972

*For list of circulars and memoranda still in force, see the current edition of *List of Departmental Circulars and Memoranda,* published by the Scottish Education Department. (available from room 323, 43 Jeffrey Street, Edinburgh EH1 1DN.)

C841	The First Two Years of Secondary Education.	1972
C848	Safety in Outdoor Pursuits.	1972
C851	Employment of Non-teaching Staff in Secondary Schools.	1972
C861	Nursery Education.	1973
C863	The School Premises (General Requirement and Standards) (Scotland) Amendment Regulations and the Further Education (Scotland) Amendment Regulations.	1973
C879	Organisation of School Year.	1973
C895	Education (Work Experience) Act.	1973
C898	Organisation of Secondary Education.	1974
C915	Local Government (Scotland) Act 1973: School and College Councils.	1974
C916	Religious Education in Scottish Schools.	1974
C917	Health and Safety at Work Act 1974.	1975
C929	College Councils for Further Education.	1975
C930	Ill Treatment of Children.	1975
C931	Differences of Provision for Boys and Girls in Scottish Secondary Schools — A Report by HM Inspector of Schools.	1975
C947	Sex Discrimination Act 1975.	1976
C948	Courses for School Pupils in Further Education Colleges.	1976
C949	Regulations under the Employment of Children Act 1973.	1976
C956	The Education (Scotland) Act 1976: School Leaving Arrangements.	1976
C965	Seminar on Educational Disadvantage.	1976
C979	Race Relations Act 1976.	1977
C991	Employment of Additional Teachers in Schools Serving Urban Areas of Deprivation.	1977
C1021	Admission of Overseas Students.	1978
C1044	Further Relaxation of Procedure for Approval of Education etc Building Projects.	1979
C1052	Milk and Meals: administration of the Education Act 1980.	1980
C1057	Special Educational Needs in Scotland.	1980
C1058	Education (Scotland) Act 1980.	1980
C1071	Directive of the Council of the European Community on the Education of the Children of Migrant Workers.	1981
C1072	The Staffing of Primary and Secondary Schools.	1981
C1074	Education (Scotland) Act 1981.	1981
C1080	Education (Scotland) Act 1981: Second	1982

	Commencement Order	
C1083	Education (Scotland) Act 1981 as Amended: Education (Record of Needs) (Scotland) Regulations 1982.	1982
C1084	The "21 Hours Rule": Part Time Education and Supplementary Benefit.	1982
C1085	The Educational Implications of the Youth Training Scheme.	1982
C1087	Education (Scotland) Act 1981—Implementation	1982
C1089	Teaching and Learning in the Senior Stages of the Scottish Secondary School.	1983
C1090	16-18s in Scotland: an Action Plan.	1983
C1093	The Munn and Dunning Reports: Implementation of the Government's Proposals.	1983
C1095	Publication of Reports by Her Majesty's Inspectors of Schools.	1983
C1100	Corporal punishment in schools.	1983
C1107	Implementation of the Government's proposals for the reform of the curriculum and assessment in S3-S4.	1983
C1108	Placing Requests for Under Age Children.	1984
C1112	Education for 16-18s in Scotland: Implementation of the Government's Action Plan.	1984
C1120	Education (Fees and Awards) (S) Amendment Regulations 1984.	1984
C1133	Education Authority Bursaries (S) Regulations	1985

(b) MEMORANDA

Year/Serial No.	Title
M57/48	Education of Children in Hospital.
M1/68	Careers Literature in Schools.
M3/68	Elimination of Corporal Punishment in Schools. Statement of Principles and Code of Practice.
M22/70	Safety Precautions in Schools.
M13/71	Assistance to Student Trainees with Expenses Incurred in Attending Part-time Vocational Day and Block-release Courses and Full-time Integrated Courses at FE Colleges.
M8/73	Amendments to the School and FE Building Codes.
M14/74	Local Government (Scotland) Act 1973: School and College Councils.

Educational and legal terms explained

Ability — how capable children are of doing something, usually in such things as reading, writing and mathematical work but also in other areas of school work as well.

Achievement — how well pupils do in various school activities, often shown by marks awarded for classwork, in tests, exams, etc. Children may "over" or "underachieve" if they do better or worse than expected.

Action Plan — see under Sixteen-plus Development Programme.

Adviser — a person employed by the education authority, usually an experienced teacher, to provide guidance, support and training for teachers.

Aptitude — usually refers to capability in a particular skill, such as drawing, playing a musical instrument, conducting a scientific experiment, and so on. It may also refer to general ability as well.

Assessment — finding out how well a child is doing at school, mainly through examinations and the marking or grading of work done in class. "Continuous assessment" means that the teacher watches over the educational progress of each child in day-to-day classwork.

Assisted Places — places at independent schools for children whose fees and other costs are wholly or partly paid for out of public funds.

Attendance order — a notice sent to parents ordering them to send their child to the school named in the order.

Audio-visual aids — equipment and materials like cassette recorders, films and film projectors, radio and TV, and so on.

Banding — grouping pupils into broad levels of ability, such as "high" "medium" and "low". Each band may comprise one or more classes of pupils. Pupils usually belong to the same band for different school subjects, but they may be allowed to move up or down between bands, depending on their progress. Banding has been replaced by "setting" in many schools.

Bilingual education — education of pupils in two languages, for example English and Gaelic.

Bursary — a sum of money, usually awarded by an education authority, covering all or part of the maintenance costs and any fees charged for education mainly after school leaving age.

Capitation allowance — the amount per pupil spent on books, equipment and materials by the education authority.

Catchment area — the residential area from which a school normally draws its pupils (also referred to as 'zoning' or the school's 'delineated area').

Central institution — a college directly funded by the Scottish Education Department and offering various degree, diploma and other advanced courses.

Certificate of Secondary Education (CSE) — a public exam mainly taken by pupils in England and Wales but also taken by pupils in some Scottish Schools. The CSE will be merged with the General Certificate of Education (GCE) to form a new General Certificate of Secondary Education exam (GCSE) in due course.

Certificate of Sixth Year Studies (CSYS) — a certificate awarded for private study in up to three subjects during the sixth year of secondary school (usually after 'Highers' have been taken).

Child guidance service — A service staffed by psychologists employed by the education authority to help children who have difficulties with learning, problems with behaviour or other special needs.

Co-educational school — a school which takes in both boys and girls. Boys and girls at co-educational schools may still be taught in separate classes for some subjects, such as physical education.

Common course or curriculum — courses or subjects taken by all pupils, as generally happens in primary school and in the first and second years of secondary school.

Community school — schools which usually try to involve members of the local community, including parents, in the life of the school, for example, by allowing adults to attend the same classes as pupils.

Comprehensive school — a secondary school meant to cater for pupils in the whole ability range. Most secondary schools in Scotland are comprehensive. Pupils with severe learning difficulties may attend special schools instead, however.

Compulsory education — education is compulsory between about the age of five to sixteen, although this need not necessarily involve compulsory attendance at school as some children may be educated at home or in hospital.

Consultative Committee on the Curriculum — a body appointed by the Secretary of State to advise on what is taught in schools.

Core curriculum — the compulsory areas of study which all pupils must normally follow. Pupils may be allowed to choose other courses or subjects outside 'the core'.

Curriculum — the range of subjects or areas of study taught at school.

Denominational school — a school run by or on behalf of a religious body. Most denominational schools in Scotland are Roman Catholic and funded and managed by education authorities.

Department of Education and Science (DES) — the central government body responsible for education in England and Wales (but not Scotland, except Scottish universities).

Director of Education — the most senior official employed by the education authority to look after the running of educational services in its area.

Education authority — the local government body (regional or islands council) responsible for the running of education services in its area.

Exclusion — barring a pupil from entering school, often for reasons of discipline. This is sometimes referred to as suspension.

Extra-curricular activities — activities run by the school, mainly through school clubs and sports teams outside the ordinary school day or timetable, to promote new interests, hobbies and pastimes, among pupils.

General Certificate of Education (GCE) — the main public examination taken by pupils in England and Wales from about the age of 15 or 16. GCE subjects are taken either at ordinary and advanced levels. Some Scottish schools also let pupils take the exam. It will shortly be replaced by a new Certificate of Secondary Education (GCSE) catering for most of the ability range (the GCE was meant for the most able 20 per cent of pupils).

234

General Teaching Council for Scotland (GTC) — the body which controls entry into the teaching profession in Scotland. Teachers must normally be registered with the GTC before they can teach in most schools and in various subjects.

Governing body — a body of various representatives, including parents, responsible for the general running of a school in England and Wales and independent schools in Scotland. Most Scottish schools have school councils instead.

Grammar school — in England and Wales, this refers to a secondary school which caters only for more academically able pupils. There are also some 'grammar schools' in Scotland, but most of these are in fact comprehensive schools.

Highers — Higher Grade of the Scottish Certificate of Education, usually taken in the fifth and sixth years of secondary school or at a college of further education.

Independent School — a privately-run school providing education for five or more pupils. Independent schools must be registered with the Scottish Education Department.

In loco parentis — a Latin term meaning "in place of the parent" and applied to schools and teachers whenever they are left in charge of your child.

Inspectors — officials, more properly known as Her Majesty's Inspectors (HMI's), employed by the Scottish Education Department to inspect schools and colleges, advise staff and promote educational developments.

Integration — educating children with "special educational needs", in ordinary schools or classrooms alongside pupils without these needs, instead of at a special school.

Intermediate treatment — a sort of halfway house between taking children who have been in trouble or have other difficulties into full-time residential care, and putting them under compulsory social work supervision while they remain at home. It takes various forms but usually consists of individual or group counselling or community work done in the evenings, at weekends or during school holidays, possibly including short stays away from home.

Intelligence/intelligence tests — there are many varied and conflicting views about what is meant by "intelligence", some saying it is simply what intelligence tests measure! Most intelligence tests deal with reasoning, memory, numerical and other abilities to give a child's IQ (intelligence quotient). With the introduction of comprehensive schooling intelligence testing is now less common.

List D school — see under "Residential Schools".

Mixed ability grouping teaching — pupils of different abilities being taught in the same class or group. Most pupils are taught this way at primary school and in the first few years of secondary school.

Mixed classes — classes of boys and girls taught together.

Modern maths — a general approach to maths placing greater emphasis on mathematical ideas and reasoning than on mechanical, repetitive number work.

Module/modular course — a short-course lasting about 40 hours. Modules may be taken in different combinations of subjects to suit learners' preferences, as under the "Sixteen Plus Development Programme".

Munn and Dunning Development Programme — see under "Standard Grade".

Nursery education/school — education for children between about the ages of three and five.

Open plan schooling — instead of the school being divided into separate classrooms, pupils share a common work area, sometimes with partitions. This gives greater freedom of movement between one part of the area to another. It is usually found in primary schools.

Parent-teacher/parents' association (PTA/PA) — voluntary groups of parents and teachers who meet in order to get to know each other and support the work of the school.

Primary education — education from about the age of five to twelve years.

Progressive education — education based on the needs and interests of the individual pupil and often associated with informal teaching methods and a flexible curriculum.

Progress reports/records — confidential documents kept by or on behalf of the education authority containing information about individual pupils' progress in schoolwork, attendance record, medical condition, home background and other details.

Public school — the legal term used to describe any school in Scotland managed by an education authority. In England and Wales, it means the opposite, a private or independent school, often taking in boarders.

Pupil-teacher ratio (PTR) — the number of pupils in relation to teachers at a school, including teachers without a class (e.g. 25:1 or 25 pupils to a teacher).

Record of needs — an official document saying what a child's or young person's special educational needs are and how they should be catered for.

Remedial education — education for children with learning difficulties e.g. in reading.

Residential (former 'List D') Schools — schools providing education and personal care for children who have been in trouble or have other serious difficulties.

School age — ages 5 to 16 approximately. Education is compulsory for all children of school age. Compulsory education starts at the age of 5 or at the next school starting date (if later).

School council — a body of parents', teachers and other representatives which must be set up by the education authority to help with the management of a school or group of schools.

School day — this normally lasts from about 8.45-9.00 in the morning to about 3.15 to 3.45 in the afternoon, with a lunch break in between (the actual starting and finishing times vary from area to area or school to school). The school may stay open for out of school activities once the school day is over.

School handbook (brochure or prospectus) — a booklet written for and given to parents with information about the school, including what is taught there.

School report — a document issued to parents normally at least once a year saying how well their child is doing at school, drawing attention to any difficulties their child is having and remarking on their general conduct.

School year or 'session' — this runs from about the middle of August to the end of June or early July.

Scottish Certificate of Education (SCE) — the main public exam taken by Scottish secondary school pupils. It is taken at two levels: Ordinary Grade or Standard Grade (from the fourth year) and Higher Grade (from the fifth year).

Scottish Education Department — the central government department forming part of the Scottish Office and dealing with educational matters in Scotland (except Scottish Universities, which come under the Department of Education and Science).

Scottish Joint Negotiating Committee (SJNC) — the official body responsible for negotiating teachers' salaries and conditions of service.

Secondary education — education for children aged from 12 to 18 years. It is not compulsory after about age 16.

Secretary of State for Scotland — the Cabinet Minister in overall charge of Scottish Affairs, including Scottish education. A junior non-Cabinet Minister is given special responsibility for Scottish education.

Selective school — a school which only takes pupils from the upper academic ability range. Most schools in Scotland are non-selective.

Setting — putting pupils into different classes or groups for various activities, like reading and maths, according to their abilities in these. Pupils might therefore be in the 'top' set for some subjects and in the 'middle' or 'bottom' set for others.

Sixteen-plus Development Programme (or 'Action Plan') — a range of short courses, called 'modules', in technical, vocational and other subjects mainly intended for pupils and students at school or college from about the age of 16. Completion of these courses leads to a 16+ National Certificate awarded by the Scottish Vocational Education Council.

Social education — education for personal development, such as learning to handle relationships with others, reach decisions properly, or deal with various practical matters.

Special educational needs — children such as physically disabled or mentally handicapped children, are said to have special educational needs if they need additional or special help with their education compared with a majority of children of their age. Help may cover special tuition, medical support, therapy or special adaptations. Their needs and what should be done about them may be entered on a 'Record of Needs'.

Special schools/classes — schools or classes catering wholly or mainly for pupils with a 'Record of Needs' (see under "Special Educational Needs" above).

Standard Grade — the exam due to replace the Ordinary Grade of the Scottish Certificate of Education as part of the Munn and Dunning development programme. It is taken at three general but overlapping ability levels.

Streaming — Putting pupils into separate classes or groups according to their general level of ability. Pupils will normally stay in the same 'stream' for different subjects (compared with setting).

Syllabus — a plan or programme showing what topics or activities will be covered within a school subject or examination course at a particular level or stage of education.

Team teaching — two or more teachers working together with a class or group of pupils, pooling their knowledge and expertise.

Timetable — a plan or chart showing what subjects and other activities pupils are doing at different times of the school day, usually divided into 35-40 minute 'periods' or longer 'double periods' in the case of secondary schools.

TVEI — Technical and Vocational Education Initiative — the name given to a series of government-sponsored projects run by education authorities to prepare 14-18 year olds for working life.

Vocational education — education leading to a specific job or career and preparing pupils for adult living in general.

Young person — a person over school age (age 16 approx) but not yet 18.

Periodicals and other publications

Periodicals and other publications of general interest to parents
(see also under **Where to Find Out More** at the end of different topics for more specialist information.)

ACE Bulletin (every two months), Advisory Centre for Education Contains news, comment and advice and a digest of recent reports to do with education and of concern to parents.

British Education Index The British Library, Bibliographic Services Division, annual edition. Comprehensive annual listing of all published articles of educational interest in over 300 English-language periodicals in alphabetical order of topics.

Childright (ten times a year) Children's Legal Centre.

Dictionary of Education by Derek Rowntree, Harper and Row, 1981 Thousands of educational terms defined.

Education Year Book, Longman, annual edition Comprehensive UK listing of all education authorities, secondary schools, special schools, colleges, universities, careers centres and specialist educational bodies.

History of Scottish Education by James Scotland, University of London Press, 1979 (2 vols).

International Encyclopaedia of Education, ed. Torsten Husen and T. Neville Postlethwaite, Pergamon, 1985 (10 vols). Brings together the latest scholarship through 1,448 articles on educational topics, in alphabetical order.

Parents and Schools (three times a year), Campaign for the Advancement of State Education.

Primary Education Directory (annually), School Government Publishing Co., Ltd. Lists name, address and headteacher of every primary school in the UK.

SCAN (monthly), Scottish Community Education Council.

Scottish Education, Scottish Information Office, current edition.

SCOLAG (monthly), Scottish Legal Action Group.

The Scottish Child (four times a year), Scottish Child Publications, 56 Albany Street, Edinburgh.

Scots Law Times (weekly), W. Green & Co. Includes reports on selected sheriff court cases.

SPTC Newspaper (3 times a year), Scottish Parent Teacher Council.

Statistical Bulletin, Scottish Education Department, obtainable from Room 265, Scottish Office Library. Periodical publication covering several different educational topics.

The Times Educational Supplement Scotland (weekly).

Education A-Z: where to look things up, compiled by Elizabeth Wallis, Advisory Centre for Education, current edition. Quick access to relevant addresses, publications, and terminology on a large number of educational topics, listed alphabetically.

You and Your Rights: an A-Z guide to the law in Scotland, Readers' Digest Association Ltd., 1984.

Children, Parents and the Law, Consumers' Association, 1985. Includes sections on the law applying to children in Scotland.

Useful addresses

EDUCATION AUTHORITIES

Borders Regional Council
Director of Education, Education Department, Borders Regional Council, Regional Headquarters, Newtown St. Boswells TD6 0SA (08352 3301).

Central Regional Council
Director of Education, Education Department, Central Regional Council, Regional Headquarters, Viewforth, Stirling FH8 2ET (0786 3111).

Dumfries and Galloway Regional Council
Director of Education, Education Offices, Dumfries & Galloway Regional Council, 30 Edinburgh Road, Dumfries DG1 1JQ (0387 63822).

Fife Regional Council
Director of Education, Education Department, Fife Regional Council, Regional Headquarters, Fife House, North Street, Glenrothes KY7 5LT (0592 754411).

Grampian Regional Council
Director of Education, Education Department, Grampian Regional Council, Regional Headquarters, Woodhill House, Ashgrove Road West, Aberdeen (0224 682222).

Highland Regional Council
Director of Education, Education Department, Highland Regional Council, Regional Building, Glenurquart Road, Inverness IV3 5NX (0463 34121).

Lothian Regional Council
Director of Education, Education Department, Lothian Regional Council, 40 Torphichen Street, Edinburgh EH3 8JJ (031 229 9166).

Strathclyde Regional Council
Director of Education, Regional Education Office, Strathclyde Regional Council, 20 India Street, Glasgow G2 4PF (041 227 2847).

Strathclyde Regional Council (Argyll Division)
Divisional Education Officer, Argyll Division, Argyll House, Alexandra Parade, Dunoon DA28 8AJ (0369 4000).

Strathclyde Regional Council (Ayr Division)
Divisional Education Officer, Ayr Division, Regional Offices, Ayr KA7 1DR (0292 66922).

Strathclyde Regional Council (Dumbarton Division)
Divisional Education Officer, Dumbarton Division, Regional Council Offices, Dumbarton G82 3PU (0389 65151).

Strathclyde Regional Council (Glasgow Division)
Divisional Education Officer, Glasgow Division, Education Offices, 129 Bath Street, Glasgow G2 4SY (041 204 2900).

Strathclyde Regional Council (Lanark Division)
Divisional Education Officer, Lanark Division, Regional Offices, Hamilton ML3 0AE (0698 282828).

Strathclyde Regional Council (Renfrew Division)
Divisional Education Officer, Renfrew Division, Regional Offices, Cotton Street, Paisley PA1 1LE (041 889 5454).

Tayside Regional Council
Director of Education, Regional Education Office, Tayside Regional Council, Tayside House, 28 Crichton Street, Dundee DD1 3RJ (0382 23281).

Orkney Islands Council
Director of Education, Education Department, Orkney Islands Council, Albert Street, Kirkwall KW15 1NY (0856 3535).

Shetlands Islands Council
Director of Education, Education Offices, Shetlands Islands Council, 1 Harbour Street, Lerwick ZE1 0LS (0595 3535).

Western Isles Islands Council
Director of Education, Education Office, Western Isles Council, Sandwick Road, Stornoway, Lewis PA87 2BW (0851 3992).

LEGAL ORGANISATIONS

Law Society of Scotland	26 Drumheugh Gardens, Edinburgh EH3 7YR (031 226 7411).
Law Centres Federation	18-19 Warren Street, London WC1P 5DB (01 387 8570).
Legal Aid Central Committee (Scotland)	41 Drumsheugh Gardens, Edinburgh EH3 7SW (031 226 7061).
Scottish Courts Administration	26/27 Royal Terrace, Edinburgh EH7 5AH (031 556 0755).
Scottish Law Commission	140 Causewayside, Edinburgh EH9 1PR (031 668 2131).
Scottish Legal Action Group (SCOLAG)	c/o Dept. of Scots Law, Edinburgh University, Edinburgh
Lay Observer	30 Castle Street, Edinburgh EH2 3HT (031 226 2503).

OFFICIAL AND PROFESSIONAL EDUCATIONAL ORGANISATIONS

Association of Directors of Education Scotland	c/o Director of Education, Lothian Regional Council, 40 Torphichen Street, Edinburgh EH3 8JJ (031 229 9166).
Association of Educational Advisers in Scotland	c/o Dean Education Centre, Belford Road, Edinburgh EH4 3DS (031 343 1931).
British Educational Management and Administration Society	Moray House College, Edinburgh EH8 8AQ (031 556 8455).
Chartered Institute of Public Finance and Accountancy, Scottish Branch	Strathclyde House, 20 India Street, Glasgow G2 4PF (041 227 3174).
Commission for Local Authority Accounts in Scotland	18 George Street, Edinburgh EH2 1QU (031 226 7346).
Commissioner for Local Administration in Scotland (Local Ombudsman)	5 Shandwick Place, Edinburgh EH2 4RG (031 229 4472).
Commission for Racial Equality (CRE)	Elliot House, 10-12 Allington Street, London SW1E 5EH (01 828 7022).
Consultative Committee on the Curriculum (CCC)	*See* Scottish Education Department
Convention of Scottish Local Authorities (COSLA)	Rosebery House, 9 Haymarket Terrace, Edinburgh EH12 5XZ (031 346 1222).
Council for National Academic Awards (CNAA)	344-384 Gray's Inn Road, London WC1X 8BP.
Department of Education and Science (DES) (Schools in E & W and Universities in the UK)	Elizabeth House. York Road, London SE1 7PH (01 928 9222).
Educational Institute of Scotland (EIS)	46 Moray Place, Edinburgh EH3 6BH (031 225 6244).
Educational Publishers Council (EPC)	19 Bedford Square, London WC1 (01 580 6321).
Equal Opportunities Commission (EOC)	249 West George Street, Glasgow G2 4QE (041 226 4591).
General Teaching Council for Scotland (GTC)	5 Royal Terrace, Edinburgh (031 556 0072).
Houses of Parliament	Westminster, London SW1 (01 219 3000).
National Children's Bureau	8 Wakely Street, London EC1V 7QE (01 278 9441).
National Union of Teachers	Hamilton House, Mabledon Place, London WC1H 9BD (01 387 2442).

Professional Association of Teachers (PAT)	22 Rutland Street, Edinburgh EH1 2AN (031 229 7868).
School Broadcasting Council for Scotland	5 Queen Street, Edinburgh EH2 1JF (031 225 3131).
Scottish Catholic Education Commission	43 Greenhill Road, Rutherglen, Glasgow G73 2SW (041 647 2986).
Scottish Centre for Studies in School Administration	Moray House College, Holyrood Road, Edinburgh EH2 8TS (031 556 8455).
Scottish Centre for the Tuition of the Disabled	Queen Margaret College, 36 Clerwood Terrace, Edinburgh EH2 8TS (031 339 5408).
Scottish Community Education Council (SCEC)	Atholl House, 2 Canning Street, Edinburgh EH3 7EG (031 229 2433).
Scottish Council for Educational Technology (SCET)	Dowanhill, 74 Victoria Crescent Road, Glasgow G12 9JN (041 334 9314).
Scottish Council for Research in Education (SCRE)	Moray House College, 15 St John Street, Edinburgh EH8 8JR (031 557 2944)
Scottish Education Department (SED)	New St. Andrew's House, St. James Centre, Edinburgh EH1 2SX (031 556 8400).
Scottish Examination Board (SEB)	Iron Mills Road, Dalkeith, Midlothian (031 663 6601).
Scottish Information Office	New St. Andrew's House, Edinburgh EH1 3TD (031 557 0557).
Scottish Institute of Adult and Continuing Education	30 Rutland Square, Edinburgh EH1 2BW (031 229 0311).
Scottish Joint Negotiating Committee (SJNC)	6 Coates Crescent, Edinburgh EH3 7AL (031 226 7214).
Scottish Secondary Teachers' Association (SSTA)	15 Dundas Street, Edinburgh EH3 6QG (031 556 5919).
Scottish Vocational Education Council	38 Queen Street, Glasgow G1 3DY (041 248 7900).
Universities Central Council on Admissions (UCCA)	PO Box 28, Cheltenham, Gloucestershire GL50 1HY (0242 519091).

VOLUNTARY ORGANISATIONS INVOLVED WITH EDUCATION

Advisory Centre for Education	18 Victoria Park Square, London E2 9PB (01 980 4596).
Advisory Committee for the Education of Romany and other Travellers	Mary Ward Centre, 42 Queen Square, London WC1N 3AJ.
An Comunn Gaidhealach	Abertarff House, Church Street, Inverness IV1 1EU (0463 31226).
British Association for Early Childhood Education	Montgomery Hall, Kennington Oval, London SE11 5SW (01 582 8744).
British Youth Council (Scotland)	Atholl House, 2 Canning Place, Edinburgh EH3 8EG (031 229 6111).
Campaign for the Advancement of State Education (CASE)	4 Hill Road, Carshalton Beeches, Surrey (01 669 5929).
Campaign Against Sexism and Sexual Oppression in Education	7 Pickwick Court, London SE7 4SA (01 857 3793).

Campaign for Freedom of Information	3 Endsleigh Street, London WC1H 0DD (01 278 9686); Scottish Campaign for Freedom of Information — c/o Scottish Consumer Council.
Centre for Studies in Integration in Education	The Spastics Society, 16 Fitzroy Square, London W1P 5RQ (01 387 9571).
Child Poverty Action Group	1 Macklin Street, London WC2B 8NH (01 405 5942).
Children's Legal Centre	20 Compton Terrace, London N1 2UN (01 359 6251).
Consumers' Association	14 Buckingham Street, London WC2N 6DS (01 839 1222).
Co-operative Union	Scottish Branch, 95 Morrison Street, Glasgow (041 429 2556).
Education Otherwise	25 Common Lane, Hemingford Abbots, Cambridgeshire PE18 9AN (0480 63130).
European Parents Association	EPA Secretariat, c/o Office for Co-operation in Education, 51 rue de la concorde, B1050, Brussels, Belgium.
Gifted Children's Information Centre	21 Hampton Lane, Solihull, West Midlands (021 705 4547).
Gingerbread (one-parent families)	13 Elmbank Street, Glasgow G2 4QA (041 226 4541)
Hyperactive Children's Support Group	59 Meadowside, Angmering, Sussex BN16 4BW (090 64 725182).
Independent Schools' Information Service	22 Hanover Street, Edinburgh EH2 (031 225 7202).
Invalid Children's Aid Association	126 Buckingham Palace Road, London SW1W 9SB (01 703 9891).
Justice for Children	35 Wellington Street, London WX2E 7BN (01 836 5917).
National Association for Gifted Children	1 South Audley Street, London W1Y 5DQ (01 499 1188).
National Association for Maternal and Child Welfare	1 South Audley Street, London W1Y 6JS (01 491 1315).
National Association for Multiracial Education	86 Station Road, Mickleover, Derby DE3 5FP (0332 511751).
National Association for Pastoral Care in Education	Faculty of Education, Warwick University, Coventry CV4 7AC (0203 24011).
National Association for Support of Small Schools	91 King Street, Norwich (0603 613088).
National Association for the Welfare of Children in Hospital (Scotland)	94 Murrayfield Gardens, Edinburgh EH12 6DJ (031 337 6412).
National Campaign for Nursery Education	33 Hugh Street, London SW1V 1QJ (SAE for reply).
National Committee on Racism in Children's Books	7 Denbigh Road, London W1 2SJ (01 221 1353).
National Council for Special Education	1 Wood Street, Stratford upon Avon, Warwickshire CV37 6JE (0789 5332).
National Confederation of Parent-Teacher Associations	43 Stonebridge Road, Northfleet, Gravesend DA11 9DS (0474 60618).
National Child Care Campaign	17 Victoria Park Square, London E2 9PB (01 981 1221).
National Consumer Council	20 Grosvenor Gardens, London SW1W 0DH (01 730 3469).
National Council for Civil Liberties	21 Tabard Street, London SE1 (01 403 3888).
National Council for Educational Standards	1 Hinchley Way, Esher, Surrey KT10 0BD (01 398 1253).

National Council for Mother Tongue Teaching	5 Musgrave Crescent, London SW6 4PT (01 736 2134).
National Gypsy Education Council	Sociology Department, Thames Polytechnic, Wellington Street, London SE18 6PF (01 854 2030).
National Out of School Alliance	Oxford House, Derbyshire Street, London E2 6HG (01 739 4787).
National Union of Students	12 Dublin Street, Edinburgh (031 556 6598).
Right to Comprehensive Education	36 Broxash Road, London SW11 6AB (01 228 9732).
Royal Association for Disability and Rehabilitation	25 Mortimer Street, London NW1 8AB (01 637 5400).
Royal Scottish Society of Prevention of Cruelty to Children	Melville House, 41 Polwarth Terrace, Edinburgh EH11 1NU (031 337 8539).
Rural Forum Scotland	c/o Scottish Council for Voluntary Organisations (see below).
School Bookshop Association	1 Effingham Road, London SE12 8NZ (01 852 4953).
Scottish Association of Citizens Advice Bureaux	82 Nicolson Street, Edinburgh EH8 9EW (031 667 0156).
Scottish Child and Family Alliance	56 Albany Street, Edinburgh (031 557 2780).
Scottish Children's Book Association	1 Beaumont Gate, Glasgow G12 9EE (041 339 2802).
Scottish Consumer Council	314 St. Vincent Street, Glasgow G3 8XW (041 226 5261).
Scottish Council for Civil Liberties	146 Holland Street, Glasgow G1 4NG (041 332 5960).
Scottish Council on Disability (SCD)	Princes House, 5 Shandwick Place, Edinburgh EH2 4RG (031 229 8632) (see also SCD's Directory of Voluntary Organisations on Disability in Scotland.)
Scottish Council for Opportunity in Play Experience (SCOPE)	16 Sandyford Place, Glasgow G3 7NB (041 221 4148).
Scottish Council for Racial Equality	12 Bowmont Gardens, Glasgow G12 9LR.
Scottish Council for Single Parents	13 Gayfield Square, Edinburgh EH7 3NX (031 556 3899).
Scottish Council for Voluntary Organisations	18/19 Claremont Crescent, Edinburgh EH4 4QD (031 556 3882).
Scottish Council for Spastics	Rhuemore, 22 Corstorphine Road, Edinburgh EH12 6HP (031 337 2804)
Scottish Down's Syndrome Association	48 Govan Road, Glasgow G51 1JL (041 427 4911).
Scottish Dyslexia Association	c/o Department of Education, Dundee University, Dundee DD1 4HN
Scottish Education Action for Development (SEAD)	29 Nicolson Square, Edinburgh EH8 9BX (031 667 0129).
Scottish Parent Teacher Council	Atholl House, 2 Canning Street, Edinburgh EH3 8EG (031 229 2433).
Scottish Pre-School Playgroups Association	16 Sandyford Place, Glasgow G3 7NB (041 221 4148).
Scottish Society for Autistic Children	2nd Floor. 12 Picardy Place, Edinburgh EH1 3JT (031 557 0474).
Scottish Society for the Mentally Handicapped	13 Elmbank Street, Glasgow G2 4QA (041 226 4541).

Scottish Sports Council	1 St. Colme Street, Edinburgh EH3 6AA (031 225 8411).
Society of Teachers opposed to Corporal Punishment	18 Victoria Park Square, London E2 9PB (01 980 8523).
Scottish Telephone Referral Advice and Information Network	Dowanhill, 74 Victoria Park Road, Glasgow G12 9JN (041 357 1774).
Welsh Consumer Council	Castle Buildings, Womanby Street, Cardiff CF1 2BN (0222 396056).
Workers' Educational Association	212 Bath Street, Glasgow G2 4HW (041 332 0176).

Index

accidents to child in school 173, 174-5
acoustics of school building 177
activities
  extra-curricular 16
  out of school 41, 50, 75, 89, 129, 181
Acts of Parliament 227
admission to school 17-19
  age for 17-18, 128
  changes, consultation 180-5
  denominational schools 79
  education authority guidelines 52-56, 128,
    130-1
  information for parents 130-1
  racial discrimination illegal 161-2
  sex discrimination 197-8
  under five 18-19, 128
adult education 89, 110, 111, 153, 195
advice and assistance
  further education 154
  legal action by parents 139-40
  publications 23-24, 240-1
  racial discrimination 163
  where to go for help 20-24
advisory councils on education matters 195
age, ability and aptitude 13, 50, 54, 88, 96,
  121, 162, 202
appeals
  admissions under age 19
  attendance order 32, 122
  children's hearing decision 48, 49
  choice of school 52, 55-60, 130, 139, 194
  examinations, SCE results 98-99
  exclusion 15, 67, 101, 103, 104, 190-1
  legal aid not applicable 22
  parental rights taken away 44
  residential school placement 168
  secure accommodation rights 169
  special educational needs 15, 21, 131, 139,
    194, 206, 214-19
  transfer of child to another school 85
arbitration panel
  class size disputes 61
artistic aptitude 201-2
assault on child 86, 139
assessment centre
  residential school placement 168
assessment of pupils
  education authority powers 89
  legal requirement 95
  methods 95
  progress record see progress record

assessment of special needs 207-10
Assisted Places Scheme 25-29, 107, 125, 128,
  166, 189, 195, 225
attendance at school
  age 14, permission to stay away 30
  attendance order 31-32, 33
  authorised absences 33
  beyond school leaving age 137
  duty of education authority 88
  exclusion counts as absence 31, 33, 101
  failure to attend 31-32
  failure to benefit from schooling 101-2
  family holidays 119-20
  industrial action by teachers 222
  information for parents 129
  legal advice to parents 140
  parental responsibility 14, 16, 18, 30-33,
    40, 92
  punctuality 92, 129
  reasonable excuses for non-attendance
    30-31, 119-20
  registration of daily attendance 33
  truancy 31, 32-33, 43, 46, 167
attendance order 31-32, 122

behaviour problems 43, 46, 204
"belt" for punishment 84
bi-lingual education 34-35, 73, 88
boarding accommodation
  changes to, consultation 181
  children of mobile workers 147
  duty of education authority 88
  grants 15, 36-37
  religious observance rights 37, 79, 166
  sex discrimination 198-9
  see also residential school
booklets
  starting school 19
  subject options in secondary schools 116
  written information about schools 75
books
  capitation allowance 107
  charging for, illegal 89
  damage and loss liability 38, 158-60
  duty of education authority to provide 88,
    105
  expenditure on, statistics 109
  free to pupils 38
  sex discrimination 198
  stirring racial prejudice 161, 161
  storage space for 177

bullying 117, 173
bursaries *see* grants

camp sites
    educational provision for travellers'
        children 147-8
capitation allowance 38, 107
careers guidance 116, 117-18, 198
catchment area
    alteration to, consultation 180
charitable bequests 108
child benefit 114
child development 155
child guidance
    availability of service 15, 23, 117
    children's hearing reports 48
    disruptive pupils 85
    under-age admissions 19
childminding 155, 156
children
    abuse of 40
    assault on 86, 139
    educational rights 40-42
    encouragement by parents 13, 124, 155,
        201-2
    freedom of thought 41
    freedom to run organisations 41
    legal binding agreements, age for 42
    liberty and freedom of movement 41
children in care
    advice and assistance 23
    compulsory care 43-44, 47-48, 49
    parents' rights 43 45
    voluntary care 43, 44, 47
children's hearing 44, 46-49
    appeal to sheriff 48, 49
    assault arising from corporal punishment
        139
    disruptive children referred to 85, 86, 167
    "place of safety" order 169
    Reporter 31, 32, 46-48, 85, 86, 139
    residential school placement 167, 168, 169
    reviews 49
    secure accommodation rights 169
children's home 43, 44, 45
children's panel 47
choice of school 13, 14-15, 17, 19, 32, 50-60, 88
    appeal 52, 55-60, 130, 139, 194
    changes to general guidelines 182
    information for parents 128, 130, 132
    placing request 51-56
    special educational needs 50, 51, 207,
        213-14
    transfer request 52, 53
Church of Scotland
    education committee appointment 90
citizens' advice bureaux 21, 69

classroom
    records of size held by education
        authority 61
    standards 177
class size pupil numbers
    composite class 61-62
    disputes 61
    education authority powers 90
    primary schools 61, 62
    secondary schools 61, 62
cloakrooms and lockers 177
closure of school
    advice and assistance 20, 21
    consultation with parents 15, 88, 179-80,
        181-5
    denominational school 79-80, 179, 194
    lobbying against 185
    rural, government permission for 179, 194
clothing
    grants 15, 88
    information for parents 65
    national costume worn by ethnic
        minorities 162
    sex discrimination 199
    what to wear at school 64-65
    see also uniform
Commissioner for Local Administration 67,
    69, 70-72, 91, 184
community
    adults learning alongside pupils in
        school 76, 154
    classes for, education authority powers
        89, 111
    education oversight 195
community council
    school council representation 187
community organisations
    closure of schools and 21
    education authority powers to finance 89
complaints 16, 20, 21, 66-72
    children banned from activities in
        school 41
    child wrongfully punished 87
    councillors 69, 71
    education authority assistance with 16,
        66, 67, 68-69
    education authority failure 70-72, 76, 91,
        139
    education committee consideration 68, 69
    examination course choice 96
    failure to provide proper education 76, 202
    independent schools 126-7
    legal action 91
    local ombudsman 67, 69, 70-72, 91, 134
    MP's consideration to 69, 76
    meals at school 143
    political parties 69

complaints—contd.
  PTA/PA refused by headteacher 150
  racial discrimination 67, 162-3, 223
  residential schools 171
  school council consideration of 66, 68, 69, 76, 187-8
  school rules 193
  Secretary of State 16, 60-70, 71, 76, 139, 194
  sex discrimination 67, 199-200, 223
  teachers and headteachers 223
  voluntary organisations support with 67
  see also appeals
composite class 61-62
compulsory education 88, 153, 155
computerised records 191
corporal punishment 83, 84-85, 101, 139, 141
correspondence courses 154
  financial assistance with 111
councillors
  complaints consideration 69, 71
  school council representation 187
country schools 61-62
  closure 179, 194
courses
  advanced 153
  block release 153
  financial assistance towards 111
  non-advanced 153
  "open learning" 154
  part-time, definition of 111, 112, 114, 152
  part-time paid by employers 153
  sex discrimination 198
Court of Session
  children's hearing, conduct of case, appeal to 48
  education authority failing in statutory duty 139
  endowments, powers to alter 108
  see also legal action, sheriff courts
court order
  residential school attendance 167, 168, 169
criminal offence 43, 46, 86-87, 101
  residential school placement for 68
cultural activities 88
  charges 105
  further education 152
curriculum 73-77
  advisers 90
  articles made in school lessons 105
  charges for books and equipment illegal 89, 107
  Consultative Committee 195
  development 76, 186
  education authority powers 89
  information for parents 131
  parental wishes 75-76

curriculum—contd.
  primary education 73-74
  religious education compulsory 165-6
  school council discussion of 186
  secondary school 74
  timetable 74
custody order
  responsibility for child's education 14

day nurseries 155, 156
days in school year 33
denominational schools
  closure 79-80
  conversion into non-denominational consultation 181-5
  information for parents 79, 128, 129, 132
  management of 78-80
  open to all 166
detention for disciplinary offence 83, 84
diagnostic tests 95
Director of Education
  appointment 90
  inspectors reports, action on 136
disability
  examinations, help with 98
  special educational needs *see* special educational needs
  student allowances 113
  transport to school 224
disadvantaged areas
  additional government grants 63
  flexibility granted 62
  residential schools for children from 167
discipline 41, 81-87
  changes in, consultation 181
  Code of Practice 82, 85
  corporal punishment 83, 84-85, 101, 139, 141
  disruptive pupils 85
  education authority powers 89
  exclusion *see* exclusion
  guidance for pupils 116
  hair styles 65
  jewellery 61
  list of punishments 83-84
  make up 65
  medical, social, emotional or other problems 84
  outside school hours 85-86
  parents disagreement with 100-1
  personal belongings brought to school 158-9
  policies, parents' views on 87
  removal from classroom of child 103
  residential school 170

discipline—contd.
  school rules 14, 86, 100-1, 129, 140, 158-9, 193
  transfer of child to another school 85
  wrongdoing by child, parent responsibility for 86-87
discrimination
  racial see racial discrimination
  sex see sex discrimination
disruptive pupils
  exclusion from school 100-1, 102
  procedures for dealing with 85
  residential schools 167
  Warnock report 205
divorced parents
  child's education, responsibility for 14
doctors visiting schools 145
dramatic ability 202
drug misuse among pupils 145, 159
dyslexia, help with examinations 98

educational terms 232-9
educational welfare officer 117
education authority
  administration 90
  admission to school guidelines 52-56, 130
  advice and assistance 21
  appeal committee for choice of school 55, 57-60
  capitation allowance guidelines 107
  charging for essential items 89, 107
  choice of school appeals 52, 55-60, 130, 139
  class size disputes 61
  class size guidelines 62
  compensation for loss, damage or injury 139-40
  complaints against 70-72, 76, 91, 139
  complaints to 16, 66, 67, 68-69
  computerised records 191
  denominational school management 78
  duties 88-89
  financial expenditure 107, 108-9
  information for parents 128, 131-3
  holiday dates arrangements 119
  law, problems with interpretation 140
  legal action against 139-40
  maladministration, grounds for complaint to Ombudsman 70-72
  places in other areas, charges for 105
  policies and practices 131
  powers 89
  school closure procedures 179-85
  school council powers 186, 187
  school health and safety requirements 176
  special educational needs provision 204-20

education authority—contd.
  starting dates of schools vary 17, 18
  teaching staff at a school 62-63
wills and bequests to schools 108
education committee
  appointment 90
  complaints consideration 68, 69
  co-option of parents and pupils 90
  financial decisions 107
  open to public 90-1
  sub-committee appointments 90
  teacher misconduct and indiscipline 223
"efficient education" 13, 88, 121, 126, 139, 152
emergencies in schools, contact addresses 145, 189
emotional problems, children with 167, 204, 205
employers
  records on pupils, access to 190
employment
  children to age of sixteen 92-94
  public performances of children at school 93
  work experience 93
  young persons taking up whilst at school 137
endowments, register of 108
Episcopalian schools 78
equipment
  assistance to parents towards cost of 111
  capitation allowance 107
  damage and loss liability 38, 158-60
  duty of education authority to provide 38, 88, 105
  pupils own, permission to take to school 38
  safety requirements 174
European Convention on Human Rights 40, 41
European Court of Human Rights 22, 85, 101, 139, 140-1
European Economic Community (EEC)
  children of migrant workers 146-7
European Parents' Federation 150
evening classes, financial assistance 111
examinations
  appeal against SCE results 98-99, 140
  Certificate of Secondary Education 95
  changes in arrangements, consultation 181
  choice of subjects 96
  Common Entrance Exam 125
  complaints over choice of course 96, 140
  dates 96
  disability, provisions for 98
  dyslexia, provision for 98
  education authority powers 89

examinations—contd.
English exams 97
free entry 16
grades of SCE 97
guidance for pupils and parents 116
hospital or confined to home,
  allowed to sit 145
illness preventing completion of 98
internal in school 95, 96, 97
marks, computerised 191
non-advanced courses 153
private arrangements to take 96
public 95-99
resits 97, 152
results 130
Scottish Certificate of Education 74, 95,
  96-99, 125, 140, 166, 169
selection of pupils for 95, 130
vocational 96-97, 153
syllabuses 75
exclusion
appeals 15, 67, 101, 103, 104, 190-1
disruptive pupils 100-1, 102
last resort 85
legal advice for parents 140
legal procedures 102-3, 132
length of 102
non-attendance at school 31, 33
not an excuse from being educated 31, 33,
  101
parents preventing child from obeying
  rules 100-1
reasons for 100
record on pupil, inclusion of 84, 103-4,
  190-1
unlawful, compensation 103
young person 16, 104
see also discipline
extra-currcular activities 16

family centres 155, 156
"feeder" primary schools 130, 180, 186
fees for independent schools
Assisted Places Scheme 26
field study courses
assistance towards cost of 110
Assisted Places Scheme an 27-28
finance
annual abstract of accounts 109
education authority powers 89, 108-9
public education 107
statistics publication 109
fire drills 174
first aid 145
flexibility allowance 62
fostering 43, 44
free education 15, 88, 105, 152

fuel storage 177
fund-raising 107-8
furniture storage space 177
further education
bursaries for 110, 111, 112-13, 152
advice for 154
charges for 105, 153
college council 186
compulsory to 18 not implemented 153
courses 153
duty of education authority 89, 152
school pupils permission to attend 153

Gaelic speaking 15, 34-35, 73, 88, 131, 132,
  153
games see physical education
General Teaching Council of Scotland,
  complaints 67
gifted children 201-2
government regulations 228
grants
advice and assistance 22
community and voluntary organisations 89
duty of education authority 88, 110
flexibility allowance 62
further education bursaries 110, 111,
  112-13, 150, 152
industrial career scholarships 195
mature students for HE 113
parental contribution for further
  education awards 113
parental contribution for higher education
  awards 110, 112, 113
parent's groups 89
school trips and special courses 105, 110
sixteen plus 14, 22, 110, 112-13
student HE awards 22, 110, 111, 113-14
welfare 15, 88, 110
guardian
legally binding agreements for children,
  age for 42
guidance
careers 116, 117-18, 198
educational 116
personal 116

headteachers
power to ban on certain activities 41
complaints against 223
complaints to 67-68
setting up decisions on PTA/PAs
  establishment 150
guidance for pupils 116
holidays for children in term time,
  permission required 119-20
school council appointment 187

health and safety
  class size 61
  see also safety
health education 145
health visitors
  children at risk, support for 155
  special needs of child, advice 207
heating and ventilation of school
    building 177
higher education
  student allowances 22, 110, 111, 113-14
HM Inspectors *see* inspectors
holidays
  fixing of 119, 129
  parents taking children away in term
    time 119-20
  religious observance 120
home education
  alternative arrangement during
    industrial dispute 222
  attendance order 122
  education authority powers 89, 105,
    121-2
  parents' arrangements for 13, 14, 30, 31,
    50, 121-2
  reasons for 121
home-school relations 66, 150-1, 186
home tuition
  during convalescence 145
homework 66
  discretionary 140
  employment of child interfering with 92
  information for parents 123-4
  objection to, by parents 124
  parental encouragement 124
  reasons for 123
hospitals
  education of child in 89
  schools 145
Human Rights, European Convention
    on 140-1

independent schools
  Assisted Places Scheme 25-29, 107, 125,
    128, 166, 189, 195, 225
  bursaries and scholarships 115
  choice of 50-60, 125
  complaints about 126-7
  corporal punishment 84-85, 101
  education authority paying for 105,
    110, 111
  endowments 108
  financing of 107
  holiday arrangements 119
  information for parents 128
  information service 23, 125
  inspections 125, 134

independent schools—contd.
  payment for books and materials 39
  registration of 126
  religious discrimination 166
  sex discrimination 200
  special 125, 131, 213
  starting date 17
  uniform 27, 65
industry
  college council co-operation with 186
  grants and scholarships for careers in 195
  school council representation 187
information
  access to education committee
    minutes 90-91
  education authority expenditure 108-9
  local authorities Code of Practice 108
information for parents
  assessments of pupils, arrangements
    for 95
  basic information 128, 131-2
  clothing and uniform 65, 129, 131
  denominational school 79, 128, 129, 132
  discipline in schools 82-83, 129
  duties of education authority 88, 128,
    130-3
  examination results 95, 130
  handbook/prospectus 132
  hand delivery 133
  homework 123, 129
  independent schools 128
  languages other than English 35, 129, 133
  progress of child at school 16, 129
  school council 187
  school rules 129, 193
  secondary school 130
  specially talented children, policy
    for 202
  starting school booklets 19
  supplementary information 130-1
  where to find 131-2
  written about schools 15, 17, 75, 128-33
injuries in school 173, 174-5
inspections
  assessments 134-6
  follow-up actions 135-6
  independent schools 126, 134
  Secretary of State's powers 194, 195
inspectors
  advice and information 134
  records on pupils, access to 190
  reports on schools 75, 134-6
insurance
  loss or damage to child's personal property
    at school 159
  school trips 174
intermediate treatment 167

Jewish school 78

languages other than English
 children of migrant workers 146-7
 Gaelic 15, 34-35, 73, 88, 131, 132
 information for parents 35, 129, 133
 special classes for racial groups 162
 special educational needs 205, 206
law, educational
 discretionary 140
 problems of interpretation of 140
leaving age 13, 14, 137
legal action
 accidents or injuries to child at
  school 174-5
 charges for school education 106
 child wrongfully punished 87
 compensation for loss, damage or
  injury 139-40
 complaints 91
 industrial action, effects 222
 parental rights and responsibilities 139-41
 personal property lost or damaged at
  school 159
 racial discrimination 163
 school closure 184
 Sikh boy wearing turban to school 162
 teachers' action or inaction
  compensation 223
 see also Court of Session and sheriff court
legal aid
 children's hearing 47, 48
 European Commission 22
 scheme 22
"legal dispensary" 22
legal terms 232-9
leisure time activities
 further education 152
libraries
 education authority powers 89
lighting in schools 177
List D schools
 see residential (former 'List D') schools
local authorities
 grants for bi-lingual instruction 35
 misuse of public funds redress 109
 "parental rights resolution" 44-45
local enquiries
 Secretary of State, powers for 194

mandatory education 13
materials
 assistance to parents towards cost of 111
 capitation allowance 107
 charge for articles pupils keep 38
 duty of education authority to provide 88,
  105

materials—contd.
 free to pupils 38
 loss or damage 158-60
 pupils own, permission to take to
  school 38
 racial prejudice, discouragement of 162
 sex discrimination 198
 storage space 177
mathematical aptitude 201-2
meals
 accommodation for serving 177
 Assisted Places Scheme 27
 charges for 143, 181
 complaints 143
 free of charge, qualification for 142, 152
 grants 15, 88
 information for parents 129
 lunchtime supervision 173
 nursery schools 156
 nutritional standards 143
 special diets required by religions 166
 supervision 143
medical advice 117, 207
medical care 15, 129, 144-5
medical conditions
 children going on school trips 174
 exclusion from school 101-2
 home education because of 121
 meals and milk provision 143
medical examination of child 14, 194
 on admittance to residential school 170
 special educational needs 207, 208
medical room in school 145
Member of Parliament (MP)
 complaints to 69, 76
mental handicap
 special educational needs 204-20
migrant children
 educational provision 146-7
 EEC regulations 146-7
milk
 free provision 142-3, 152
 grants 15, 142-3
 nursery schools 156
Minister for Education, Agriculture and
 Fisheries 194
mobile workers
 educational provision for children 147
moral education 166
mother tongue teaching 146-7
museums
 education authority powers 89
musical aptitude 201
musical instruments
 assistance to parents towards cost of 111
music lessons 105

"Named Person" 205, 206, 210, 212-13, 218
nurses visiting schools 145
nursery classes 75
nursery schools 13, 16, 17
  admissions to 130
  building regulations 176
  charges not allowed 105, 156
  choice of 50, 131, 132
  links with home 156
  meals and milk charges 156
  play space regulations 176
  provision not compulsory 88, 89, 128, 140, 155-6
  special educational needs 155-6, 206, 208

Ombudsman, local 67, 69, 70-72, 91, 184
open days 151
"open learning" courses 154
Open University
  financial assistance for courses 111, 113
  "open learning" courses 154
options, subject in secondary school 75, 95, 96, 116
outdoor centres 88
out of school activities 41, 50, 75, 129, 174, 181
  education authority powers 89
  school rules 193

parents
  attendance at school of child 14, 16, 17, 30-33, 119-20
  children in care 43-45
  children to be educated according to wishes of 75-76
  child's actions, responsibilities for 86-87
  discipline of children outside school hours 85-86
  discipline of school, disagreement with 100-1
  discipline, school's policy, views on 87
  discrimination — race or sex 15
  education of child, responsibility for 13-14, 121
  encouragement of child 13, 124, 155, 201-2
  examination of child by doctor or psychologist 14
  exclusion appeals 15
  extra-curricular activities 16
  Gaelic speaking 15, 34-35
  guidance for child 15
  helping in school 76, 150-1

parents—contd.
  holiday arrangements in term-time 119-20
  home education, choice for child 13, 14, 30, 31, 50, 121-2
  information about school 15, 17, 19
  legal action to defend rights 139-41
  legally binding agreements for children, age for 42
  options for secondary schools 75, 95, 96, 116
  personal belongings taken to school 158-9
  progress of child at school 16, 75, 190-1
  religious education, right to withdraw child 15
  residential (former 'List D') school placement 170
  rights 14-16, 40, 139-41
  safety of child at school 14
  school closure consultation 15, 88, 179-80, 181-5
  school council representation 15, 88, 90, 186, 187
  school rules, responsibility for child to obey 14
  sixteen plus children, maintenance 14
  student maintenance costs, contribution to 110
  uniform or dress of child 14, 15
  visiting school 13
  welfare grants 15
parents' associations/parent-teacher associations 16, 149-51
  complaints, assistance with 68
  educational issues, discussion 76
  links with school council 150, 187
parents' groups
  advice and assistance from 21
  education authority powers to finance 89
  for each class or year group 151
  research grants 195
parent-teacher relations 66, 151
part-time courses
  definition of 111, 112, 114, 152
physical education 73, 74, 88, 152
  games and sports representation without race discrimination 162
  sex discrimination 199
places at school
  guidelines for changes, consultation 182
  requests 51-56
play
  how children learn 155
  parents with children 13
playground
  standards 177
  supervision 173
playgroups 13, 155, 156

playing fields 88
  minimum size regulations 176
police
  arrest of children 41
  exclusion from school, assistance
    with 102
  illegal articles taken from pupils 159
  records of pupils, access to 190
  school damage, property theft, report
    to 160
  school report to 86
political parties
  complaints, consideration of 69
preparatory schools
  Assisted Places Scheme 25
pre-school education 16, 89, 155-7
  special educational needs 155-6, 206, 208
  see also nursery school and playgroups
primary schools
  basic staffing complement 62
  choice of 50, 51
  capitation allowance 38, 107
  changes, consultation 180-5
  class size 61, 62
  curriculum 73-74
  "feeder" schools for secondary schools
    130, 180, 186
  guidance for pupils 116
  homework arrangements 123-4
  nursery classes 156
  parents helping in 76
  Primary Education Development
    Project 76
  toilet and washing facilities 177
  transfer to secondary school 17, 19, 116,
    129-30, 180-5
progress records
  Assisted Places Scheme holders 189
  child at school 16, 75, 95, 129, 151, 189-90
  duty of education authority 88, 129,
    189-90
  information sought from other
    professionals 190
  parents' rights 190-1
  special talents 202
  see also records on pupils
psychological tests 14, 95, 189, 207, 208
public performances by school children 93
punishment see discipline
pupils' councils 41
pupil teacher ratio 63
  see also class sizes of pupils

racial discrimination 15, 23, 161-4
  careers advice 117
  complaints 67, 162-3, 223

racial discrimination—contd.
  definition of 161
  duty of education authority 88
reading, parental encouragement,
  importance of 13'
Record of Needs 190, 204-20
records on pupils
  computerised 191
  exclusion details on 84, 103-4, 190-1
  medical information 144
  parents have no right to see 104
  psychological tests 14, 95, 189
  residential (former 'List D') schools 170
  vocational advice 117
  see also progress records
records, school 190
recreational activities 88
  charges 105
  further education 152
"Red Book" 62
registration of daily attendance 33
religious education
  boarders' rights outside school hours 37,
    79, 166
  denominational schools 78-80, 166
  education committee appointments for 90
  freedom 41
  guidelines 165
  holidays, observance 120
  independent schools 166
  legal obligation to provide 73, 165
  Roman Catholic see Roman Catholic
    schools
  school council, member representing 166
  withdrawal right 15, 73, 165
remedial classes 205
Reporter of children's hearing 31, 32, 46-48,
  85, 86, 139
reports issued to pupils and parents 75, 95,
  129, 191
research grants 195
residential (former 'List D') schools 44, 45,
  46, 48, 167-71
  appeal and review 168
  children's hearing 44, 46-49
  complaints 171
  court order to attend 167, 168, 169
  criminal offence, placement for 168
  curriculum 169
  discipline 170
  holidays and leave allowed 169
  length of stay 168-9
  management of 170
  medical exam on admittance 170
  parental rights 170
  placement of child in 167-8
  records of children 170

residential (former 'List D') schools—contd.
  run aways from 169
  secure accommodation 169
  welfare of pupils 169-71
rights
  children's 40-42
  European Convention on Human
    Rights 40, 41
  parents 14-16, 40, 139-41
  UN Declaration on Human Rights 14, 40
Roman Catholic Schools 78-80
  closure 79-80
  education committee appointment for 90
  religious education in 165
  see also religious education
rural schools 61-62
  closure 179, 194

safety
  child out of school 14, 173-4
  duty of education authority 89, 172-3
  in the classroom 172-3
  playground 173
  school building regulations 176-7
  school trips 105, 110, 145, 174
  work experience 93
  see also health and safety
scholarship awards 115
school
  acoustics 177
  classroom size records 61
  changes to, consultation 179-85
  closures see closure of school
  cloakrooms and lockers 177
  complaints 16, 20, 21, 41, 66-72, 76
  composite class 61-62
  day-to-day running 88
  heating and ventilation 177
  lighting 177
  numbers in, calculation of 131
  opening and closing times 129, 174, 181
  parents visiting 13
  property damage 158-60
  special see special school
  starting dates 17
  storage space 177
  toilet and washing facilities 177
  written information for parents 15, 17, 75,
    128-30
  see also nursery school, primary school,
    secondary school
school building
  maintenance 88
  fire risk 174
  regulations 61, 68, 174
  safety 174, 176-7

school building—contd.
  standards 176
  water supply 177
school closure see closure of school
school commencement date 17
school council
  closure of school and 21, 179, 186
  complaints consideration 66, 68, 69, 76,
    187-8
  conduct of meetings 187
  curriculum developments 186
  duty of education authority 88, 89, 90, 186
  educational issues discussion 76, 186-8
  functions 186
  future of 188
  headteacher appointment 187
  holiday dates, arrangements 119
  inspections, follow up actions 135
  links with PTA/PA 150, 187
  parental representation 15, 88, 90, 186, 187
  press and public attendance 187
  pupil representation 41, 187
  religious education representation 166,
    187
  representatives on 186-7
  school rules, complaints 193
  teacher representation 187
  written information for parents 187
school day 129, 174, 181
school premises see school building
school fund 107
school health service 144-5
school holidays 119-20
school report 33
school rolls 131
school rules
  appeals against not possible 140
  disobeying, exclusion result 100-1, 193
  each school has set 193
  information for parents 129, 193
  out of school hours 193
  parents' disagreement with 193
  parents' responsibility for child to obey 14
  personal belongings 158-9
  see also discipline
school site
  minimum size regulations 176
school staff
  advice and assistance 21
  see also headteachers and teachers
school term 119, 129
school trips 105, 110, 145, 174
school year 33, 119
Scottish Education Department 194-5
  Circulars 229-31
  Memoranda 231
Scottish Examination Board 95, 130

Scottish Office 194
secondary schools
  basic staffing complement 62
  capitation allowance 38, 107
  changes to, consultation 180-5
  choice of 50
  class size 61, 62
  curriculum 74
  curriculum developments 76
  examinations *see* examinations
  "feeder" primary schools 130, 180, 186
  guidance for pupils 116-18
  homework arrangements 123-4
  information for parents 130
  rest-room 177
  subject option and choices 75, 95, 96, 116
  toilet and washing facilities 177
  transfer from primary to secondary 17, 19,
    50, 51, 116, 129-30, 180-5
Secretary of State
  basic staffing complement for schools 62
  building standards and regulations 176
  charges for school education, decisions
    on 106
  complaints 16, 67, 69-70, 71, 76, 139, 194
  curriculum advice 195
  denominational school closures 79-80, 194
  failure to provide proper education
    complaint 76
  grants for bi-lingual teaching 35
  industrial action effect on service level 222
  powers 88, 139, 194-5
  promotion of education 195
  proper school education, failure to
    provide 202
  racial discrimination complaints 163
  residential (former 'List D') school
    placement termination 168
  secure accommodation standards 169
  sex discrimination complaints 199-200
  special educational needs appeals 139,
    194, 216-19
  wills bequests to schools powers 108
secure accommodation 169
selection of pupils
  changes in procedure, consultation 180-5
separated parents
  child's education, responsibility for 14
sex discrimination 15, 23
  admission to school 197-8
  books and materials 198
  careers advice 117
  complaints 67, 199-200, 223
  direct discrimination 197
  duty of education authority 88
  independent schools 200
  indirect discrimination 197

sheriff courts
  appeal against decision of children's
    hearing 48, 49
  attendance order appeal 32, 122
  choice of school appeal 59-60, 67, 130, 139
  legal cases in 140
  racial discrimination complaints 163
  sex discrimination cases 200
  special educational needs appeal 216, 217,
    218
  see also Court of Session *and* legal action
single sex school
  changes to, consultation 180-5
sixteen year old *see* young person
social activities 88
  charges 105
  further education 152
social education 118, 166
social problems, children with 167
social work department
  children in care 43-44
  day nurseries 156
  residential schools funding 167-8, 170
  residential school placement, review of
    child's progress 168, 170
social worker
  advice and assistance 46, 117, 207
  children at risk, support for 155
  children's hearing report 46, 47, 49
  records on pupils, access to 90
  residential (former 'List D') school,
    children in, responsibilities 168, 169
  "supervision requirement" for child 48
solicitors
  advice on the law 21-22
  see also legal action
special abilities and aptitude 201-2
special educational needs
  admissions under-age 18
  appeals 15, 21, 131, 139, 194, 206, 214-19
  child guidance advice 117
  choice of school 50, 51, 207, 213-14
  chronic medical problems 145
  duty of education authority to provide 88,
    204
  emotional and social problems 167, 204
  information for parents 132, 204-5
  future needs assessment at 14 or 15 years
    of age 219
  Named Person *see* Named Person
  post sixteen 152, 209, 211
  pre-school children 155
  Record of Needs 190, 204-20
special schools
  closure and changes consultation 180-5
  independent 125, 131, 213
  information for parents 130

special schools—contd.
    provision 205
sport *see* physical education
starting school
    age for 17-18
    arrangements 19
    guidance 116
    medical examinations 144
    see also admissions to school
student grants *see* grants
study problems 116
subject options and choices 75, 95, 96, 116
supervision *see* safety
supervision order 43, 44, 49, 168
"supervision requirement" 48
supplementary benefit 114
suspension *see* exclusion
swimming pools 88

tawse for punishment 84
teachers
    activities outside school hours of
        pupils 222
    advice and assistance 21
    basic staffing complement 62, 90
    complaints against 223
    complaints to 67-68
    conditions of service 61, 89, 221-3
    disciplinary action against 223
    education committee appointments of 90
    education authorities' duties to 89
    extra for bi-lingual teaching 35
    industrial action 222
    lunchtime duties 173, 222
    pay dispute 99
    performance of day to day duties 222
    qualifications 221
    registration 221, 223
    special educational needs advice 207
    special training 119
    training and supply 195
    "twilight" teaching duties 222
    working hours 221-2
teacher training
    standard of entry 195
technical education 96-97, 153
    textbooks *see* books
timetable 74
transfer to secondary school 17, 19, 50, 51,
    116, 129-30, 180-5
transport to school
    choice of school 50, 52-53, 225
    costs, education authorities help
        with 224, 225
    denominational school 79
    duty of education authority 88, 129, 224-5
    free 224, 225

transport to school—contd.
    further education 152
    safety and supervision 225
    school closure, consultations on 181, 183,
        184
    "statutory walking distance" 225
travelling children
    educational provision for 147-8
travelling costs to school 129
truancy 31, 32-33, 43, 46
    children's hearing 46
    residential (former 'List D') schools 167

unemployment
    vocational courses 153
    Youth Training Scheme 114, 153
uniform 14, 64-65
    Assisted Places Scheme 27, 65
    grants 15, 65
    information for parents 65, 129
    national costume by ethnic minorities 162
    refusal to wear, exclusion 101
    sex discrimination 199
    see also clothing
United Nations Declaration of Human
    Rights 14, 40
units for disruptive pupils 85
university
    extra-mural departments, adult classes 153
    Open University *see* Open University
    Secretary of State for Education and
        Science 194
    student grants 22, 110, 111, 113-14

vocational education 96-97, 153
voluntary organisations
    advice and assistance 21
    complaints, support for 67
    residential schools 167

walking distance to school 30
Warnock Committee report 206
water supply for school building 177
welfare benefits
    child benefit entitlement 114
    family credit 140
    parents dependent on 111
    part-time students eligibility 114
    supplementary benefit/income
        support 114, 142
welfare grants
    availability 110-13
    duty of education authority 15, 88, 110
    maintenance grants for school pupils 15,
        22, 110
wills
    bequests to schools 108

work experience
    last year at school 93

young person
    assessment for special educational
      needs 152, 209, 211
    definition 137
    exclusion from school 104

young person—contd.
    legal rights 42, 137
    maintenance costs, assistance with 14, 22,
      110, 112-13
    responsibility for own education 14, 137
    staying at school 152
Youth Training Scheme 114, 153
youth resource centre 168

Printed in Scotland for HMSO by McQueen Ltd., Galashiels.
Dd. 762205/4536 C80 2/87